MONTEBELLO

Robert Drewe was born in Melbourne and grew up on the West Australian coast. His novels, short stories and non-fiction have won national and international prizes, been adapted for film, television, theatre and radio, and been widely translated. He has also written plays, worked as a film critic, columnist and investigative journalist, and edited five anthologies of stories.

Praise for
Montebello

Beautifully crafted… This dazzling memoir is a perfectly integrated work of art. Drewe's literary instincts are as impeccable as his ear for the English language is unfaltering, and his latest memoir has all the more force for being set down with such a delicate hand.

The Australian

This is a beautiful book.

Sydney Morning Herald

Robert Drewe at his supple, subtle and funny best.

Peter Temple, *The Age* Books of the Year

Imaginative Australian storytelling at its best, a worthy sequel to the wonderfully evocative *The Shark Net* by one of Australia's greatest living writers.

ABC *Weekend Bookworm*

Montebello is at heart a moving and profound love story. This is a splendid memoir with many moods – delicate, tough, ironic, compassionate – that are beautifully controlled and paced.

Australian Book Review

Clear, unadorned, cool, sardonic, penetrating, incisive… The atmosphere this riveting memoir evokes is so vivid and visceral you can almost feel the fine white sand between your toes and the ferocity of the sun.

Booktopia

Drewe is a born raconteur: brilliantly funny… This memoir works such sweet and poignant charm. On sharks, parents and childhood pleasures, Drewe is the nation's undisputed laureate.

The Monthly

MONTEBELLO

a memoir

From the author of *The Shark Net*

ROBERT DREWE

PENGUIN BOOKS

Also by Robert Drewe

Fiction

The Savage Crows
A Cry in the Jungle Bar
The Bodysurfers
Fortune
The Bay of Contented Men
Our Sunshine
The Drowner
Grace
The Rip

Non-fiction

Walking Ella
The Shark Net
The Local Wildlife

Plays

The Bodysurfers – the Play
South American Barbecue

Miscellany

Sand (with John Kinsella)
Perth (with Frances Andrijich)

As Editor

The Penguin Book of the Beach
The Penguin Book of the City
The Best Australian Short Stories 2006
The Best Australian Short Stories 2007
The Best Australian Essays 2010

To Anna, Sam, Laura,
Jack, Amy, Ben and Jim

Madie and Corey
Leea and Andy

and for
Tray

In Memoriam
Bruce Bennett

1941–2012

I see it always from a small boat – not a light, not a stir, not a sound…It is all in that moment when I opened my young eyes on it. I came upon it from a tussle with the sea.

Joseph Conrad, 'Youth'

But the islanders, seeing I was really adrift, took pity on me.

H.G. Wells, *The Island of Dr Moreau*

CONTENTS

1
THE FATS DOMINO VOICE

It was that fabled occasion, a dark and stormy night, the sea just a blacker inked line in the distance, and I was lying in bed in the deep gloom of three a.m., singing *Blueberry Hill* in my Fats Domino voice.

We were on the trailing edge of a cyclone and wind buffeted the timbers of my rented cottage on the cliff edge at Broken Head. The house's rocking gave the sensation of being in a sailing ship. Palm fronds lashed and rasped against the window, more rain, endless rain, thundered on the tin roof, and I'd hardly have been surprised if the cottage, an architectural folly that resembled a nineteenth-century schooner almost as much as a house, sailed over the cliff onto the sodden sugarcane fields below.

If we're speaking of the true life, of genuine self-awareness, it was a night of pivotal moments when things could go either way. I could either plummet to the depths or shape up, brush myself down, pick myself up, pull my finger out, turn a frown upside down. Basically, get a grip. The odds at that stage favoured plummeting.

Anna, my anxious seven-year-old daughter and my youngest child, was insisting I sing to her, and had chosen the song. As the rain crashed down, she complained, 'You need to sing louder.' If I sang any louder

I'd lose the throaty timbre of Fats Domino. Anyway my breathing was still shallow and irregular because I'd just killed a brown snake by her bedroom.

She was propped up beside me in bed, clasping my left hand. I was lying on my right side, and the hand-holding and singing position twisted my old lower-back injury. I seemed to have pulled a muscle while killing the snake. How it had slithered indoors was a mystery, but on Anna's insistence (perhaps there was a nest of them under the house?) I'd closed every door and window against more invading wildlife.

The bedroom door and door-frame were so swollen with damp that I had to body-slam the door with my shoulder to shut it. I'd also closed the sliding glass door leading into the dripping tangle of bougainvillea, palms, camphor laurels, ferns, vines, lantana, cane toads, water dragons, brush turkeys, bats, owls, spiders and, obviously, snakes, that surrounded our lives this January night in the rainforest hinterland of northern New South Wales.

Storm-blown bougainvillea petals were streaming down the windows like gouts of blood. I turned off the light so we couldn't see them, and then the humid room was dark as well as stifling.

'Again,' my daughter ordered, adjusting her grip. *Blueberry Hill* was one of the four numbers in my lullaby repertoire. For the others – *Summertime, Blue Skies* and *Sentimental Journey* – songs still to be rendered this turbulent night, my normal voice would suffice.

I started over. *'Ah found ma thrill . . .'* If only she'd fall asleep so I could open the window. We'd been awake since two a.m. I'd thrown the dead snake out into the bushes. We'd drunk soothing warm milk and eaten toast and plum jam in the kitchen while I tried to get her mind off the snake.

As a going-to-bed or long-car-journey diversion she liked to enviously count the excessive number of pets of her school-friend Gemma

Frith. So once more we counted Gemma Frith's animals: forty-three, if you included ducks. As usual, Anna (six pets only) said, 'Don't you think that's too many? I don't think people should be allowed to have more than thirty-seven.' I agreed: 'That's plenty.' Now we were back in bed, having trouble falling asleep.

While I was trying to kill the snake, it had tried a desperate ruse. In one quick movement it shed its skin. The skin flew off in a single life-sized piece, landed beside the real squirming snake and wriggled alongside it, like a twin. This was nature's trick to confuse the enemy, and it worked. Then – a final defence – the real dying snake suddenly exuded a terrible acrid smell. It stank as if it had been rotting in the sun for a week. I felt a guilty nausea. I couldn't get this cadaver smell out of my sinuses.

I wasn't focussed on *Blueberry Hill* but I could have sung it in my sleep. Even as I lay twisted on my side, holding hands and singing *The wind in the willow played/Its sweet melodee/But all of those vows you made/Were never to beee*, my mind was racing backwards and forwards from the snake. My thoughts were scattering even more wildly than was customary in my pre-dawn decline of morale. Eventually they stopped and settled around an icy realisation. As of yesterday I was old. My step-mother and last surviving aunt and uncle had just died within weeks of each other (each death a heavier emotional blow than I expected) and I was now the oldest person on each side of the family.

I was shocked by the realisation. Admittedly, I was no longer young (I could see that was probably going too far), but neither was I old. I was barely middle-aged. All the parts, except for close vision and lower back, still worked well enough. I was *youngish*.

Along with cheery birthday commiserations from my brother Bill and sister Jan, eternally five and ten years younger, a letter had arrived right on cue from my insurance company. AMP Life crisply pointed out that my particular life policy had expired that very day. For obvious reasons, including seeing the words *expire* and *life* in close conjunction, this came as a blow.

Until yesterday, if any misfortune from disablement to death had occurred, my loved ones were all covered. It was an expensive policy, chosen because I'd been self-employed for twenty years, since leaving journalism to write fiction, before the days of compulsory superannuation; also because of the financial risks inherent in writing literary fiction, the second-least lucrative genre (poetry wins, hands down) in an ill-rewarded industry, in a lightly populated country of chiefly non-fiction readers.

And because, highly unusually for a writer (or anyone these days), I'd had seven children – the youngest two of whom were still at school.

A marriage break-up out of the blue had walloped me. I no longer owned a house, and it seemed unlikely I ever would again. I was also a recent arrival in a regional town of hierarchical habits and an obsession with residential longevity. My old friends and adult children, however, all lived in the cities. So, I presumed, did any potential female partner.

I envisioned a future as a melanoma-dappled pensioner in a one-room flat above the Lennox Head fish shop. If I got lucky, maybe while beach-combing, I'd meet a dolphin-tattooed old hippie chick – Frangipani Blossom or Zenith Sunbeam: someone in the colonic irrigation or tantric trades. Unless fortune struck in an improbably immediate and imaginative way, that was me in ten years. Dead or alive, I was up the proverbial creek which, thanks to this endless rain, was currently in flood. Woe was me.

My literary agent had recently asked me, 'Where do you want to be in ten years?' Well, at three a.m. that got me worrying. At that hour who mulls over their successes? 'You should have had me knocked off last week,' I remarked on my birthday to the woman who until two years before had been my partner for twenty-five years.

'Don't even think it,' she said. 'Don't send such thoughts out into the cosmos.' With New Age breeziness, she suggested a financial plan for me. I should write a letter to the angels, asking politely for riches. I should state the exact amount I needed and leave the request on the bookshelf above my work desk where the angels would be sure to see it.

'Should I include my ABN and bank details?' I wondered.

'Treat this with due respect,' she said.

This monsoonal night the cosmos was receiving all sorts of wildly depressing data from me. Self-pity. Bitterness. Sorrow. A longing for intimacy and an affectionate female touch. Two years was a long time between drinks. Granted, there was one non-related female who cared deeply about me. I was always on her mind; indeed, she was obsessed with me. Unfortunately she was a stalker.

She was a self-described psychic who'd taken to writing me devoted spidery epistles in red biro on the back of old Christmas cards. She wrote that she had regular visions of me in supermarkets 'buying tinned goods and looking pale.' How she longed for the day when we could meet 'for our mutual benefit and the consumption of fresh fruit'. She suggested her place on alternate Thursdays, when she was 'spiritually unencumbered'.

I like fruit well enough, and mutual benefits as well, and I was quite prepared to be unencumbered on Thursdays. But as my spiritual stalker had neglected to include her name, address or phone number, I guess she thought I was psychic too.

To be frank, ever since a startling moment on a certain early autumn day two years earlier, I'd been unreceptive to anything or anyone spiritual, mystical, New Age, alternative, counter-cultural, hippie, zodiacal or even standard-issue North Coast conventionally unconventional. The day before this pivotal couple of minutes I'd returned home from Writers' Week at the Adelaide Festival, Australian literature's oldest and biggest celebration, vaguely hungover from the round of publishers' parties and still chuffed at having been invited to deliver the opening address.

I'd had a quick swim in the surf, eaten dinner, made homecoming love with my wife, and gone to sleep. Next day, Monday, 13 March, I returned to the work desk – my self-satisfaction ebbing back to its normal level of vague anxiety – when something made me enter the marital bedroom and open the bedside drawer on *her* side of the bed. *Something made me.* Why? In twenty-five years I'd never felt the need to do so. And in the drawer was a handsomely bound, professionally authored, multi-paged horoscope.

This didn't seem such an unusual discovery. She was *into* astrology. I opened the book, which was headed *His Stars: Your Partner's Horoscope.* How sweet of her to get my horoscope done professionally, I thought, flipping through the swirls of charts which pointed out my sense of humour, love of family, even my love of the outdoors. Despite my distinct reservations about astrology, a topic I'd been known to mock, I had to admit the astrologer had me pretty accurately pinned down. Except in the final sentence: 'To sum up: your partner is intriguingly unconventional for a Pisces!' *Pisces?* I'm a Capricorn.

. . .

She'd already rented a white cottage on the top of the nearest hill, and she moved out of home immediately. The cottage (which to her annoyance, I would refer to bitterly as 'the love shack') was starkly visible from the veranda, the yard and most rooms of our house. Although he would nose it deep into the shrubbery, so was the Piscean's red Mercedes.

Married life, family life, imaginative working life – life as I'd known it – jolted to a halt. There was an expression used of politicians that came to mind: *rooster one minute, feather-duster the next.* The date *13 March, 13 March* rang in my mind now as the storm raged in the night and my sense of self – how pathetic and stupid was I? – was again fading by the second. Where was my life, my career going? (The career: the last card in the depressive's pack.) In my recently acquired daze, where was *I* going? This was not the *me* I was used to. *Who was this person?*

Only the week before, a woman in a Land-Rover with Queensland licence plates had stopped me in the Woolworths car park to seek directions to the Big Prawn fish and chip shop on the Pacific Highway at Ballina. Apparently she had trouble finding a bright pink, six-by-nine-metre concrete-and-fibreglass prawn which towered over Australia's main highway. She beckoned me to the car window and asked, 'Do you speak English?'

That threw me. Now I looked foreign? 'Yes – I – speak – English,' I enunciated. I gave directions to the Big Prawn very crisply and grammatically. I wanted my English to be impeccable. This Queenslander with unsophisticated dining habits should be in no doubt about me or my antecedents. The woman gave me a strange look, thanked me briskly, quickly wound up the car window, and accelerated away.

Now I lay twisted up in the humidity, the stink of dying snake in my nostrils, imitating an old New Orleans entertainer. This night of the soul was growing much darker than the usual abyss. Could this be karma? In the past I'd left women for other women. I, too, had made children unhappy.

Psychologists say you can't miss a life stage; having missed my wild-oats period by marrying at eighteen, I'd sowed a few oats in my thirties. But that was yesteryear. And not during the marriage.

Creatively, I was also tussling with something Don DeLillo wrote in his novel *Point Omega*: 'The true life is not reducible to words spoken or written, not by anyone, ever. The true life takes place when we're alone, thinking, feeling, lost in memory, dreamingly self-aware, the sub-microscopic moments.'

Fair enough. At the moment I was certainly 'lost in memory' all day long and 'dreamingly self-aware' of 'sub-microscopic moments'. But I found it hard to set any of these moments down – or anything else either – without lapsing into maudlin self-pity. The critic in me, the person who prided himself on his literary bullshit detector, was having trouble with imaginative objectivity.

Then, *then,* as often happens – and how grateful I am for this familiar habit – just when worry and longing and guilt could have swept me into a hellish vortex, a thought struck. Not an epiphany exactly, but definitely the leap of insight when an idea suggests itself. I was actually galvanised by melancholy. I stood aside and saw the snake episode and its anxious aftermath, this concurrence of fear and family-defence and sadness, from a writerly distance.

I saw the ridiculousness in the situation: the snake, the tempest, the self-absorption, the high anxiety level, the Fats Domino voice, and I felt oddly calmed. My daughter was finally asleep. Her grip relaxed, her hair and breath brushed my cheek, love – overwhelming, indescribable love – enveloped me and, for the moment, I was saved.

. . .

Over the next few days I relate the snake story over and over. Try stopping me. There's no credit coming from the country folk, however. They grumble, 'Sounds like a whip snake to me.' (Bite venomous but not fatal.) Or, 'I bet it was a tree snake.' (Harmless.) Even, 'A brown snake? Are you sure? That sounds unlikely.' But city friends all *ooh* and *ahh* and regard me as intrepid, the women among them shaking their heads in awe. One woman, unable to bear the ferocious excitement engendered by my re-enactment, even puts her hands over her ears and makes that irritating *la-la-la* noise.

The story so impresses them that I have no need to embellish it.

For the purposes of the narrative I backtrack an hour before *Blueberry Hill*, before the toast and warm milk and the tightly sealed doors and windows. Suddenly, I relate, I'm woken at 2 a.m. by a heavier than usual cloudburst thundering on the roof. Padding to the bathroom through the living room, I spot the snake wriggling across the bare floor between my daughter's bedroom and mine.

A snake! The slick floor is hampering its progress. It's unsure which way to go. On the floor-boards it stands out in sharp relief: a young brown snake, a bit longer than my forearm. Apart from being born with enough venom to kill a cart-horse, brown snakes are notoriously aggressive at any age or length. And now it's trying to crawl into her doll-house.

For a moment I stand there stupefied. I'm hardly snake-proofed. I'm barefoot, of course, and wearing only underpants. The snake is nosing into the doll-house's second floor. Its coils are tipping over tiny tables and chairs and cupboards and people: little plastic mummies and daddies and children. This is overdoing the imagery. It's like a Pedro Almodovar film about marriage breakdown.

My mind is whirling. At two o'clock in the morning I can't phone a wildlife rescuer, one of those noble volunteers who care for the region's inappropriately situated wildlife. In this greener-than-green area, snakes and goannas have greater status than horses or dogs, and the signs at my nearest beach saying *Do Not Molest the Sharks* are regularly souvenired by disbelieving tourists. However, I'm not totally immune to the local environmental ethos that a poisonous snake is a beautiful creature: forget its venomous reputation, just stand still, don't disturb it and it will silently vanish.

But I don't want this snake to silently vanish. My biggest fear is that the snake will silently vanish. I don't want it slithering off into my daughter's bedroom, or my teenage son's room upstairs, or disappearing into the melange of toys and clothes and sofa cushions. I don't want it to surprise us, reappearing at a time of its choosing to bite the children. Or, indeed, to poison Life-Policy-Expired-Only-Yesterday me.

I'm also species-territorial. *People Inside – Wildlife Outside.* Especially brown snakes that can kill you. And a brown snake is *inside the house.* And inside the doll-house. I can't wait until wildlife-rescue business hours. I'm going to have to deal with this.

How? I don't have one of those wire hooks that local snake handlers flourish so casually. I'm also lacking snake-killing weaponry. Somewhere in the monsoonal downpour outdoors, in the red mud and dripping shrubbery, is a shovel. There are grass clippers and tree trimmers. There is an axe, and a mattock with a split handle, and various bricks and heavy rocks. The axe would be best. But even if the snake waits patiently for me to find the axe, I can hardly chop up the living room.

All these thoughts flick by much more quickly than their retelling. Now I run the contents of the kitchen cutlery drawer through my mind. I decide that the only utensil in the house approaching a suitable weapon is a barbecue tool for turning steak and sausages and scraping fat off the grill of the Beefmaster.

When I race to fetch the barbecue spatula, the snake finds the doll-house too cramped, slithers toward the sofa and endeavours to creep under it. This makes my task a fraction less dangerous. I'm able to kneel on the sofa so the padded armrest is between me and the snake – as long as it doesn't rear up.

I carefully bend down, and then thrust the leading edge of the spatula down hard onto the snake's neck. I hold on, and press down, and keep holding on. There is a lot of thrashing.

Amid the thrashing and shedding and cadaver-stink, and my growing nausea and fear of the snake, Anna wakes up. Sleepy and fuzzy-haired, she pads past me to the toilet, comes back, passes by the spatula and snake activity again, then turns from the bedroom door and asks, with a frown, 'Why are you kneeling on the couch with your bum in the air?' She is carrying a teddy bear with a concertina stomach that plays Brahms' *Lullaby* when you stretch the bear out to its full length. She does so.

I'm nonchalant. 'I'm just getting rid of a snake. Why don't you pop into my bed and turn the light on.'

The barbecue spatula isn't as sharp, weighty or deadly as I'd hoped. I have to press down for a long while – years, decades, it seems – as the snake whips about. My right side is stiff and cramping but if I relax for a second the enraged and desperate snake will lurch up and bite me. It takes about twenty minutes to die. As the requiem of Brahms' *Lullaby* issues impatiently from a bear's belly in the bedroom, it seems much longer than that.

. . .

The snake episode is a turning point. It's not an Aust Lit snake. It's not the Snake of Capitalist Greed of Henry Lawson's poetry, or hardly even the Snake of the Threat of Female Otherness of Lawson's *The Drover's Wife* and *The Bush Undertaker*. If anything, it's the Snake of Male Dazedness and Foggy Indecision.

At least I've acted, taken control of events. And in the way of north-coast weather patterns, the cyclone storm cell spins out into the South Pacific by morning. Sun glistens on the wet palms and, one by one, the bougainvillea blood-gouts on the window panes dry and blow away in the breeze. The sky, the foliage and the fauna appear sharply etched and the whole passage of the day seems more optimistic.

I force myself to function. I start by writing a regular column for *The Age* newspaper. I manage to concentrate and narrow my focus by writing the column in longhand and then transcribing it onto the computer. Once I've accomplished that I find the creative and deadline

discipline involved is hugely helpful. After three columns, I'm able
to give up the handwriting and return to the laptop. I knuckle down
further and write a couple of short stories. I write more stories. They
start coming reasonably easily. I write a dozen of them, and sub-
mit them for publication, four of them to *Meanjin* magazine. (Frank
Moorhouse says *Meanjin* is Aboriginal for 'Rejected by the *New Yorker*'
but at this point their acceptance of the stories gives me a huge lift.)
Then I publish them all in a collection, *The Rip*. The title says it all.

I also begin seeing women. *Seeing* is a strange euphemism for
dating; I don't really *see* them at all. Or really feel them, or hear them,
for that matter. I'm pleased to meet attractive new women (why not?),
and happy in their intimate company (how pleasant) but only vaguely
disappointed when we break up (too bad). If I were to estimate my
capacity to wholeheartedly love anyone other than my children (for
whom my love is prodigious), or my ability to create another large work
of the imagination, a big novel like *The Drowner*, I'd put it at around
fifty per cent. Nevertheless, this is an improvement.

Time passes, time passes, and I find myself absorbed by the
countryside, the elements, the exotic flora and fauna of the northern
rainforest. Several times a day I check the weather radar online; then
I stand outside and marvel at the clouds building up just as they are
on the screen. I can stare for hours at brush turkeys nesting in the
shrubbery and water-dragons sunbaking on the septic tank. One day
there is a strong tsunami warning following an earthquake out in the
Pacific; I stand on a cliff and wait at the appointed time of impact for
the engulfing wave. Once my children are on high ground I relish the
idea. Go on, sweep everything away. Nothing happens.

To use up the constant adrenaline surges of anxiety, I impulsively
take long, fast walks along the beach and country lanes. Snakes rus-
tle away from me; a nervy nesting swamp-hen darts out of Emigrant
Creek and bites my shin. I swim and gym for the same adrenaline

reason (I can't stop myself frenetically exercising), and quickly lose seven kilos without dieting. Waiting for my daughter at the school gate, tension momentarily flattened by lifting weights, I'm strangely, calmly, impressed by the smell of camphor laurels, the way palm fronds bisect the sky, and the high altitude attained by soaring pelicans. My new columns and stories throng with lizards and swamp-hens and silky-oaks and palm trees and relationship breakups. Obviously, I'm not yet out of the woods.

Those friends close to me professionally, my publisher, Julie Gibbs, and my agent, Fiona Inglis, start asking, 'What's next?'

Good question.

2
THE BARGE

The barge finally left for the islands just after midnight, its departure delayed by a drunken fisherman who'd fallen into the harbour while trying to tie up his dinghy alongside us. Luckily, a crewman who was loading our supplies heard his splashing and choking cries, ran to the barge's bow and saw the man floundering half-submerged and tangled in his mooring rope, and hauled him out before he drowned.

I sat on my backpack and watched from the end of the wharf while the paramedics worked methodically on the semi-conscious fisherman. Moths and mosquitoes swarmed around the ambulance lights and the medics had to keep brushing them off. The ambulance was parked beside the barge and it was another half hour before the man sat up, swore, coughed violently and vomited. Then the ambulance left for the hospital, and the loading of the crates of stores and heavy equipment, and the six passengers, continued.

Now I stood at the stern rail as the lights of Dampier fell behind and we threaded our way through the near-shore Intercourse Islands. Was the explorer Captain Phillip Parker King, many months away from home comforts, stuck on a theme when naming them in 1818? There is Intercourse Island itself, then East Intercourse Island and West

Intercourse Island, as well as East Mid-Intercourse Island and West Mid-Intercourse island. Familiar to iron-ore miners today, the islands are also remembered by generations of sniggering Perth geography students, who thought that name better suited to Rottnest Island, Perth's favourite romantic holiday spot.

The engines throbbed at a steady pitch and strings of phosphorescence streamed and glowed in the barge's wake. It was still early October, but even in spring the temperature on the Pilbara coast of Western Australia easily reaches 35 degrees Celsius. The easterly wind was warm and smelled of red deserts.

A landing barge doesn't sail or roll so much as surge slowly and methodically through the water at about seven knots. The gentle swell of the ocean beyond the harbour was barely noticeable as the *Tom Welsby* ploughed along. The uncommon situation: spending the night on deck in the Indian Ocean, with the desert breeze on my face, the mixed marine whiffs of fuel and salt, suddenly struck me with a jolt of nervous enthusiasm.

It was difficult to explain to my companions why I was aboard the *Tom Welsby* with them this night, bound for a barren Indian Ocean archipelago of uninhabited, government-controlled islands with a notorious past. So I didn't try. I hoped the trip would amount to something, even though the *what exactly?* wasn't clear to me. It wasn't only that I'd returned to the original backdrop of my writing – the West Australian coast – and that I was probably an islomaniac as well (I'd only recently heard of the term *islomania* – a fascination with islands), it was that ever since I was nine years old I'd been alarmed by the Montebello Islands.

With permission to stay on the islands during an important experiment finally granted by the West Australian Government, I felt the familiar thrill tinged with anxiety I get when embarking on a new experience. The word *romance* covered it, in the sense of an inexplicable adventurous enthusiasm. To be honest, romance in the usual sense was also on my mind.

I was visiting Western Australia more and more regularly lately. I told myself I was flying back and forth for research purposes. True enough, but I'd recently met someone. To be accurate, I'd re-connected with a woman I'd known and admired since she was a girl. The fact that she was unavailable and innocent of the extent of my interest seemed hardly daunting. When you're hugging a passionate emotion to your chest, life's possibilities seem boundless. I would fly three thousand kilometres on the chance of a meal with her, a kitchen conversation, a drink on the veranda in the company of others: her family; her husband. A glimpse even.

· · ·

My fellow passengers bound for the Montebellos were five govern-ment conservationists: a team of three men and two women. They'd picked me up from Karratha airport in a packed Land-Rover and then driven straight to the pub. No-one spoke or made to get out of the car, but from the cartons of beer already crammed in the back, I sensed I should buy a personal supply for the next fortnight.

'Cans, mate. Not bottles,' I was advised.

I entered the public-bar hubbub of beards, work-boots and tat-toos – miners and fishermen vying to out-yell, out-laugh, out-muscle and out-drink each other – and, from a young, strung-out barmaid with nose and eyebrow studs, for double its price in the southern cities (boutique beers were off the scale) bought a load of Victoria Bitter.

In my buoyant mood, I thought how fitting it was to be leaving from a port named after William Dampier. From his initial landing in the *Cygnet* in 1688, and again in 1699, the old pirate and navigator extensively explored and chronicled this coast, writing in *A New Voyage*

Round the World the first account of Australia in English, indeed the world's very first travel book, 'New Holland is a very large Tract of Land. It is not yet determined whether it is an Island or a main Continent, but I am certain that it joins neither to Asia, Africa nor America.'

In Miss Doris Langridge's Grade Two class, Dampier's saturnine face glowered down on us from the classroom wall. On either side of him, the standard heroic and bewigged Anglo portraits of Captain Cook and Clive of India barely kept him in check. Dampier seemed to be straining against their disapproval.

During ink-writing lessons, Miss Langridge insisted that the blunt ends of our pens pointed towards William Dampier. She enforced this regulation by rapping our knuckles with her savage ruler, a notorious metal-edged, fifteen-inch weapon inlaid with rectangles of West Australian timbers: jarrah, karri, wandoo and tuart. Tough luck if you were left-handed. Piracy, penmanship and punishment thus combined in our seven-year-old minds, ensuring thereafter both a crabbed writing style and an antipathy to English explorers.

Frowning impatiently down on us, all gaunt, pock-marked cheeks and lank tresses, Dampier looked as if he'd been painted while suffering from scurvy or something nasty picked up while sacking the coast of Boca del Drago. Like a Disney pirate captain, he out-menaced the classroom's other English historical celebrities, the Royal family, and was easily confused with *Peter Pan's* Captain Hook.

He was certainly an enigma: a pirate who collected botanical specimens as his booty? Of course, when it was carried out against the Spanish enemy, its allies, ships and territories, piracy was an acceptable occupation: 'profiteering'. Pirates sought financial backing from big business before entering the profiteering industry, and a plundering licence was required.

Few other explorers have been so honoured in the Yellow Pages, and few historical figures have featured so prominently in both the nation's geography and everyday commerce. On the Pilbara and Kimberley coasts his turbulent career is marked by place-names and businesses, from archipelagos to pubs and pizza shops. The geographical naming honours again rested with Philip Parker King, a great admirer. More than a century later he retraced Dampier's *Cygnet* and *Roebuck* voyages, and always travelled with copies of his books.

Dampier's fame as a best-selling author and natural historian, whose vivid descriptions, maps and drawings fascinated generations of scientists, navigators, scholars and writers – influencing Defoe's *Robinson Crusoe* and Swift's *Gulliver's Travels* – is largely forgotten in Australia, except by botanists. More fitting than commemoration by beer and pizzas, his name is given to three plant genera: *Dampiera, Eucalyptus dampieri* and *Willdampia formosa*.

However, his local popularity depends on his buccaneering career. There's an improbable north-west myth that he buried a sea-chest of treasure on Buccaneer Rock, off the shoreline at Broome. But Indian Ocean tides wash over the rock every day. And why would he hide respectably gained loot, especially treasure stolen oceans away, in the Caribbean and along the Pacific coast of South America?

It's impossible to miss his legendary presence in these parts. Just for a start we have the port of Dampier and Dampier Peninsula, Hill, Terrace, Land, Creek, Archipelago, Monument, Road, Downs and Hotel. There's Roebuck Bay, Deep, Town, Plains and Hotel. And Cygnet Bay and Hill. And Buccaneer Archipelago and Rock.

This celebration of his alternate raffish profession is ironic given his scientific and literary impact, and his initially pessimistic view of New Holland, the land that would become Australia: its indigenous population ('the miserablest People in the World') and available foodstuffs ('neither Herb, Root, Pulse, nor any sort of Grain . . . no Trees bore Fruit or Berries').

As the first English explorer to set foot on Australian shores, however, more than eighty years before Captain James Cook arrived on the east coast, his voyages resulted in an astonishing collection of journals, illustrations and specimens of plants, sea and land animals, insects and shells, driving a European imagination eager for news of 'other worlds'.

What he couldn't know was that under this 'dry, sandy Soil, destitute of Water', and beneath its coastal seabeds, were mineral, oil and natural gas deposits worth many trillions of dollars. Four centuries later, here lay a fortune at the outer limits of calculation and consciousness in any century, and the corporations and individuals who uncovered it, though of certain shared sensibilities with William Dampier, would be enriched beyond the imagination of the shrewdest pirate.

. . .

Vivid signal fires now pinpointed this treasure as our barge ploughed westward into the night. They were the waste-gas flares from oil rigs and natural-gas platforms. At the same time, a brilliant blaze of light, as wide and high as any dawn or sunset, radiated out from Barrow Island and spread over the sea and across the night horizon.

This roseate glow illuminated a massive industrial development abounding in financial superlatives. 'The biggest in the nation's history.' Corporations as well as State and Federal governments of all political hues proudly spruiked that it encompassed both the country's biggest-ever oil field and its largest natural gas development.

With an industrial project so gigantic, conservationists didn't know where to start with their misgivings. So they began with turtles. They complained that the all-night glare already played havoc with the island's turtle hatchery, bewildering the pregnant turtles and then their just-hatched offspring. Both mothers and babies were normally directed by the moon's reflection on the ocean. This endless over-whelming glare: was it day or night? They had to return to the sea. But where exactly was the sea?

Turtles had been commercially 'fished' or 'harvested' on Barrow Island from the mid-nineteenth century until 1973, but over the years Barrow had made other canny entrepreneurs – among them whalers, pearlers, and guano miners – piles of money. Even slavers. Until he was arrested and removed from the Swan River Colony in 1876, Captain William Cadell had used the island as a base for trading in Aboriginal slaves, who were used as divers in the pearling industry.

More recently, West Australian Petroleum had discovered oil there in 1964, and Barrow went on to become Australia's leading producer of oil. By 1995 there were 430 wells producing oil and natural gas across the southern half of the island in a lacework of pipelines and outcrops of nodding, oil-pumping 'donkeys'. Oil tankers were filled by a submarine pipeline that extended ten kilometres out into the ocean.

In 2009 a consortium of Chevron, ExxonMobil and Shell had received environmental approval from the Western Australian Government to develop natural gas reserves, known as the Gorgon Project, sixty kilo-metres north of the island. It was Australia's largest resource project and began producing 40 trillion cubic feet of gas from mid-2011.

Was it a misguided public-relations effort, or intentionally pro-vocative, that Barrow Island's central endeavour was named after the three grisly sisters of Greek myth, the terrifying monsters with hair of writhing, venomous snakes and fierce frowns that turned their challengers to stone?

. . .

As the ocean streamed past and the *Tom Welsby* pressed on into the night, we ate takeaway fried chicken and bread rolls, and cracked open cans of beer from our supplies. The barge's skipper and crew, Boxhead, Grommet and Glenn, had accepted a beer before departure but said they didn't drink while at sea. So it had to be their cheery natures that caused me to wake periodically throughout the night to bursts of convivial laughter.

Of our team, we four males slept on camp stretchers on deck, the two women in bunks in an indoor cabin. In the temperate weather, I saw the open deck as a bonus for us men. However, the women were advantaged in the toilet by a sign over the lavatory demanding *Men Please Piss Overboard*. This seemed a reasonable enough request, to ease pressure on the sewage tank, but the barge's sides and bow were solid metal, with no gaps, from the deck to the chin-high rail. Only the stern was open to the elements – widely, gapingly open, with no safety rail, right down to the deck. And it faced east, and a strong easterly wind was blowing.

The balmy night air and the steady thrum of the engines soon encouraged sleep in the other passengers. But not me. The glow in the west made the eastern sky intensely dark and starless. The sky did not press down, however; it was limitless. The ocean was limitless. The unattainable was possible.

At school we'd studied Joseph Conrad's stories, 'Typhoon' and 'Youth', and 'Youth' now came vividly to mind. Over a bottle, an old sea-dog recalls his adventures as a twenty-year-old sailor: 'I see a bay, a wide bay, smooth as glass and polished like ice, shimmering in the dark. A red light burns far off upon the gloom of the land, and the night is soft and warm.'

It's not an unwelcome feeling, if only for a few hours, to feel romantically intrepid. My thoughts kept returning to the new but long-known woman back on the mainland and suddenly the voyage had all the anticipatory fantasy of a tryst.

3
THE HARBOUR STORY

To cover my flights from my home in northern New South Wales down to Sydney, across the continent to Perth and then north to Karratha, and hence to Dampier and the islands – the dates conveniently coincided – I'd accepted a gig as guest speaker at the Albany writers' festival. Among the amiable hosts and visiting writers, a woman from Victoria got chatting to me, and cloistered indoors for much of the time by the damp weather cloaking King George Sound, we gradually exchanged basic personal information.

On the second afternoon we played truant from the festival to get some air. We went for a walk in the sea-mist and ended up in a coffee shop by the harbour. She said she was emotionally exhausted. The last time she'd been away from home was two years ago, and then only to Sydney. As she spoke (she needed to talk), the coffee cup shook in her hand. For various reasons her Sydney Harbour story was fresh in my mind when I arrived in the Montebellos a week later. On a quiet afternoon there I wrote it down.

No matter the hour, whenever they chanced to look down from their hotel room at the grey harbour swell lapping below, there was a ragged group of people fishing with hand lines from the adjacent pier.

The hotel was built over the water, a converted shipping wharf with a heritage listing, and their room's décor made a feature of the plain wooden beams and thick planks and unadorned metalwork of the original structure. The light off Sydney Harbour was clear and vivid. For an assignation, especially at this stage of their relationship, it would be hard to find a more pure setting.

Stephen (let's call him) was a long-divorced architect from Brisbane, she ('Claire') was a Melbourne writer, unhappily married to a chef ('Nigel'), and their affair was two years old. Their friendship, however, went back twenty-odd years, indeed since the day of Claire's wedding to Nigel, and for most of that time, Stephen had since told her, he'd secretly loved her.

Two New Year's Eves ago, with midnight's alcohol and courage aboard, he'd finally told her. By then she'd suffered enough of Nigel's excessive drinking and constant infidelities, his savage temper, his belittling control over her and, lately (since, thanks to television, he'd assumed cooking celebrity), his increasingly expensive cocaine habit. In her view, these were no longer excusable as classic chef's idiosyncrasies and she was open to Stephen's declaration.

Under a Fitzroy jacaranda with two or three late blossoms still clinging tenaciously to its branches they kissed like teenagers, and a relationship began based on snatched phone calls and texts and romantic bi-monthly liaisons. And now, deeply involved, they met halfway between their home cities, in a hotel built over the water, to plan a future together.

She knew her food and her restaurants, of course, and the first night she suggested they dine at Spice Temple. The exciting food flavours, the restaurant's shadowy ambience suggesting opium dens, could not have been more suited to the adventure ahead.

Walking back to the hotel along the harbour shore, lips still numbed by chilli, they kissed in the sea breeze and pointed out waterside apartments they would like to live in together, and admired the play of lights on the sleek harbour like the eager tourists they were.

Stephen indicated warning signs along the harbour railing: 'No fish or crustaceans caught west of the Sydney Harbour Bridge should be eaten.' The signs, in a dozen languages, warned of elevated dioxin levels in harbour fishes, caused by a century of industrial pollution. Commercial fishing was banned and, for recreational fishers, only fish caught east of the bridge, towards the open sea of the Heads, could safely be eaten. And no more than 150 grams per month. Otherwise 'Catch and Release.'

Back in their hotel room, as he closed the curtains before undressing, he spotted the clump of scruffy fisher folk hunkered down under a street lamp on the next pier. Where the light pooled on the water, their dipping and rising fishing lines resembled the parallel strands of a spider's web and shone with phosphorescence.

'Our friends are fishing *west* of the bridge,' he said, and shook his head.

On their second day, in a mood of serious optimism, their heads full of forthcoming plans, they rose late and decided on a brisk walk before lunch. He was curious to check out the pier fishermen. They'd still been there when he opened the curtains that morning. Surely they weren't the same individuals, homeless people driven to catch and eat contaminated fish?

The fishers turned out to be women as well as men, with several children who should have been at school among them. Though Vietnamese, Aboriginal and Caucasian, their solemn weathered faces gave them the uniform appearance of family members from one distinct lost race. They fished in silence. Someone had hung a plastic shopping bag of bait on one of the dioxin warning signs.

'Let's go,' Claire said, and they stopped for coffee nearby. His hand rested on the table-top and she suddenly placed both of hers over it. 'Well,' she said, and her eyes watered. She had some news.

When Nigel had begun losing his sense of taste and smell, a drastic enough occurrence for a chef, he had seen the doctor. The heavy-drinking and coke-imbibing chef's lifestyle had finally taken its toll. The prognosis wasn't good.

Stephen stared out across the harbour. One of the fishermen was hauling in a very small fish. *Catch and release,* he thought. The man unhooked it and placed it in his bag.

'Where does that leave us?' Stephen asked.

She began sobbing. 'Until this morning I swear I was leaving him. But I can't. Have you ever heard of a wife leaving a husband with cancer? In the history of the world? It just doesn't happen.'

The Albany coffee shop had amateurs' paintings of whales on its walls, reference to the town's old industry. Whales breaching at dawn, whales breaching at sunset, whales arced by rainbows, whale-mothers and calves; sentimental New Age whales, not a harpoon in sight. I glanced at the whale pictures for a few moments, then in the sudden intimacy her confession had provided, I asked this new festival acquaintance what happened next.

Her eyes, too, roamed the room before she was able to look in my direction, and they were still unfocussed as she reached for a tissue. Her words were a staccato passage of misery.

'Husband still very much around,' she said. Wordlessly, she stretched out the neck of her sweater to reveal a yellowing bruise on her neck. 'Not going out gracefully.' She must have been attractive once but now she looked sick herself. 'Love of my life gone for good.'

4
THE FEARSOME DEPTH
OF THE SEA

Viewed from a ship's rail, the boundless breadth of the open sea, and especially the idea of its fearsome depth, always registers on me as if I'm seven years old again, crossing the Great Australian Bight on the coastal liner *Manoora,* and struggling with the knowledge that the sea rolling around and beneath me is four kilometres deep.

It was my first sea voyage, travelling with my parents and three-year-old brother Billy from Fremantle to Melbourne to spend the Christmas holidays with my grandparents.

We returned on the *Manoora,* too, and the next year we repeated the week-long journey there and back, again on the *Manoora.* Even by the fourth voyage, when everything about the ship was familiar, from the ingrained aroma of coffee in the saloon to the humid porridge smell of the children's dining room, the idea that the ocean-bed was so far down was still exquisitely frightening.

I'd stand at the ship's rail, chipping off paint bubbles with my fingernails, and imagine measuring that distance on land – it would extend from our house all the way up the hill and down the highway to the coast. Then I'd visualise the same distance vertically: down, down in the darkness to the bottom of the sea. It beggared belief.

How come the enormity of this depth didn't stagger all these amiable adults patting Billy's fair head as they strode the salty promenade deck, their rubber soles squeaking and chirping? ('Nine Times Around the Deck Equals One Mile', stated a varnished wooden sign.) As if it were of no concern, they blithely amassed deck miles, played quoits, ate ice-cream sundaes, and discussed the crepe-paper hats they'd make for the Mad Hatter's Ball.

There was a morning on the first *Manoora* voyage when both Billy's and my heads were patted by a friendly man, and suddenly we were in his cabin sipping lemonade. I can't remember how or why we'd been left unsupervised. It can't have been for more than a minute or two. Nor do I recall what he said to us, or why we went with him to his cabin so quickly. He must have seized his chance.

What I remember is the man's friendly smile, and Billy and I sitting side-by-side on the edge of the man's bunk, and the man chatting cheerfully as he poured the lemonade, and him passing the glasses to us, and us taking barely a sip before our angry parents burst into the room and took us away.

I remember the man's smile turning sheepish. 'I was just giving them a lemonade,' he said.

. . .

My most vivid memory of that voyage was of my parents dressing for the Fancy Dress Ball. My mother went as the Great Australian Bite. Her punning costume was just a set of dentures she'd borrowed from the infirmary and stuck to the strap of her evening gown. She looked glamorously un-costumed and she had to pin a sign to her dress saying what she was.

But my father got into the spirit of it. He went as a drunken reveller, an Upper-Class Twit sort of partygoer. He wore his dinner suit, with his shirt and bow-tie all dishevelled, and lipstick kisses on his cheeks and collar and shirt front. My mother applied the kisses enthusiastically while they laughed and fooled about.

She was excited to be returning to Melbourne and her family. It was the most affectionate I would ever see them. To complete his costume, he held an empty champagne bottle (maybe they had emptied it beforehand) and dragged a crayfish on a string.

. . .

These annual voyages back to Melbourne were sentimental and welcome homecomings for my mother. But for us children, Western Australia had quickly become home, especially in summer when Perth's river and ocean attractions were overwhelming for a child.

Whenever I consider the notion of *home-town* – not the place where I happen to live now, or Melbourne where I was born, or even Sydney, the city where I've spent most of my adult life, I vividly recall a particular Sunday during our first summer in Perth, before the family had properly settled in.

Nothing spectacular happened this hot February day and it mightn't have stuck in my mind if the way-of-life, the arid landscape and the blistering weather hadn't still been new to us. In late spring my mother, Billy and I had left Melbourne and followed my father across the country to a better job, and the summer heatwave that rolled across our sandy suburb was a novel experience.

Both my parents were heat-dazed and short-tempered. The most recent return visit to Melbourne had revived my mother's homesickness, and the appearance of a small grass snake under the clothesline in the back yard made her agitated and weepy for a week. With an axe kept by the back door she saw herself as a Henry Lawson character, a lone wife grimly facing the dangers of the outback. (In reality my father was only ten kilometres away, at work in the city.)

None of this bothered me. My sole concern was the stout and crimson-faced Miss Langridge, who seemed to detest me. For some reason she was sarcastic about me coming from Melbourne, and she appeared always on the verge of violence. She had a dowager's hump and her bad posture meant she could easily thrust her face down to a child's level.

Her most recent attack had revealed as much self-loathing as it did a dislike of seven-year-old boys, and me in particular. As her Ruler of Many Local Timbers whacked my knuckles once more, this time for not sitting up straight, she yelled, 'You're slumping. You must not slump!' And then she hissed, 'Do you want to end up looking like me?'

Looking like Miss Langridge! That confusing nightmare image, coming on top of her fierce actions, meant that Sundays now mightily depressed me. They'd turned into a worrying forerunner to Mondays. All Sunday I anticipated Monday morning and the savage face of Miss Langridge glowering close to mine, her heavily rouged cheeks quivering with fury.

This day was another typical summer Sunday. I was home from Sunday school and waiting for lunch in the hiatus between morning and afternoon. Flattened by the heat, and by the Presbyterian teacher, Mr Hand's earnest interpretation of Jesus's relentless niceness (for some reason that morning it had involved lambs), I flopped down on the grass in the front yard.

Insects hummed and clicked in the bushes. In the kitchen, Garner Ted Armstrong, the American radio evangelist, was haranguing West Australians from some far-off place with a rowdier view of Jesus than Mr Hand's. Indoors, someone switched stations, first to a dirge of organ music, then to a local country and western program where a man and woman were yodelling competitively, then back to Garner

Ted. They gave up then and turned off the radio. Monday and Miss Langridge were looming up fast.

I stretched out on my back in the thin shade of a Geraldton-wax bush. At once I became aware of the lawn under me; the grass whose name, I already knew, was buffalo. I could feel the blunt grass blades pressing insistently against my bare arms and legs and on the back of my neck and head. I could feel their concentrated buoyancy under my shirt and shorts. I was lying on a buffalo mattress.

Maybe only an unusual small boy pays attention to grass. But after the fine soft lawn of our old Melbourne house I was impressed by the buffalo grass. It was sturdy. Each broad blade left an indentation on the skin. I liked the independence of the lawn's individual runners, the way they struck out optimistically into the dry sandy soil, forever seeking new territory. I liked how the matted strands sprang back after you trod on them. But mostly I liked the name. It was tough and cowboy-ish. If a person was suddenly and magically turned into grass, I thought, how much better to be buffalo rather than couch or bent.

As I lay spreadeagled, I felt completely supported by the grass. I let myself sink and it held me up. Magpies burbled nearby, trilling *Pop Goes the Weasel* as usual. I closed my eyes against the sunlight, and felt its heat on my eyelids, and for the first time became aware of those amoeba shapes, the kaleidoscope of patterns, swimming in my eyes.

I was conscious of a sensation out of the ordinary: a meeting of body and mind and environment. The word for this first sensual reverie wasn't one in that seven-year-old's vocabulary. *Perfection* comes close. The buffalo under my back, the warmth of the sun, the sky's clarity, the self-satisfied ruckus of the magpies, the aroma of the Sunday roast wafting from the kitchen: this place where we were now living was – at that moment – simply perfect.

I was called in for lunch then. Although I was hungry I was loath to break the spell. I felt hypnotised. I had to will myself to get up from the grass. And with the feeling of regret that accompanied rousing myself, I had a flash – and this is not a retrospective sensation – that this was a valuable feeling, one worth remembering.

For the time being, my Sunday mood, the anxious anticipation of Monday and Miss Langridge faded away. My whole attitude to life and my place in it was transformed in that drowsy quarter-hour on the buffalo. This was my place. Rarely have I been more contented than I was for that fifteen minutes. Perhaps I've never got off the grass.

5
THE SECOND ARK

My head lay on my backpack; my feet rested against a new aluminium dinghy bound for the islands; my cheek nestled against a rear tyre of a new quad bike. The new-rubber smell brought back my rubber childhood: rubber products from bicycle tyres to bathplugs were strewn all around our everyday existence as the family of a Dunlop man.

One side of my stretcher abutted a neatly crated desalination plant. On the other, mysteriously, loomed many boxes of breakfast rolled-oats and six big buckets marked *Peanut Butter*. That didn't augur well for the next fortnight's meals. Did the conservationists live on this stuff?

They appeared a quiet lot. Each member had silently sloped off to his or her bed until I realised – after a perilous urination visit to the windy gap in the stern rail, that I was the only passenger still up.

Already none of these professional ecologists fitted the greener-than-green image of an environmentalist that I was used to, living in Byron Bay. There was nothing earnest, precious or proselytising about them. No-one seemed to be on a 'personal journey'. Despite the vast supplies of peanut butter and porridge they'd brought with them, they also didn't appear an overly vegetarian or tree-hugging bunch. We'd just scoffed fried chicken.

Brent Johnson, the team leader, who'd agreed to my request to join their island project, had the build and amiably brisk manner of the Australian Rules footballer. And Andy Smith, the tall senior research scientist, would turn out to be a droll Liverpudlian with a fund of African wildlife adventure stories. They were good-humoured and efficient and I could easily imagine being friends with them in 'real life'. The other team workers were Karen, the very solemn bird specialist, and two post-graduate members, Sean, an American technical assistant, and Kelly, the fauna assistant.

These younger two, in their early twenties, lean and athletic, were wary of me, alternately shy and vaguely disconcerted to have a writer foisted on their project. For a fortnight my conversational openings to them would go nowhere. Was it just a generational matter, or had these young public servants been cautioned about talking to me? Maybe a 'loose-lips-sink-ships' warning?

Perhaps politics was a concern. We'd all be dossing down in a hut in the sand dunes together, but they were twenty-four-hours-a-day government employees. And this was a sensitive political-ecological endeavour involving strange bedfellows. It was a challenge, with the spectre of 'trillions' of dollars (I always find it hard to write that word without feeling guilty of exaggeration) hanging over proceedings.

How could I explain to people a curiosity about these particular desert islands that had begun when I was a child, continued through my teens, and had recently become an obsession?

The Montebellos had an unfavourable history, one that nevertheless excited me. Friends asked why I intended to go there. After all, I wasn't a keen fisherman any longer, and only men on week-long matey fishing trips, living aboard their hired cruisers, went anywhere near there. I'd answer, rather lamely, that I needed to get the feeling of a place where powerful events had happened when I was young.

'Like what?'

Back in 1952 the Australian Prime Minister, Robert Menzies, without formal consultation, had agreed at once to a telegrammed request from Britain's Clement Attlee to allow Britain to use the islands as a site for testing its first atom bombs.

When dissident voices were raised, the Minister for Supply, Howard Beale, issued a statement proclaiming, 'The whole project is a striking example of inter-Commonwealth co-operation on a grand scale. England has the bomb and the know-how, we have the open spaces, much technical skill and a great willingness to help the Motherland.'

So on 3 October 1952, Britain's first-ever nuclear bomb, as big as Hiroshima's, was detonated below the waterline in an old navy frigate, HMS *Plym,* anchored just off Trimouille Island. In 1956 Britain exploded a second bomb at the northern end of Trimouille, and a third on Alpha Island. Stated at the time to have a yield of 60 kilotons, the Alpha Island weapon was actually far bigger. The real yield was 98 kilotons, five times greater than the bomb that devastated Hiroshima.

The third test broke an assurance made personally by Prime Minister Anthony Eden to Menzies that the yield would not exceed 2.5 times that of the 1952 bomb (thus about 62 kilotons). The lie of its true nuclear load was concealed until 1984.

During the bomb tests, the Montebellos were occupied by British forces, backed up by hundreds of Australian servicemen, who constructed many kilometres of temporary roads, jetties and other facilities. Some structures and nuclear rubbish from the tests remained on the islands ever after.

The explosions were celebrated as great successes. Britain had triumphantly joined the United States and Russia in the Nuclear Club. Meanwhile, the radioactive fallout swept across the continent from Western Australia to Queensland's inland and coastal towns, crops and pastures, its grazing animals and populace, and out over the Pacific as far as Fiji.

. . .

'Really?' This was news to almost everyone.

Some acquaintances recalled that Maralinga in South Australia was a British bomb test site on the mainland a decade later. But no-one I knew outside Western Australia – and not many people there either – had heard of these three nuclear bombs being exploded in their own country.

The Montebello bombs were an historic monument to the dominant global political mentality of the day. And like many occurrences in 1950s and 60s Australia, their detonation was a case of *Keep quiet. Keep your head down. Don't rock the boat. The authorities must know what they're doing.*

But that was yesteryear. There was a reason for my current interest. The islands were part of an innovative twenty-first century environmental experiment to bring together the mining industry and the ecologists. The Bogeymen and the Angels. Any rapprochement between the Black Hats and the White Hats was usually pretty one-sided. Would it be any different this time?

The islands stood for the two major human preoccupations in my life to this point. At one end was the Cold War, the arms race and the prospect of nuclear annihilation; at the other, the fragile Global Economy, so intricately bound up with the environment and global warming and an economic survival dependent on digging up minerals and fuels from the earth and the sea-bed and selling them.

That was the Big Picture.

. . .

The islands were officially a prohibited area controlled by the Commonwealth until 1992 when the Australian Government gladly handed them back to Western Australia. With a new designation as the Montebello Islands Conservation Park, they were no longer a totally prohibited area, but neither were they a sensual summery playground. There was still residual, low-level radiation on Trimouille and Alpha Islands. Landings there were restricted to one hour, no soil disturbance was allowed, and no metal objects could be handled or removed.

Even discounting their history, the islands' isolation, the absence of facilities, the landing restrictions (no jetty or airstrip), not to mention the regular fierce tropical cyclones, did not exactly encourage tourists.

One obstacle after another got in the way of my visiting the islands. A back injury, the changing of state governments and consequent departmental shifts and deferred permissions; torn knee ligaments requiring an operation, a last-minute stolen wallet and credit cards, and eleventh-hour Perth-to-Karratha airline booking errors, all seemed destined to stymie my efforts. If anything, the complications made the journey even more of a fixation. I was determined to get there.

Finally, the State Department of Environment and Conservation agreed to my request to accompany an animal relocation team to the Montebellos. I said I wanted to write a book about the islands. I couldn't expect the government's conservation team to understand that islomania came close to being my personal narrative.

. . .

The island venture that I joined was the final stage of a 'groundbreaking' sixteen-year endeavour called the Montebello Renewal Project, which was turning the islands into an Australian Ark.

To be accurate, it was an Ark once removed, a second-stage Ark. The initial Ark, likened by conservationists to Galapagos Island –

a place where many delicate mammal, bird and invertebrate species that were extinct or threatened on the mainland had long thrived in peace and isolation – was for many years Barrow Island.

Then to Barrow Island came the American Chevron Corporation and its partners, Shell and ExxonMobil, with their giant Gorgon gas project, the nation's biggest-ever industrial development. It meant a huge and complex infrastructure, a large workforce and the construction of a completely new port in what was now a marine park. And – wouldn't you know it? – the site of the liquefied natural gas plant had all these endangered native animals living on it.

Around its shores, whose coral reefs would be dredged for shipping lanes, were breeding sites for dugongs and green, hawksbill and flat-back turtles. On its grasslands lived many species already vulnerable to extinction: Australia's largest lizard, the perentie; the Barrow Island euro; the spectacled hare-wallaby; the bettong; the golden bandicoot; and the Barrow Island mouse. The bushes sheltered the aptly named spinifex bird and the black-and-white fairy wren.

As well, a whole subterranean ecological community of rare invertebrates crept and slithered around the island's limestone caves. There were crustaceans, blind snakes and spider-like creatures so unusual they had only their imaginative Latin names to identify them.

Any cave-dweller called *Draculoides bramstokeri* (Bram Stoker of course being the author of *Dracula*) probably deserves respect. Not surprisingly, this arachnid has fang-like pincers to grasp its prey and crunch it into pieces before it sucks out its victims' bodily juices. Fortunately it's only five millimetres long.

Fretting over the destiny of the golden bandicoot and spectacled hare-wallaby, the joint creative minds of the mining industry and government came up with a scheme called the Threatened Species Translocation and Reintroduction Program. As part of the Gorgon deal with the Western Australian Government, it would be funded by Chevron. And Hermite Island in the Montebello Islands, named by the French navigator and naturalist Nicolas Baudin after Admiral Jean-Marthe-Adrien L'Hermite, hero of Napoleonic battles against the English fleet, would become the second Ark.

6
ISLOMANIA

I read that islomania was first identified and understood by Lawrence Durrell in *Prospero's Cell,* set on Corfu. He described it as a condition of the psyche. 'Islomania is a rare affliction of spirit. There are people who find islands somehow irresistible. The mere knowledge that they are in a little world surrounded by sea fills them with an indescribable intoxication.'

He wrote in *Reflections on a Marine Venus* that in the notebooks of Gideon – judge of the Hebrews and the person responsible for that Bible in the drawer by your hotel bed – he'd found a list of diseases unclassified by medical science. They included islomania. 'Gideon believed that we are the direct descendents of the Atlanteans, and it is to the lost Atlantis that our subconscious is drawn. This means that we find islands irresistible.'

While I found islands irresistible, by no means did I see this as an affliction. Islands had loomed as powerfully in my life as they had in my imagination. As a child I was drawn to castaway stories: *Robinson Crusoe,* of course, *Treasure Island, Swiss Family Robinson* and *The Coral Island,* which William Golding turned into *Lord of the Flies*; and especially thrilling to me, *The Island of Dr Moreau.*

I also loved Ion Idriess's adventurous yarns of the islands and tropical coast of northern Australia, featuring cannibalism, devious pearl dealers, ravenous sharks, and gropers with mouths so wide, Idriess's books informed me, they could swallow a pearl diver whole – heavy metal-and-glass helmet, canvas suit, lead boots and all. What made his stories so thrilling to me as a boy was that they often happened right here, in my own State. I saw myself partaking in these adventures one day.

I even pored over desert-island cartoons, and the American magazines my father brought home from his office were full of them. The magazines were part of my childhood worship of all things American. My favourite was the *Saturday Evening Post*. I admired its sentimental Norman Rockwell covers of freckly, jug-eared kids playing baseball, squirming in the dentist's chair, or selling lemonade on street corners. Then I'd turn to the advertisements for Hershey Bars and Pontiacs and Buicks and Camel cigarettes ('More Doctors Smoke Camels Than Any Other Brand!'). I was hungry for this American stuff.

As if they were stories, I'd peruse these glossy ads for their real meaning. To me, they *were* stories. They definitely told of lives more entertainingly parented, more interestingly shod (their shoes were sharp sneakers; mine were plain old Dunlop Volleys or, worse, Dunlop Bumpers), fashionably crew-cutted, smarter-jeaned, more dangerously toyed and more deliciously confected than mine. (Daisy air-rifles! Schwinn Phantom bikes! Whitman's Sampler Chocolates!) And then, trying to fathom why they were supposed to be funny, I'd analyse the *Post* cartoons.

I was serious about my magazine analysis, as avid as any child computer nerd today. I detected four main cartoon categories: Heaven, Cannibal Cooking Pots, Exhausted Husbands Coming Home From Work, and Desert Islands. The heaven cartoons also split into two sub-categories: St Peter Frowning at the Pearly Gates (sitting at a receptionist's desk with copious files and a quill pen, weighing up some new candidate's unlikely chances of entry) and Men Sitting on Clouds, Wisecracking About Their Past Lives. God never put in an appearance. Presumably he was in residence a few clouds away, beyond the angels with haloes and harps, and too serious for the *Post* to joke about.

The 'Honey, I'm Home' cartoons were boring. I didn't find the heaven cartoons funny either. Their hints of a questionable afterlife disturbed me. The same went for the cooking-pot cartoons. Forget the chubby black cannibals with their chef hats and bones in their noses. How could they joke about *death* – now, or as soon as that goofy white explorer in the pith helmet was nicely stewed?

On the other hand, I saw something appealing in desert-island cartoons. Granted, the ragged castaways, sitting on those little round islands with their single coconut palm, did look dejected, and the encircling dorsal fins didn't help. But I'd consider ways they could improve their lot. Build a signal fire or a raft from the palm tree. Eat coconuts and crabs. Make fishing lines from palm-leaf strips. Climb the tree and wave their tattered shirts.

There was a point to desert-island cartoons. Sooner or later a ship would come over the horizon and spot them. No matter how serious the castaways' hardships, at least they weren't in heaven or a cannibal's cooking pot. *Things could definitely be worse.*

· · ·

Islomania is usually associated with writers and painters because they're the most likely to depict their condition. Immediately you think of Robert Louis Stevenson and Paul Gaughin. But there have been many other famous sufferers, from Tiberius, tiring of Rome and retreating to rule the Empire from Capri, to Captain Cook, hero-explorer of the Pacific. Cook's third and fatal voyage is seen by psychologically inclined historians as a last wistful tour around the tropical islands before his melancholy attempt to return to England.

Obviously Fletcher Christian and the *Bounty* mutineers fell heavily under the sensual spell of islomania. So did the actors portraying Christian in Hollywood films based on the mutiny. After playing the role, Marlon Brando became enraptured by Tahiti, purchased Tetiaroa, one of the Society Islands, and another nearby islet, Onetahi, and started a Tahitian family. Mel Gibson bought Mago Island in Fiji. None of the Captain Blighs felt so inclined.

7
ROTTNEST ISLAND

If I'd been a budding sufferer before, my islomania soared when as a teenager I discovered Rottnest Island and ever after associated islands with summer and romance.

Rottnest was where West Australians lost their virginity. Or, in the case of boys, alleged they had. Thereafter they (well, I) imbued this particular desert island twenty kilometres off the mainland with a sensual quality not immediately evident to foreigners or Eastern Staters.

Arriving on Rottnest, boys and girls stepped self-consciously off the ferry (under the curious eyes of earlier, already tanned and scruffy holidaymakers, present at the jetty to check out the new arrivals), found their lodgings or camping ground, dropped off their backpacks and camping gear, promenaded in groups, shrugged off their newness, mingled, joked, and gradually, hopefully, paired off.

Around every headland lay limpid and deserted lagoons. There was a moon over Rottnest that I'd never noticed before, and glistening stars, too, obviously of recent origin. Crushed by our bare feet, fallen figs from the island's Moreton Bay trees released a heady seminal aroma over the settlement. At night, the day's salt washed from their hair, all the strolling girls smelled of Sunsilk shampoo.

Rottnest was so popular a holiday destination that accommodation needed to be booked a year ahead. Teenage campers, however, could pitch their tents for free in the dusty camping ground. To outsiders, the island's attractions seemed limited: small furry marsupials called quokkas hopping everywhere, rundown bungalows and cottages, a tin-and-fibro cinema playing dated movies (*High Society* five summers in a row), the weather-beaten Hotel Rottnest, nicknamed the Quokka Arms, and dilapidated tearooms with a limited menu of hamburgers, sandwiches, tea and instant coffee. In summer, bush-flies stuck to every damp patch of skin and crows woke you at dawn. None of this mattered. No, that's wrong. It did matter: all this was good and we adored it.

To us young islomaniacs nothing on the island ever registered as discomfort or aggravation. The white beaches and turquoise bays, egalitarian attitudes and brown-limbed girls, drove inconvenience from our minds and suffused the island with a golden summery glow of sensual promise.

Although first sexual experiences on Rottnest tended to occur *al fresco* or on a rickety camp stretcher, such was the island's allure that recalling those youthful island holidays brings to mind the words of Bill Murray in *Groundhog Day*: 'I was in the Virgin Islands once. I met a girl. We ate lobster, drank Pina Coladas. At sunset we made love like sea otters. *That* was a pretty good day. Why couldn't I get *that* day over and over and over?'

So enchanting was Rottnest's attraction, so powerful its sense of distance from the Australian land-mass and suburbia's strict moral inhibitions, that any boy and girl finding themselves swimming at a deserted Little Parakeet Bay, say, were bound to try to mimic sea otters.

Of course, most of Rottnest's magic lies in nostalgia for youth. Much of its charm is illusory, like the way the island, viewed from the mainland, often appears as a mirage. In certain weather conditions the island can spend days as an optical illusion, breaking and blurring into separate smaller islands which drift with one's memories into the wider ocean.

. . .

The nostalgic pull of Rottnest was so strong that I wrote the sensation into 'The Manageress and the Mirage', the story that led my first short-fiction collection, *The Bodysurfers*.

The experience of writing and publishing *The Bodysurfers* with my friend James Fraser was the most fun I've had in my career. We were both young, it was the first book James published, and the whole process was a combined seat-of-the-pants operation involving many lunches and drinks and late-night discussions. Part of the book's success, I'm sure, was the now-famous 1940 jacket painting by Charles Meere, *Australian Beach Patterns* (all those perfect Teutonic bodies frolicking on Bondi beach), which I found languishing in the bowels of the Art Gallery of New South Wales.

That a book of short stories should become a best-seller, never out of print since 1983, and eventually be made a BBC and ABC television mini-series, a play, a British radio series and a Penguin Classic, flew in the face of publishing lore that short stories didn't sell and helped break a few other shibboleths as well, including the accepted wisdom of the bush's overwhelming primacy over the coast as an Australian literary backdrop.

Importantly for my family, it would be the most financially successful of all my books. Literary writers rarely mention the financial side. It's bad form; leave the money talk to the airport novelists with their yachts and Maseratis. Strange, since we're the ones who are always struggling. But I owe a lot to those stories about the coast, which kept the wolf from my family's door, if not the gate, for many years.

. . .

The voyage to Rottnest – if you boarded in Perth there was twenty kilometres of river, then the same distance of ocean from Fremantle – was an important part of the experience. Depending on who was on board, wishful thinking could take place and hopeful plans be made.

When I think of the island I always think of the boats that took us there: the *Islander,* the *Triton,* the *Zephyr,* the *Temeraire* and the *Wandoo.* (These ferries made such an impression on me that I mentally transported the *Islander* across the continent in my novel *Grace* and put it down in an estuary on the central coast of New South Wales.) As a teenager, I wanted the ferry that could get me to Rottnest fastest, so I usually chose the *Islander*. The *Islander* carried the most passengers but there was such intense rivalry between the ferries that it led to open warfare.

There were two departure points for the island, the first at the Barrack Street jetty in Perth and the second at the river mouth at Fremantle, and it was always exciting to see the boats racing each other neck-and-neck down-river to be first to the waiting passengers at Fremantle. It wouldn't have been too surprising to see them firing cannonballs at each other.

The ferry wars waged for twenty-five years, from the late 1950s to the 1980s, with the ferry owners regularly accusing each other of sabotage and business shenanigans. There were countless legal wrangles and the various companies and their wars were the subject of several marine courts of inquiry. Always popular with their passengers were the one-on-one fist fights on the wharf.

With ferry sabotage, timing was everything. On 1 March 1963, the day before the Labor Day holiday weekend, a fire caused considerable damage to the *Islander*. The fire, which began in the women's lounge of the boat, was the second in successive years in the ferry's lounge. The first fire had broken out on the day before the Easter holidays.

And the year before that, the ferry had been flooded a day ahead of the Easter holidays.

After the 1963 fire on the *Islander,* the body of John Herbert Turner, 62, who owned the rival ferry, the *Triton,* was found four hours later in a partly submerged dinghy near the Narrows Bridge. In the dinghy the police found two empty four-gallon petrol drums and a jemmy. The City Coroner, Pat Rodriguez, found that Turner had died of a heart attack after deliberately lighting the fire in the *Islander.*

The *Triton* had suffered its own sabotage troubles from the beginning of its career. In October 1959, two weeks before it was due to start on the Rottnest run, it mysteriously sank on its mooring at North Fremantle. A wooden plug below water level had been forcibly removed.

As the older ferries were eventually phased out, a modern boat entered the Rottnest Island run. It was intended to be the beginning of a faster and more sophisticated ferry service, an end to the old bitter rivalries. Alas, on 8 June 1975, the *Hydroplane* was completely destroyed by fire.

. . .

There was another Rottnest burning-boat story that held me, as well as West Australian society and the academic, arts and Catholic church establishments, in its thrall for twenty years. This was because successive State administrations kept its details under wraps. Media coverage, too, was strangely almost non-existent.

It fitted Perth's image of Rottnest as a scene of adult sexual intrigue as well as adolescent romance. The story concerned the murder-suicide in 1991 of Veronica 'Bobbi' Cullen, a vivacious woman who was a kindergarten teacher and a budding poet, and a leading Perth architect, Ernest Rossen, who made a speciality of designing Catholic churches.

Contrary to established court practice, the inquest into their deaths was not open to the public and Press at the time, and my enquiries even two decades later through the Coroner's Court, the police and Freedom of Information provisions were either stalled or denied.

After four months of inquiries, the final correspondence from FOI officers stated, confusingly: 'As the Case File could not be located in relation to your application I have made the decision to refuse you access. Notwithstanding this, an Offence Report was located, consisting of four folios. Exempt matter has been removed in accordance with Section 24 of the Act because these folios contain matter which is considered personal to third parties.'

When I replied that this defied the Freedom of Information Act, the FOI officer then 'elaborated' thus: 'In this scenario the BLANK has caused the death of his BLANK after evidence of her BLANK. He has then terminated his own life by subsequently torching his vessel at sea off Carnac Island. Extensive air and sea searches failed to locate them until weeks later when the bodies were located.'

What actually happened was that early on Saturday, 21 September 1991 Ernest Rossen, aged sixty-three, and his partner Bobbi Cullen, fifty, left their home in Subiaco and went to sea in Rossen's six-metre fibreglass runabout. The boat left the Fremantle Sailing Club at 6 a.m. with three full containers of fuel.

A short time later, when the boat was fourteen kilometres off the coast, Rossen bound Bobbi Cullen in chains and threw her overboard. Then he blew up the boat and killed himself. The intensity of the explosion burnt the boat down to the waterline, reducing it to a charred shell.

Bobbi Cullen's body, wrapped in three metres of chains, was found in the ocean near Rottnest over a week later and identified by dental records. Rossen's torso was found by a fishing boat floating in the sea off Ocean Reef. He had left behind several letters.

Both of them had been married to others. Ernest and Iris Rossen, also an architect, were the parents of nine children. Bobbi had married when she was seventeen and had four children. After a career in early-childhood education she returned to university in her forties, gained a Bachelor of Education degree and studied English literature and creative writing. The week before her death she gave her first public reading of her own work. A memorial prize for women's poetry has since been established in her name through the English Department of Curtin University. Funeral notices mentioned Bobbi Cullen's grace, humour and loving and nurturing nature.

Ernest Rossen specialised in designing Catholic churches, including Our Lady of Mercy Church, St Anthony's Memorial Church and St Denis' Catholic Church in Joondanna, which was named in 2007 as one of the State's finest examples of architecture.

A death notice in the *West Australian* for Ernest Rossen said 'Died At Sea 21st September'. A Memorial Mass was held for him at the Holy Rosary Church, Nedlands, a week to the day after the murder and the boat explosion.

Died At Sea? The way this dramatic murder-suicide was presented to the community, it appeared that Ernest Rossen had unfortunately been struck by a sudden marine malady which made him accidentally bind his partner in chains and throw her into the Indian Ocean just before he and his boat spontaneously combusted.

In the absence of official disclosures about the murder-suicide, the Perth gossip-mill went into overdrive. Most rumours mentioned that Rossen was in the habit of taking younger women out in his boat to Rottnest. Then Bobbi had shocked him with the revelation that she was in love with someone else.

Rossen digested this unwelcome news. In a letter left behind, he is supposed to have written, 'We're having a last boat cruise. And then . . .'

. . .

The summer before travelling to the Montebellos I took my youngest daughter to Rottnest. The vessel carrying Anna and me was a missile-shaped craft called the *Star Flyte Express*. The words 'boat' or 'ferry' scarcely applied to this sleek craft. It was vivid scarlet and white and it looked like a cross between a tourist bus and a weapon.

The old ferryboats took one hour to race each other down-river from Perth to Fremantle, and then another hour, weather permitting, to cross to the island. Once you were out in the open ocean, the usual rowdies headed for the bar and a couple of nauseous day-trippers hung over the rail, but while you had the wind and spray in your face you could sit on your kitbag and believe you were on a *voyage*.

On my first visit to the island for twenty-five years, Anna's and my journey took twenty minutes from Fremantle and the sensation, all the passengers accommodated buttock to buttock on the moulded plastic seating indoors, was like travelling in a speeding bus.

She was nine now, and homesick, but the island loomed so quickly out of the swell, and I'd talked it up so much to her, that she cheered up on arrival. She wasn't fazed, as I was, by the surprising appearance in the old limestone settlement of boutiques and coffee shops and Red Rooster chicken as well as many nanny-ish signs warning against feeding the seagulls and quokkas (bad for their health) and walking on the sea-wall, not wearing a bicycle helmet, and riding bikes in the settlement (possibly injurious to holidaymakers).

Her spirits dropped again as we entered our small room in the Rottnest Lodge. Seeing she was already a bit limp I kept quiet for the moment about our room's past as a cell in the old Aboriginal prison or she would've started worrying about ghosts.

When I was a teenager the Lodge was called the Hostel and this quadrangle of thick-walled limestone cells was known as the Quod. We were unaware that some four thousand men and boys were imprisoned there from 1838 to 1903. There was some vague inkling that it had been a prison of some sort, but its history of Aboriginal misery and disease was unknown to us.

If a proper awareness of the dismal past had existed, we would probably have shrugged and dismissed it as clearly a pretty soft punishment, occurring in the most relaxing island in the world, a democratic place advertised as 'The Isle of Girls', with crayfish you could pluck with your hands from the reef and great beaches and the nation's best jam doughnuts.

Now that the island's prison past was recognised and token deference was paid, the Quod's past was even promoted to tourists. The cells' 'heritage' stone walls, constructed by the prisoners to keep themselves confined, were so thick they kept guests cool in summer and warm in winter. It was mid-summer now and I must say my daughter and I were perfectly comfortable.

. . .

Some of us had already regarded the Quod with awe over the years. My first entrance through its grim stone arch was like entering a harem of disdainful teenage girls guarded by suspicious fathers. Once inside, all supercilious holidaying eyes were on you. As a foolish sixteen-year-old I'd even tried to impress one guest, the tanned and flashing-eyed Roberta, by appearing there with a recently speared and bleeding wobbegong shark strung over my shoulders.

Next year I was swept away at Rottnest by a blonde convent-girl named Ruth. And two years after that, I honeymooned with her at the Quod, where her panicky complaints to a poker-faced housemaid that she'd spotted a flea on the bed-cover provided the first hint that my new and pregnant first wife suffered from a fear of fleas, ants, mosquitoes, itches, stings, spiders and bees. And some others.

The half-hour flea hunt was unsuccessful but the reason for these phobias soon became clear: unluckily, she was an uncanny attractor of anything that stung, chafed, nipped or smelled odd. Bluebottles, wasps, hornets and many allergens that rarely bothered others sought her out personally to attack.

The Rottnest nurse eventually convinced her that a bluebottle sting didn't require an emergency air-rescue across the ocean to Royal Perth Hospital, just immersion in hot water. Thankfully, the flea had fled. And our honeymoon continued.

. . .

Early one morning my daughter and I packed water bottles and potato chips, left the settlement and rode our bikes through specks of wind-blown spume from the island's salt lakes, up and down hills, until we reached Little Parrakeet Bay. I was keen to show her a beach cove that meant much to me.

At eight a.m. the bay was still deserted and pristine and unchanged from my memory. It made me happy that no footprints marred the beach. I wanted Anna to be impressed by its uniqueness. 'Isn't this great?' I said. The sand remained as pale and powdery as talc and the limestone cliffs still crumbled and tumbled into the sea and became reefs.

Already the shade was retreating and the cliffs and dunes behind us formed an amphitheatre of heat. We swam in a reef pool where I'd swum with several companions over the years. The last one had been the woman who would become Anna's mother, although that day nothing had been further from our minds than children.

The temperature contrast between beach and sea felt extreme, like entering another climatic region. Little Parrakeet Bay was both colder and saltier than I remembered, much cooler than our stretch of Pacific Ocean in northern New South Wales. The bay still had the chill of the night on it and we shivered where twenty-five years before her mother and I had made love in the warm water. (And, dropping our bikes on our way back to our lodgings, also in the gritty scrub, where we disturbed a dugite that, fortunately, rustled away from us.) Back then we'd chosen many unlikely outdoor sites when the mood struck us.

We were together for ten years, then split up for six months, got back together and were married. I'd thought we were anchored; our mooring totally secure. Another fifteen years passed during which we had two much-loved children, Sam and then, unexpectedly, Anna.

How do you pin down when a relationship changes tack? I can guess the day, the minute when I got an inkling. At least that's the sensation that engendered my short story 'The Water Person and the Tree Person' in *The Rip*. A middle-aged man paddles his new kayak, a Christmas present from his wife, out to a small island opposite their holiday cottage. Exhausted but boyishly proud of himself, feeling young again, he turns to face the cottage veranda, ready to wave to her and bask in her affectionate approval. The veranda is empty.

Now Anna and I lay spreadeagled on the sand to get warm again. She crushed rocks in her fingers and I heaped and patted damp sand over her legs so it looked as if she was driving a speedboat, then a racing car. This was really a game for younger children but she liked having my full attention. No longer homesick, she was enjoying herself.

I was trying to impart to her by osmosis what this little cove, the island, our holiday, and she, above all, meant to me. But gradually a noisy crowd arrived on bicycles and we left by ten.

8
WHALE MEAT

Despite interrupted sleep on board the barge and the vague concern that a sudden ocean swell would cause a rolling quad bike or rampant peanut-butter bucket to crush me in my stretcher, there was something to be said for waking – even five or six times – on deck, on a moonlit tropical sea.

I stood at the rail in the cool stillness under the stars and thought of the woman on the mainland and hoped we had a future together. Other women I'd finally begun to see after the break-up had been jealous of the time I wanted to give my youngest son and daughter. This one wasn't; she was warm and welcoming. The other women, already bruised and needy when we'd met, wanted instantly voiced commitment and firm arrangements to set up new households. A *future* occurred to them but not yet to me.

I didn't blame them but I was unable to make moving-in plans. I was only capable of a browsing, skimming fondness. One woman had said abruptly and accusingly, 'You're not enchanted with me.' She was attractive and intelligent and her remark took me aback. At the time I thought we were 'seeing' each other, and enjoying each other's company. We were eating calamari and flathead at a beach café. I was watching snappy waves breaking on the sand and imaginative cloud formations over the Nightcap Range and I wasn't prepared.

I laughed in nervous surprise. *Enchanted?*

'Yes, I am,' I said. It was too late.

I was turning such thoughts over in my mind as dawn broke over the ocean and a humpback breached in the low swell. Where the whale submerged again, the sea arched and rolled in on itself, slippery as mercury. Then the surface flattened into the quivery sheen of gin, and I wished my long-time friend and new hoped-for lover was sharing the experience.

Perhaps that was a test of enchantment: the wish to share experiences with a specific woman and by doing so turn them into adventures. The desire to share a whale sighting at sea, a moon-bright deck, a night on the ocean, far from land.

Up on the bridge, Grommet, the only other person awake, had spotted the whale from a distance. As it crossed our bows we smiled and mutually adored nature and simultaneously gave each other the thumbs up.

As I made this *aren't-we-blessed-to-see-a-whale* gesture, I was struck by how dramatically things had changed in a single generation. Whales first entered my consciousness as cat's meat.

It's a sacrilegious admission now, but in my Perth childhood my nightly chore was to cut up a slab of whale for Jimpy, our ginger half-Persian. The whale meat was firm, dark and fibrous, and oily and strong-smelling as well. It took a lot of pressure for a ten-year-old to cut it into cat-bite-size cubes. I'm not sure why my mother bought whale meat. I suppose it was cheap. Maybe she was loyally supporting the main industry of Albany, where we sometimes spent summer holidays at Middleton Beach. Whale-consciousness certainly didn't exist.

I doubt she thought of *Moby-Dick*. With literary whales, you think first of Herman Melville, and maybe outdoorsy writers like Jack

London and Walt Whitman. But everyone from Dostoyevsky, Joyce, Proust, Garcia Marquez, Orwell and Kipling to Bob Dylan and Tim Winton has heeded the whale's siren call.

My school English lessons ignored the literary whale in favour of *Hamlet, As You Like It,* Byron, Wordsworth and Conrad, but in geography class whaling matched such vital West Australian industries as pearling, timber and asbestos. Whaling was presented more dramatically than Collie coal or Donnybrook apples. In our Commonwealth Bank project books we glued photographs of men in woollen beanies aiming harpoon guns and brandishing flensing knives. The classic workers' pose was to stand, gumbooted, inside a dead whale. I remember Jimpy preferred sheep's liver.

The cat's-meat recollection struck me recently as I watched the dreamy-eyed folks thronging the headlands and gazing wistfully out to sea at Byron Bay, near my home. The whales, mostly mothers and calves, were returning south for the summer. As whale-watchers rushed from their cars with their binoculars, something happened to their faces. They softened. They smiled. They looked mesmerised. Grandparents and children held hands and shared a sentimental moment.

Not so long ago, from 1954 to 1962, whale-watchers were those who came to see humpback whales being winched ashore and sliced up. Whaling was Byron Bay's first tourism experience. Motorists diverted off the main highway to take in the spectacle, and excited children from Lismore and Casino were bussed into town on school excursions with the expectation of educational mayhem.

Byron Bay was far from a fashionable holiday town back then. A miasma of surf 'n' turf slaughter hung over the beach. A cattle abattoir was the other major industry and as the school buses came down the hill into town all the children would gag and cough theatrically and hold their noses. Then they crowded the jetty – later destroyed by a cyclone – to watch whales being despatched.

This educational excursion was guaranteed to hold the students' attention. The whaling station and abattoir pumped the whale and cattle offal and blood through a pipe on the jetty directly into the Pacific Ocean. This attracted schools of sharks.

The period of the Byron Bay Whaling Company's existence coincided with the beginning of surfboard riding in Australia and the town's teenage boys perfected a particular surfing routine. They would lie sunbaking on the whaling jetty, waiting for an ideal set of waves. As the sets began to roll in, they threw sheets of newspaper into the sea. This was the dramatic test. If sharks were about, the newspaper would disappear in a frenzy of foam. If the newspaper gently floated and sank untouched, the boys would throw their Malibus off the jetty and jump the four metres down into the ocean, retrieve the boards, paddle into the take-off zone and catch a wave into shore.

For onlookers there was an entertainment bonus if tiger and whaler sharks were clinging like leeches to a dead whale when it was winched ashore. To the delighted squeals of the audience, maddened sharks leapt and writhed on the jetty, snapping and tearing chunks out of the carcass. Adding to the pandemonium, boys with .303 rifles were employed to protect the catch. Amid the chaos of shark-shooting and shouting, further down the beach other teenagers would be stolidly swimming out to sea and around the ocean buoys, practising lifesaving drills for their bronze lifesaving medallions.

The town's former Whaling Inspector, Stan Nolan, paints an affecting picture of those gruesome days. The whales' survival impulses were either protective or realistic, he says, depending on their gender. 'The whales travelling north in pairs, male and female, were vulnerable for a double capture if the female was shot first.' The worried male would remain in the area and become an easy second kill. 'If the male was shot first, the female kept going because she was heading north to give birth.'

Nowadays whales trouble people's tender emotions. Not long ago a female pygmy sperm whale washed up on Broken Head, my nearest beach. The Whales Alive people and the Marine Mammals Rescue Team from the National Parks and Wildlife Service were quickly on the scene, but the whale died. An autopsy showed an abnormal growth in its uterus, and it was riddled with parasites.

Beached whales have autopsies these days and the death was described in the local Press as 'a tragedy'. The whale was buried ceremonially in the Arakwal National Park. Around the graveside people held hands and sobbed.

. . .

During the morning, trolling a heavy line in the barge's wake, Glenn caught a barracuda, two big Spanish mackerel and a pink coral trout. He cut the troublesome and toothy barracuda loose but put the other fish in the deck-wash to stay fresh until they could be cleaned and filleted. They lay flapping and bleeding on the deck, tossed back and forth in the deck-tide, their gill workings exposed and vibrating like red anemones. It became unbearable to watch them. The gasping mackerel took the longest to die.

It reminded me why I gave up fishing. I spent my childhood and early adolescence keenly fishing the Swan River and ocean coast around Perth. One day my hook caught in a tailor's eye, not for the first time. I was acutely aware of the time it took to remove the hook – and the eye came too. For once I felt sorry for the fish, and I hardly fished again. With customary double standards, however, I still ate them.

Around the barge, three more humpbacks breached in mid-morning, and dolphins surfaced, too. Several mating sea-snakes, some striped, some golden, floated past. Transported by their sexual activity, oblivious to the barge and its churning wake, they slowly writhed together on the surface like strands of the Gorgon's hair.

Then in mid-afternoon, as the heat cooked the steel deck and the sky above the horizon faded in the ocean haze from sharpest azure to slate, and we'd been at sea for thirteen hours and travelled a hundred and twenty kilometres, a line of stark, flat islands suddenly appeared in the distance.

9
THE MAYFAIR AND THE BOMB

I'm nine years old. It's an afternoon in early October when I call my mother after school from a public phone box in West Perth to make a plea. My friends are going to the Mayfair. Instead of immediately catching the 3.40 p.m. bus home as usual, can I go too?

The Mayfair Theatrette in downtown Hay Street runs a sixty-minute looped program of *Movietone* news, MGM cartoons, James A. Fitzpatrick *Traveltalks, Pete Smith* comedy shorts and dramatised documentaries. Despite the *Crime Does Not Pay* and *Pathe Pictorial* episodes being more than twenty years old (their characters sport unfamiliar hats, loud wide ties and double-breasted suits), they're entertaining in a sharply monochrome, American cops-and-robbers way that I enjoy.

The Mayfair is a popular spot. Adults and children with time to kill drop in for an hour's cheap, varied – although often dated – entertainment. The theatrette is usually well attended. It doesn't matter when you come into the Mayfair. The program has no beginning or end. Because you enter in the dark, sit there until something you recognise comes around again, and leave in the dark, there are always audience members coming and going.

One thing I like to do is buy a ham and salad horseshoe roll at the deli next door and eat it during the show. If people are constantly squeezing past you to their seats or to the exit, this can be a messy performance involving poppy-seeds, crumbs, shredded lettuce and especially beetroot.

But my visits to the pictures – and Captain Marvel, Dick Tracy and Phantom comics, and Choo-Choo and OK and White Knight bars, for that matter – are strictly rationed. I'm allowed to visit the Mayfair and the local Saturday afternoon matinees only after a suitably self-denying interval of at least two weeks between sessions.

I can't understand why my pleasures have to be staggered. My parents are fearful that if I'm indulged by two consecutive Saturdays of Tarzan, or Dean Martin and Jerry Lewis, or Choo-Choo bars, I'll become 'spoilt'. Spoilt children (generally 'only' children) are anathema to them, and it's their primary role as parents to prevent this happening. So if I spend all my pocket money at once on four comics, they're confiscated and doled out to me at the rate of one a week. Better that I play outside in the baking sun as usual.

However, as gratification has been successfully delayed of late, and I haven't been to the Mayfair for ages – and I've picked up a few helpful dish-washing and garden-weeding credits – I don't think I need to plead this afternoon. But my mother's voice sounds unusually panicky. 'No. I want you to come straight home. Hurry up or you'll miss your bus.'

Further begging is useless. 'Listen to me,' she says. Her voice becomes firm and serious. 'They've let off an atom bomb today. Right here in W.A.' I can visualise her anxiously blowing cigarette smoke out the side of her mouth so it doesn't pollute the telephone mouthpiece. 'Atom bombs worry the blazes out of me, and I want you at home.'

This first Montebello bomb was code-named *Operation Hurricane*. Within one minute the local sands were activated by neutrons, and a fall-out plume of contaminated rain and mud, activated particles and a liquefied navy frigate fell directly downwind of Ground Zero on to all the other Montebello islands except Hermite Island.

My mother needn't have worried though about fall-out striking the Mayfair Theatrette, 1500 kilometres south. Instead it was blown due east by the notoriously strong westerlies, and its radioactive particles spread across Australia.

A fortnight later, no complaints of nuclear nuisance having issued from the Perth suburbs, and mollified by Federal politicians' soothings that the British nuclear test was 'helpful' for Australia's international status, and State politicians' provincial optimism that 'this will put Western Australia on the map', my mother relents and allows me to visit the Mayfair again.

On the *Movietone* news I see the nuclear cloud rising and unrolling dramatically from the Montebellos' shores. The voiceover announcer, though Australian, is Britishly upbeat and plum-toned about the atomic event. Matching his optimism, the *Operation Hurricane* personnel, wearing shorts and sunglasses, stroll earnestly about with clipboards, appearing for all the world like entertainment officers on the *Manoora*.

10
A FRIEND TO ALL PEOPLES

The Montebello archipelago appeared like a maze stuck in the middle of the ocean. The barge slowly threaded its way around flat islets of bare limestone edged with concave, sharp shorelines. These boat-repelling platforms encircled the central islands in a protective labyrinth, and on each islet platoons of cormorants stood drying their wings in the wind. On the sandy inner islands, silently watchful, scores of high pink termite mounds, shaped like wigwams and sentry boxes, stood guard.

The archipelago would have looked exactly like this to Nicolas Baudin in 1801, and named by him in honour of Marshal Jean Lannes, whom Napoleon had created the first Duke of Montebello for his bellicose endeavours against the English.

'Beautiful mountain' doesn't even faintly describe these one hundred and eighty horizontal islands and islets of limestone and white sand plains. So liltingly does *Montebello* trip off the tongue, however, that it graces not only the original small medieval fortress village in Italy but a string of international locales and hotels, hilly and otherwise, from New York to Guadalupe.

It had looked decidedly bare and uninteresting to the morose William Dampier a century before. 'The Part of it that we saw is all low, even Land with sandy Banks against the Sea. Only the Points are rocky, and so are some of the Islands in this Bay.'

The Montebellos have a six-metre tidal range. Lime-green shallows drop abruptly to indigo depths, then just as quickly merge into turquoise sand banks. When the tide rushes in, surging through narrow channels into the lagoons, so do the bait fish, impatient as rush-hour commuters, followed by bigger reef fish, stingrays, turtles and sharks.

Our arrival was timed for high tide so the *Tom Welsby* could lower its bow door directly onto the rock-ledge shore of the biggest island in the group. This was Hermite Island, one thousand hectares of rock, sand dunes, acacia and spinifex. Here the stores and equipment could be easily unloaded, and we stepped ashore.

. . .

So this was the place that had burst into my nine-year-old brain, and was still detonating when I turned thirteen, the year of the next Montebello atomic blast, *Operation Mosaic*. This particular bomb was the reason I'd joined the Eureka Youth League. As the League's manifesto, boldly outlined in its magazine, *Spotlight,* pointed out, its immediate aim was to ban atom bomb tests in the Montebello Islands.

This accomplished, the League and I would strive to become friends to all peoples. Being 'friends to all peoples' was the League's overarching aim. I saw us as a cooler, more dramatic and courageous version of boy scouts: Baden Powell crossed with Ned Kelly; with, in my case, a touch of Louis Armstrong.

At thirteen I was looking ahead. I couldn't wait to be older and shaving and wooing long-legged girls with *La Vie En Rose* on the trumpet. Hearing Satchmo play that tune filled me with an exquisite longing and envy. I was labouring to learn the instrument from a musician with the perfect jazz name of Sammy Sharp, whose studio was just down the road from Eureka Youth League HQ, in a rundown part of Perth's central business district.

Sammy had a distinguished musical past. He'd played the London Coliseum with Ted Heath's Band and his trumpet had headed the brass section of two English orchestras. Back home, he'd led the band at the Embassy Ballroom while recording three weekly radio programs: *Sunday Serenade, Sammy Sharp's Rhythm Five* and *Thursday Night at Eight*.

By the time I met him twenty-five years later, however, up two flights of stairs in a bare, dusty warehouse, Elvis's *Heartbreak Hotel* and Bill Haley's *Rock Around the Clock* had long since arrived and swept Perth's teenagers before them. Sammy, no longer young and dapper, was grumpily resigned to teaching the trumpet to those few remaining adolescent boys with jazz aspirations and copies of *Downbeat* in their pockets.

'Here,' he said, handing me a dented cornet. 'Blow it like you're spitting a piece of tissue paper off your lips. Take this home and practise every day. Give the neighbours a thrill.' The neighbours were not delighted. There were two protesting deputations to my parents and there was no doubt they represented a wider range of opinion.

Now that I live in the country, there's a sound I often hear at night: the plaintive bellow of a cow after her just-weaned calf has been removed from her. It's a sharp moan, a sudden sorrowful blast in the dark. That's the closest sound to my trumpet playing. Apart from my ear-splitting and mournful bursts, the cornet mouthpiece painfully pressed my lip onto my irregular front teeth. The bloody spit dribbling out the bell-end during my attempt at *Cry Me a River* marred any cool jazz-lick effect.

I knew Satchmo carried a hanky for his trumpet dribble, but it somehow had a stylish effect which I couldn't manage. After six weeks I wiped my chin and regretfully farewelled Sammy Sharp. I handed him the battered cornet. 'It cuts my lip,' I explained.

Sammy didn't get up from his chair. 'Rock 'n' roll, is it?' he sighed.

I couldn't say how much I'd always loved *Heartbreak Hotel*. And in my gut I knew the Beatles and Rolling Stones and Bob Dylan loomed ahead. 'I really like Miles Davis,' I said to him.

He frowned at the condescension. 'Is that so? You better push off, son.'

If my triumphant trumpet solos couldn't lead the Eureka Youth League parade, I could still march, shoulder-to-shoulder with my fellows, against the atom bomb. The League and I were for world disarmament, more swimming pools and recreation activities for young West Australians, the vote for eighteen-year-olds, equal pay for women, equal rights for Aborigines, an end to whipping and capital punishment (hanging was still popular in Western Australia) and – last but apparently not least – a People's Government to Build Socialism in Australia.

Whatever that was. Being a friend to all peoples?

I was watching *Gunsmoke* when my father spotted a copy of *Spotlight* on the kitchen table, and his face, his eyes, his neck, his whole bald head – though not his attitudes – immediately turned red.

If I was in the room too, the generous décolletage of Miss Kitty, the dance-hall hostess in *Gunsmoke,* always made him turn slightly pink, but I'd never seen him this crimson. I thought he was having a seizure. But he knew what *being a friend to all peoples* was, and he was having none of the youth wing of the Communist Party of Australia, thank you. *Spotlight* was ripped into confetti.

Before I'd marched in a single ban-the-bomb demonstration he had a word to friends in the police force. The Party office in Stirling Street abruptly received a visit from the cops and my name was taken off the books.

I was sorry West Australian kids wouldn't be getting any swimming pools and that long-legged girls wouldn't be swooning at my *La Vie En Rose* any time soon. No-one could make me like atom bombs though.

11
HURRICANE HILL

On top of Hermite's nearest dune, beyond the reach of king tides, three basic buildings perched in the sand and spinifex. The two smaller outlying structures, former ship's containers, were storage and tool sheds. Squatting between them on the highest point of the dune was a salt-corroded hut the size of a one-car garage. This was the base camp.

As I dumped my backpack on the hut's narrow veranda, a serene tropical lagoon opened up before me. It was a perfectly formed sandy beach that reminded me of my favourite inlet, Little Parrakeet Bay on Rottnest Island. How fortunate we were to have such a crystalline swimming spot barely fifty metres below the camp.

I skidded down the dune to the water, my enthusiasm quickly vanishing as I approached the shore. Barely a metre from the beach – their wingtips, long barbed stingers, and even their pale undersides exposed – scores of stingrays calmly cruised the shallows. There were so many parading the shoreline that they brushed and unfolded against each other in a neat, ever-moving choreography. Parting the stingray schools, meanwhile, cutting back and forth across the lagoon with manic bursts of speed, were the dorsal fins of a dozen sharks.

Previous conservationist teams had dubbed the hut *Hurricane*

Hill. Not only was it built on a hill, and therefore often ravaged by cyclonic winds, but *Operation Hurricane* had been the code name of the first bomb test. The hut had two rooms: the bigger one served as the kitchen, team-leader's bedroom and office, with public-service-issue whiteboard and emergency satellite phone, and the other was a tiny door-less storeroom which also contained a bed. Instead of having to assemble a camp stretcher on the open veranda with the others, I was given this storeroom bed. Generous of them, I thought: a bed rather than a stretcher – and indoors.

Lying beneath shelves weighed down with supplies: institution-size cans of Nescafé, Four Bean Mix, Carnation Milk and Mortein insect spray, it soon dawned on me that those sleeping outside on stretchers were several degrees cooler, and had mosquito nets. And that my 'real' bed indoors gave a plangent drawn-out squeak with every fractional movement of my body.

Though barely classifiable as buildings, there were two more significant structures on the island. Downwind and downhill, squatting in the sand behind a camouflaging clump of acacia, its sides chained to the ground to prevent it flying away in a Wizard of Oz-style cyclone, was a pit-toilet, its door banging in the breeze.

More dramatically positioned a kilometre to the south-east, on Hermite's highest point and with a vantage point over the whole island group, stood the austere weathered skeleton of the old British nuclear operational headquarters.

Back in September-October 1952, this observation post ringed by sea, termite mounds and spinifex bushes was the world headquarters of British prestige. Its operations set off a year of patriotic derring-do and celebration which included the conquest of Mount Everest and the coronation of Elizabeth II. On top of this prickly sand dune, the British joined the United States and Russia in their exclusive club and proudly watched the detonation of their first, second and third nuclear bombs.

Against the cloudless sky the operational headquarters now looked less an historic building than a stark Cubist arrangement of blackened rectangles. But its grim composition still dominated the landscape as well as the skyline. I made up my mind to climb the hill to inspect it as soon as possible. In the meantime, the conservation team was quickly and efficiently settling in, unpacking everything from the barge, so I felt bound to help cart buckets of peanut butter up the hill.

Absorbed by the sight of the lagoon and the observation post, I'd initially missed the display directly in front of our accommodation. Now I noticed it. On the flat patch of sand dune in front of the camp lay a big dolphin skull, and fixed to a rough rock plinth nearby, above a sign saying 'Ginger Mick', its teeth bared in its last defiant grimace, was the skull of a big cat.

. . .

Hermite was a mere twenty kilometres from Barrow, within the same bio-geographical region and easy helicopter animal-transport range, and with much the same habitat. There were only two problems. Since the nineteenth century the Montebellos had been over-run by black rats and feral cats.

Rattus rattus and *Felis catus* were the tough, wily and wild descend-ents of old shipwreck survivors and of animals brought to the islands by Asian fishing boats and pearling luggers. A natural-history report back in 1912, correctly predicting their impact on the native animals, observed: 'There was not one rock on the whole of Hermite Island that did not have a rat sitting upon it.'

Like rival creatures in a fable, by the 1920s the cats and rats had eaten every wallaby and bandicoot, indeed every native mammal on the island. And the birds as well. Gone were the flocks of Horsfield's bronze cuckoos, fairy wrens, spinifex birds, rufous whistlers, crimson chats, Mongolian plovers and thirty-five other species of native birds. Unusually for an island, it was even made seagull-less. Sea-birds no longer bred there; the rats hung around their nests and ate their eggs as soon as they were laid.

My first question to the conservationists seemed too obvious to ask. I thought of old fairy tales, of Dick Whittington's cat, and the line from the nursery rhyme: *This is the cat that ate the rat that lived in the house that Jack built.* Cats eating rats was a given.

'OK, they've eaten everything else. The island is now populated only by cats and rats. Am I missing something here? They're natural enemies and there's nothing else to eat. Why wouldn't the cats polish off the rats?'

Brent was patient with my questions. 'For the simple reason that the rats were far more prolific breeders, turning out a monthly litter of ten to fifteen young, while these feral island cats bred twice a year, for four kittens a litter.'

Unlike cats, the rats were also keen swimmers, capable of fleeing to neighbouring cat-free outcrops and reefs. And they were omnivorous, able to thrive on the plentiful termites, seeds, grasses and shoreline flotsam that were beneath a carnivore's dignity. So while there were heaps of rats to feed the cats, there were also thousands left over, to breed. This was like Hamelin before the Pied Piper.

OK, I had another seemingly obvious question. '*Ahem*. Three nuclear bombs were exploded here, in the sea and on the land. Wouldn't the blasts and the radiation have eliminated *all* the animals?

Not quite. The nuclear fallout plumes missed Hermite Island, for one thing. Of course, like the fish, birds, dolphins, dugongs and bigger animals such as the green and hawksbill turtles, hundreds of rats and cats also died. But, in the same stealthy way as had the crabs, lizards, snakes and goannas, enough survived on Hermite and in the sheltering rocky crevices of outlying islands to build up the populations again over fifty years.

This is what the conservation team did. In 1996, with rats spread over every speck of land in the Montebello group, they hand-baited the 180 islands, islets and rocks with pellets of *Pestoff*, a cereal-based bait containing the anti-coagulent toxin Brodifacoum. The massive logistical operation, involving boats and helicopters, took them three months and, at first, seemed successful. But some devious rats survived because of Hermite Island's size and convoluted terrain. The survivors escaped the baiting, swam back to the other islands and began re-colonising them.

So in 2001 the team took to the air and bombed the rat target-spots with bigger, stronger dollops of bait. This time – to their knowledge – they got them all.

The feral cat war began in earnest in 1999. Over six weeks, helicopters dropped kangaroo-meat sausages containing 1080 poison. These baits eventually killed all but four females and one tom. Using traps which attracted them with audio and odour lures: either a cat mating call or a blended mixture of cat faeces and urine, the conservationists finally captured the rest. After outwitting the team for more than a year, Ginger Mick – he of the menacing totemic skull – was the last to be killed, in August 2000.

Then the conservationists waited ten years to ensure the islands were indeed cat-and-rat free, and no longer toxic. The first ark-load of animals and birds – 161 golden bandicoots, 111 hare-wallabies, thirty-one black-and-white fairy-wrens and thirty-eight spinifex birds – were gathered from Barrow Island and brought by helicopter to Hermite Island.

Had the second-stage Ark been successful? Nine months later, the purpose of our visit to the Montebello Islands was to see if the eradication, emigration, resettling and new breeding had actually worked.

12
THE BUSHES OF DOOM

At first light next morning we set off in Indian file into the dunes. The day was already hot and still. We were still a month away from the start of the cyclone season but cyclones are a constant preoccupation in the region. In 1996 the Montebello and Barrow islands experienced the strongest wind gust ever recorded on earth: 408 km/h (253 mph) during Tropical Cyclone Olivia. No wonder the lavatory was chained to the ground.

Surprisingly, the fierce year-round westerlies that blow across the continent, which were the bane of the Dutch East India Company's trading vessels in the seventeenth century, feared by seafarers for centuries and responsible for more than 1400 known shipwrecks along the 20,000 kilometre length of the west coast (and which even these days make the Perth-Sydney air route nearly one hour faster than Sydney–Perth) did not deter British scientists from detonating three nuclear bombs here. It couldn't possibly be windy every day, they imagined.

On the conservationists' advice, I was wearing a long-sleeved shirt and jeans as protection against the spinifex spikes. There was no small-talk as we trudged over the sand-hills. Hunched under their backpacks and bush hats, everyone looked tired and drawn.

I sensed a certain reserve. Was it just early-morning reticence or did their silence have anything to do with my endlessly squeaking bed during the night? Maybe I had even snored, as had been alleged in the past? The possibility embarrassed me. I hoped the heavy silence was caused by the heat and sudden physical activity. Within minutes there was a dark patch of sweat on the back of every shirt. We plodded on.

Everywhere in the sand there were clear animal tracks, from tiny scratches to bigger claw marks, but no actual mammals or reptiles to be seen. In the rosy dawn, bush-flies woke to breakfast on our damp skin. Perhaps optimistic that our trudging would flush out a sleepy bandicoot from the bushes, a lone sea-eagle soared above us.

Spread widely in the undergrowth lay corroded drums, sheets of rusty galvanised iron, broken concrete bunkers, coils of barbed wire and the occasional broken Tennent's beer bottle from the long-ago British incursion. Their bomb squads, sailors and scientists hadn't bothered to clean up after themselves. They occupied a strangely submissive country for many months, exploded three nuclear bombs, surveyed the atomic blasts with satisfaction, officially received the Mountbattens, celebrated with extra ale rations, left behind their military and nuclear trash, and sailed home into the wind.

. . .

We got to work marking out a grid system with metal stakes and sledge-hammers. Here, later that afternoon, the team would set regularly spaced cage-traps for bandicoots and wallabies. Marsupials come out to eat at night. The traps were baited with a tasty lure they couldn't resist: pellets made of peanut butter and rolled oats. The peanut-butter mystery was solved.

When staking out a grid pattern in the tropics, on rough ter-rain, measuring distances and hammering stakes in precise spots fifty metres apart, you still endeavour to work, and walk, in straight lines. Unless it's impossible to tramp through an obstacle, there is no going around it. Perhaps you're also keen to show these outdoor types, these conservationists who spend half their lives in the rugged, sandy landscape of Western Australia, that you're not just a desk-bound writer fazed by the physical stuff. Pathetically, this is especially the case when you're partnered with a woman.

My grid partner was Karen, the stolid and uncomplaining bird specialist. She directed the positioning of the stakes. I was the labourer, carrying the stakes and wielding the sledgehammer.

I slammed heedlessly into the spinifex bushes. These *triodia,* to give them their botanical name, grew in hummocks, sometimes in an artistic circle formation, as if they'd been arranged by sculptors or extra-terrestrials. Some hummocks were head-high and igloo-sized, some cleverly masked a deep ditch or nuclear-test debris. Their leaves are stiff and pointed because they contain silica, the mineral contained in sand. They're an impregnable shelter for spinifex birds and lizards, and prevent sand-dune erosion. On the mainland, only the alternative of starvation will entice cattle to eat them; they're about as nourishing as cardboard. Termites, however, enjoy their leaves; and lizards like eating termites.

The leaves are the size and sharpness of gramophone needles. I quickly learned that ordinary Levis weren't thick enough to shield you from these spinifex spikes. Five days later, when I'd finally forgotten the itchy sting of the first day's spinifex encounter, I noticed that the pin-cushion effect had gone into reverse. The spikes were starting to work their way out of my flesh, via lividly infected pustules. On their journey out of my skin, they were passing new spikes working their way in. I soon thought of the spinifex as the Bushes of Doom.

. . .

As I crashed along though the sand and spinifex, I barely avoided falling into a crumbling cement blockhouse half hidden by wirewood and kapok bushes. I wondered at the building's purpose. Some sort of observation post, I supposed. I remembered that the British had a big defence system here back in the 1950s amongst the grit and prickles, alongside the black rats and feral cats.

It was Britain's main post-war military and scientific endeavour, a highly sensitive operation. They were at daggers drawn with the Americans. The nuclear competition between the allies had become a bit testy. It was already a badly kept secret and both countries were jealous of each other's nuclear knowledge.

Kicking aside a Cold War beer bottle, I hammered a stake into the rubble of the blockhouse, and we moved to the next point on the grid.

13
THE GAS MASK INCIDENT

It's a Saturday afternoon in late spring when my friend Tony and I stumble upon a World War II bomb shelter hidden in the sand and bamboos under the limestone cliffs of the Swan River estuary.

The war was vague and distant history, only ever brought to mind by a discovery such as this, but before I was born the city of Perth was worried it would be bombed. The Japanese had already targeted Darwin and Broome in 1942, killing hundreds of people. And then they attacked other northern West Australian towns: Wyndham, Derby and Port Hedland.

The government kept secret the numbers of casualties in case it affected morale. But down south in the suburbs of Perth, people hastily dug air-raid shelters in their back yards, bricked them in, and fitted them out with torches, spare batteries and spare sets of keys, water bottles, reading matter, and emergency tins of spaghetti, tobacco, matches, chicory coffee, camp pie and Tate & Lyle's golden syrup, for energy under fire.

These underground caverns often still remained into the 1950s and 60s, their contents unopened and rusting on mouldy shelves, sand seeping through their walls, and inhabited by red-back spiders.

The brick bomb shelter we've found by the river is scrawled with swear words and exaggerated drawings of genitalia. Now I'm twelve I pretend not to be surprised, although the sudden ferocity of this visual attack of penises, vaginas and breasts makes my head spin.

At the lowest level of its cobwebby, urine-smelling interior is a pool of inky water teeming with tadpoles. The tadpoles, fat and tar-black, are sharing their pool with cigarette butts and what seem to be elongated jellyfish.

'Frenchies!' Tony sniggers.

I agree. They're frenchies all right. I've never actually seen a frenchie before. I don't really know what they are. But somehow the frenchies, the piss smell, Tony's sniggering, the cigarette butts and giant dicks and tits and dark female triangles all seem to be mysteriously connected. The atmosphere is pressing down on me and I suddenly guess what the frenchies are for.

In a desultory way, avoiding the condoms, we start scooping up tadpoles in a golden-syrup tin. But in the atmosphere of stink and sexual mayhem we have no heart for it, and let them go. On our way out of the shelter, we spot two old gas masks on a shelf behind some rusty Player's tobacco tins. Of course we grab them, and as soon as we're outside in the fresh air we decide to adapt them into underwater masks.

We strip down to our underpants and try out the masks in the river. The water is chilly and full of jellyfish, and the masks have lost their war-time gas-resisting apparatus, but by holding the thick corrugated rubber tubes out of the water like snorkels we can breathe well enough. When I reach out to touch a rock or a shell, or a globe algae that resembles a tiny lemon-coloured brain, the riverbed turns concave and looms away out of reach. But although the lenses distort everything and the air tastes of old tyres, the masks work. I can see under water.

Before river water seeps in and the novelty wears off, the glass visors provide a unique sensation that has fascinated me ever since: of being able to see above and below water simultaneously. And of being able to see at eye level the river's actual surface skin, the liquid dividing line. Though distorted into a curve this particular day, the line looks measurable and is actually grey, not colourless. The sensation conjures up that archaic but accurate poetic description of the contrasting air and water worlds as differing 'realms'.

On shore again, if you're shivering in the afternoon spring breeze, waiting for the wind to dry you, semi-naked and vaguely bored twelve-year-old boys, the corrugated rubber tubing dares one mask handler to stretch out the tubing to its full length. And, in a nonchalant, experimental sort of way, to fire the mask at his companion's buttocks.

This is what Tony does. He fires it at close quarters. And as I turn slightly to see what's happening, the heavy glass and rubber gas mask hits me smack in the cold, contracted testes and drives the left one up into my pelvis.

. . .

Out of embarrassment, until the aching nausea gets worse, I don't mention the gas-mask incident to my parents for several days. Then they have the local GP poke inquiringly into my scrotum with his long fingers. Even more embarrassingly, at the Mount Hospital a week later, a gingery freckled nurse, wielding a frightening razor and a bowl of soapy water over my downy groin, begins to shave the four or five hairs down below while cautioning, 'Don't get excited now or I'll have to get the cold spoon!' The warning is unnecessary.

A Perth specialist, Hector Stewart, is called on to operate on me. For reasons to do with medical status – as if willing Perth's windy St George's Terrace to be London's Harley Street – a couple of local surgeons with Royal College of Surgeons' degrees have gone beyond mere 'doctor' and have travelled around the title cycle again to be called 'Mister'.

'Don't forget to call him Mister,' my mother says.

Mr-not-Dr Stewart subsequently retrieves the gas-mask-shunted ball and, apparently to keep it in place, sews my scrotum to my left thigh – a quarter of the way down.

The discomforting weirdness of this hernia-correction procedure is surreal enough to blight change-rooms and public showers for my entire adolescence. I'm beyond mortification. In the agony of cadet-camp, beach and after-sport shower stalls thereafter – if I dare shower at all – I stand in right profile so my elongated scrotum is, hopefully, not seen.

Months later, the stitches removed, the stretched and sinewy scrotum freed, I survey myself warily in the mirror and discover that the lopsided, now-thirteen-year-old boy standing in front of me has a vigorous growth of pubic hair and three testicles.

14
DRINKS

Having come this far and delivered us to the Montebello Islands, the *Tom Welsby*'s captain and crew, Boxhead, Grommet and Glenn, decided to have several days break in the islands. They moored nearby in a deeper lagoon from which music and convivial laughter issued each night. One evening they came to our camp for drinks and dinner, generously bringing with them fillets from the fish they'd caught on our voyage out.

So how did the skipper come by the nickname 'Boxhead'? It was explained that he had a German ancestor. *Oh*. 'Grommet' of course was a surfers' term for a young surfer, even though in this case the grommet was a weather-beaten, laid-back *old* surfer – and, back in port, had been the modest rescuer of the drowning fisherman.

In one of those rare moments guaranteed to cheer up an author, it was the un-nicknamed Glenn who endeared himself to me, however, by producing a salt-stained hardcover copy of *The Shark Net* for me to sign. Not since 23 September 2010 had I felt so chuffed, when the salesman in Reece's Plumbing Supplies in South Fremantle, noting my name on my credit card, praised my book while I was buying a new toilet seat.

I learned later that rather than my brusque description of the *Tom Welsby* as a 'barge', in Department of Transport terminology it was registered as a 'bow-door landing craft'. As for the barge's name, Tom Welsby had been an early twentieth-century Queensland business-man, politician and sportsman known as 'Bung Bung'.

Interestingly, his maiden speech in State Parliament deplored the passage of the Liquor Act of 1912, which specified that no longer could any person from the age of fourteen purchase liquor. Bung Bung was in favour of everyone, regardless of age, enjoying alcohol.

Bung Bung would have been right at home in this part of Australia, especially in this generation. The heat, the isolation, the fly-in, fly-out mining-shift structure, the absence of family life, made heavy drinking, and its chaotic results, inevitable. At the Karratha airport bar, I'd seen the sign: *Spirits or Full Strength Beer No Longer Sold.* I also noticed that the police station was situated next door to the pub. Sensible Wild West thinking: placing the sheriff's office alongside the saloon.

None of this would surprise a team of researchers from Queensland's University of Technology, whose three-year study entitled *Booze, Blokes and Brawls,* appeared in the British Journal of Criminology the month I was on the island. It said Australia's mining industry was propagat-ing 'a dark underbelly of alcohol-fuelled violence and social disorder'.

The study was the first to examine the social impact of Australia's mining boom. The report's author, Professor Kerry Carrington, claimed that the thousands of men constantly flying into and out of regional mining sites in Western Australia and Queensland were 'catastrophi-cally denigrating' nearby towns. The rotating rosters of fly-in, fly-out workers had no allegiances to the local communities, large disposable incomes and few entertainment options except the pub. There was a hugely disproportionate ratio of men to women.

Professor Carrington described a culture of 'organised drunken-ness', with the mining camps bussing the men to the pub at the end of a twelve-hour shift, where they were surrounded by concrete and steel mesh to keep them contained. The low numbers of women and the high alcohol intake had resulted in twice the national rate of violence. Prostitution was rife and there were problems of mental health and sexually transmitted diseases. The industry and governments were turning a blind eye, the professor complained.

The report was immediately rebuffed by the West Australian government and mining companies as 'ill-informed'.

Nevertheless, alcohol is never far from your mind here. Seeing there were few named features on the charts to aid their navigation during the bomb tests, the British took it on themselves to name the Montebellos' bays. They named them all after booze: Hock, Claret, Whisky, Stout, Cider, Champagne, Chartreuse, Burgundy, Chianti, Drambuie, Moselle and Sach bays. They also named Rum Cove and Sherry and Vermouth lagoons. Appropriately, there is a promontory named Hungover Head.

Not content with naming this Australian territory after alcoholic beverages (without local opposition, the names became official), the Royal navy then gave the most substantial islands in the Montebellos – apart from the two biggest, Hermite and Trimouille, named by Nicolas Baudin – the names of gentle English flowers.

This arid, sandy, tropically cyclonic and post-nuclear environment, as far removed from an English country garden as is possible on the planet, now has islands called Primrose, Bluebell, Crocus, Buttercup, Aster, Carnation, Dahlia, Daisy, Dandelion, Foxglove, Gardenia, Jonquil, Ivy, Hollyhock, Marigold, Pansy, Rose and Violet.

The Royal navy cartographers weren't done yet. Next they named the Montebellos' hills after zoo animals, such as Giraffe and Lion, the headlands after British Prime Ministers (Atlee, Churchill, and so on) and the channels after scientists (Bunsen, Wheatstone and Faraday).

One day in 1994 when strong winds forced the West Australian cat

and rat eradication team indoors in the hut on Hurricane Hill, the conservationists decided to strike back against the English flowers. On the
west side of the archipelago there were still many smaller un-named
islands. They named them after Australian plants. Most of these are
now official and include Eucalyptus, Waratah, Boab, Spinifex, Banksia,
Marri, Karri, Wattle, Mulga, Snakewood, Bloodwood and Snappy
Gum islands.

15
WALLABY WORLD

Birds bathing noisily in the dew puddles on the roof woke us long before the camp alarm clock went off at five next morning. The birds' racket seemed to please everyone, especially Karen, the bird observer. Until five months before, when they were transported here, Hermite Island had hardly any birds.

Karen had the most onerous job of all, rising at four a.m. to set off into the dark scrubland. There were no real trees on the islands and she had to catch sight of the birds as they rose from the bushes with the dawn. Her job was to confirm whether breeding had happened. Guesswork was involved, and she had to try to spot them before the chaos of their rooftop shower.

Birds are hard to count, particularly timid ones that hide in the shrubbery. The spinifex birds were especially hard to locate and monitor, as they were, in conservationist-speak, 'a cryptic species'. As thirty-one fairy-wrens had been brought across the sea from Barrow Island, and Karen could tell which sex was which, it was possible (for her, at least) to ascertain that this species' numbers were increasing.

'How do you know you're not counting the same ones twice?' I asked her. She gave me a cryptic look. 'Because I see them in widely different habitats.' Karen had to do more walking and squinting into the sun than anyone else. On the second day she was struck by a wicked migraine which put her to bed for two days with a towel over her eyes.

The heavy nightly dew-fall in these parts left puddles on the roof and on the rocks of the shoreline. For the birds and animals it made up for the absence of streams and springs and the long dry season on the island. As for the humans' water supply, the team efficiently managed to put the desalination plant together, and within thirty-six hours we were gulping cold glasses of ocean.

Even though the Indian Ocean is the world's second saltiest sea, after the Atlantic, the desalination process made the water from the bay taste less salty than water from any Perth suburban tap. It also occurred to me that the first bomb, *Operation Hurricane,* was exploded in the sea nearby. Fallout from all three bombs had occurred over the ocean. Still radioactive? Let's hope not.

In the early dawn our solemn Indian file shuffled over the dunes and through the nuclear-test rubble and gramophone needles, this time to check the soft-catch traps that had been placed at every grid stake the evening before.

There was a reason for the early-morning starts: to avoid heat-stressing any trapped animals. It was the first example I noticed of the team's respectful but businesslike attitude towards their wildlife charges. It was an approach best described as 'brisk tenderness'.

About half the traps had been successful. The peanut butter and rolled oats had worked their magic, and each victorious trap had either an anxious wallaby kicking and hissing inside, or a docile plump bandicoot cowering and snuffling. Often a skink or bigger lizard had gate-crashed a trap as well.

The trapped marsupials were each measured and weighed, Brent and Kelly holding them firmly to their chests, and had their new particulars checked against their previously micro-chipped details.

Then they were released. If an animal had been born since the ark landed, its handlers were immensely pleased and the newcomer was also micro-chipped.

Satisfyingly to the team, every one of the Barrow Island emigrants had put on weight since their translocation, and most of the females were either pregnant or had raw pink babies in their pouches. In the wallabies' case, their gangly hairless offspring resembled Jar Jar Binks from *Star Wars,* while the baby bandicoots, attached to nipples bigger than their bodies, looked like shiny shelled peanuts.

Life can be rough in Wallaby World. There was a moment of group uneasiness while I was solemnly advised not to be upset by what I might see there. Female wallabies and kangaroos, I was informed, were not overly maternal. If stressed, a mother was apt to expel her offspring from her pouch without a qualm. This was because Nature was always pressing forward. There was always another baby growing in the womb, ready to pop into the pouch.

'Best not to be squeamish if we have to euthanase a baby that she's ejected and won't take back,' said Brent. 'One that's too young to cope in the outside world.'

The verb 'euthanase' seemed to often crop up in their conversation. It was the first time I'd heard it applied to anything other than old, sick humans caught up in legal-political-medical-religious controversy. It was an even more euphemistic term than the veterinarians' 'putting down'. I had an unsettling image of them wringing the neck of Jar Jar Binks or crushing him underfoot.

As it happened, one trap shortly afterwards did contain a mother and infant pair. This particular baby was three-quarters out of the pouch, and she soon ejected him out of it. He squirmed, helpless, in the bottom of the cage. His eyes weren't yet open and he had no hair. He was surprisingly raw-looking and angular and big-eared and unpre-possessing, and it shocked me when Brent, who needed to measure and weigh the mother, abruptly passed him to me.

'Hold on to him,' he instructed. 'Hug him close to your chest for your body warmth.' A vast and embarrassing responsibility suddenly fell on me. The creature's eyes were still shut, yet protruding, and showing bright blue behind the translucent closed lids. More than anything he looked like something embryonic created by science fiction.

The sun was rising over the hill and with the first rays the bush-flies arrived and zoomed in on the moist baby wallaby. Slightly discomfited at the mandatory tenderness, I brushed away the flies and nestled him close to me. I hate forced emotion yet in seconds I felt sentimental about Jar Jar Binks. Suddenly the future of Australia's threatened wild-life was in my hands. I didn't voice anything but my mind screamed, *'The little tyke must live!'*

Silence, then deep sighs all round. A decision was made. Brent sat down on his portable stool and gripped the struggling mother wallaby with his knees and one elbow. He took Jar Jar Binks from me. Painstakingly, and with some difficulty, he began gently folding and pushing him head-first back inside the pouch.

Had the mother's instincts already moved on? The pouch seemed to have lost its tension. It was prolapsed and cramped in there, and it took some time to insert him. There must have been maternal mus-cular resistance because no sooner did Brent manage to get one of his legs inside than the other leg, or his tail, or a paw, would pop out. But eventually he managed to prod all of Jar Jar Binks back inside. Then he carefully secured the pouch with surgical tape.

'That'll hold him for a little while. Maybe she'll accept him, maybe she won't. Fingers crossed.'

He released the mother and she bounded off erratically, pro-grammed to elude and confuse a pursuing enemy. Zig-zagging madly over the sandy scrub as if the hounds of hell were after her, she carried her sealed issue over the dunes and far away.

16
THE OBSERVATION POST

Hermite Island was far too remote for my laptop to get broadband reception. And I'd been told that mobile phones also didn't work here. But I'd promised Anna I'd try to phone her nightly before bed.

The bedtime Fats Domino *Blueberry Hill* phase had recently been superseded by a sing-song chant in place of prayers that this small animal-lover had composed herself, and insisted on delivering and receiving to and from each of her parents. The sweet and zany two-way mantra stressed that her love for her mother and father, and ours for her, exceeded the tweets and moos, hops and poos of all the birds, cows, kangaroos and guinea-pigs in the world.

In her needy state since the break-up, this was an important ritual. I had to persevere, to try to pick up a phone signal from Barrow Island. By trial and error, on one particular dune abutting the camp, I finally found a five-minute communications window each afternoon when Telstra enabled me to get through to her. Because Daylight Saving in New South Wales put her three hours ahead, the call fortunately coincided with her bed-time. On the island, it also coincided with the team's afternoon rest period on the veranda before the evening's trap-baiting.

To my family, my daughter's ditty had long since ceased to be unusual. To anyone else, however, the sight of a man standing beside the grimacing skull of a cat, atop a sand dune on a remote island in the Indian Ocean, flies crawling on his sweating face and ants over his legs, holding his phone high in the air to ensure a signal while shouting into the wind a lullaby about guinea-pig poo, might have seemed deranged.

The conservationists definitely looked intrigued at the daily performance. Silent glances passed between them, and the occasional meaningful cough, but no-one said anything.

. . .

There was one place in the archipelago where the phone reception might be clear and constant: the highest point, the old British nuclear operational headquarters and observation post. One day I decided to make the climb before the afternoon heat was at its height. But even before noon it was a sweaty, stiff ascent up the jagged and prickly fifty-degree slope.

Kelly accompanied me, in a fashion. I had the feeling the youngest party member had been quickly assigned to see the writer didn't trip in a bandicoot hole, break his neck and bring bad publicity to the Threatened Species Translocation and Reintroduction Program. However, as either shyness or embarrassment prevented her approaching any closer to me than 100 metres, she could hardly have broken my fall if I'd tumbled down the hill onto the jagged limestone teeth of the shore.

It was difficult enough picturing the nuclear boffins and uniformed admirals and generals, including the First Sea Lord, Admiral Mountbatten, hauling themselves up through the rocks and the Bushes of Doom to observe the tests. It was impossible to imagine a perspiring

Lady Mountbatten making the climb in hat, frock and high heels. Either a clear, gently winding path to the building had once existed or – of course – everyone was helicoptered in and out.

The observation post was bigger than I'd imagined: the size of a suburban house. Although several kilometres from the Ground Zero sites, it looked bomb-blasted itself. It was gutted and surrounded by rubble, its metal skeleton darkly crusted and holed by corrosion. A loose window frame banged in the wind, as it probably had for five decades. Rusty barbed wire and the webs of generations of orb spiders still barred entry at the door, but anyone could walk through where the walls had once been.

Its site was well chosen. From here the whole Montebello archipelago unfolded in the sun like a pirate's treasure chart, a vivid map of hills, sandy coves, lagoons, mangrove thickets and island upon island stretching into the distant haze. It was hard to imagine a more beautiful or tranquil nuclear test site.

. . .

From my position now at the old observation post and detonation point the only sign of human existence was a lone yacht sheltered at anchor in the lagoon immediately below. Pristinely white, it appeared strangely vulnerable, a spotless toy boat alone in the ocean.

A tiny man in a hat sat fishing on the stern. Dark specks and smears – scattered shadowy sharks and rays – nosed through the shallows. Two rounder silhouettes indicated a pair of turtles. Then abruptly out of the north the shadow of a giant dragonfly passed diagonally across the white boat in the lagoon. The mining-company chopper clattered over my head and vanished in the direction of Barrow Island.

In the sudden silence the wind banged the old window frame and whistled through the wreckage. Two *ta-ta* lizards, miniature *Jurassic*

Park velociraptors, peeked out of the rubble, studied me crossly, and ran urgently down the hill on their back legs, as if spreading news of the interloper.

I discovered excellent reception on my mobile phone, and eagerly called friends in Sydney. I was in adventurous outdoor mode, keen to share my enthusiasm for my uncommon surroundings. 'Guess where I am?'

The calls were anticlimactic: 'Monty-where? Are you outdoors? It sounds very windy there.' Not one of them had heard of the Montebellos and their bombs.

It was still too early to ring my daughter for the guinea-pig poo lullaby. The phone signal wasn't wasted though. For five minutes I was able to reach my new, not quite unattainable, love. She was interested in what I had to say.

On my tortuous way down the slope, grasping at bushes to keep from falling, another aircraft materialised from the north, circling low over the islands. This was the coast-watch plane, on the lookout for the boats of asylum seekers and shark-fin and trochus-shell poachers. It paid me close attention for a minute, then continued on its way.

17
THAT SPRING

That spring we would meet of an afternoon at my rented house in Fremantle and drink a glass of wine and swing between moods of animation and stillness, and deliberately not go to bed, deliberately not make love, because she was married and unattainable. Unhappily and unwillingly unattainable, but unattainable nonetheless.

We'd remain sitting on straight-backed wooden chairs in the kitchen, the kitchen – decorated with holiday-cottage driftwood, carved fish and faux Mediterranean knickknacks – being the safest, most rigid room in a house, our knees touching, while the bedroom across the corridor – the room that was the Elephant in the Room – pulsated and beckoned but stayed unentered.

Our friendship was of long standing and our conversation was about anything and everything, from Pliny the Elder to the female obsession with Colin Firth as Mr Darcy. We had a matching sense of humour. Once we even avidly discussed string – the way shop assistants in the past used to wrap parcels and snap the string with a deft flick of the wrist – and with our amazed laughter at our conversation (we were both suddenly fascinated by *string*) we knew we were in love.

We were alternately animated by trivia and stilled by reality, overwhelmed at the discovery of rare kindred spirits, and when she left, with her single farewell kiss still on my mouth, I would have to take a long walk around the boat harbour.

I'd tramp through the dandelions, veldt grass and pigface along the verges of the breakwater, the breakwater littered with anglers' cigarette butts and rubbish. No-one was less environmentally conscious than fishermen, I'd think, becoming angry with their butts, plastic bait packets, prawn heads and nylon line tangles always crossly left behind when the sky was overcast and the fish weren't biting. Unfulfilled people could be bitter, reckless and disorderly.

Yacht stays tinkled in the sea breeze and oily work boats swayed on their buoys and I thought of my feelings for my passionate not-quite lover and of the growing impossibility of the kitchen-and-Pliny-and-string situation and of the possibility of life together.

One morning that particular grey spring I experienced the novel sensation of raindrops falling on my eyeballs. I was swimming backstroke lengths in the Fremantle public pool, staring up at the clouds gusting past while *Volare* and *Thriller* and *Que Sera Sera* seeped into my thoughts. In the adjoining lanes, elderly bouncing women were performing water gymnastics to taped music.

I swam a couple of Dean Martin laps and two Michael Jackson laps and a Doris Day lap and then the aquarobics instructor told the women to applaud themselves for their morning's efforts and, chattering away, they left the water.

In the sudden silence I reached the end of the pool and kicked off again with the renewed resolve of the fresh lap. It was simple. Life now had three necessities: my children and my writing. And her.

. . .

93

We went back so far that when I first saw her she was wearing the uniform of an army officer. She was a student funding her way through university in the Army Reserve. Some scientific or pharmaceutical branch of the military: Bunsen burners rather than Bren guns. Anyway there wasn't much marching or weaponry involved.

Strange clothing for a beautiful young woman, I thought, even the lightweight summer khaki. Two pips on the epaulettes. The uniform not masking her breasts; her pale blonde hair just flicking her collar. Her skin, too, was pale, Nordic, and without a freckle or blemish. Undoubtedly, she was the most attractive second-lieutenant in the service.

Even the unexpected uniform couldn't draw my attention away from her most noticeable feature, her Scandinavian hair.

Except for the one who was her boyfriend, who treated her casually – not looking up, secure in his ownership – all the males in the room stopped talking when she came in. A few seconds of silence passed before anyone could gather their wits and then, as one, we all came to attention and saluted.

· · ·

That spring when she visited me every afternoon, and we sat chastely in the kitchen and drank wine, the view from the house veranda was the same nineteenth-century skyline of pine trees and limestone you saw in historic photographs of the port.

You could see over the old prison walls to Fremantle harbour and beyond, where the live-animal ship for the Middle East halal-meat trade was crammed with sheep and all lit up like a city block at night, and the lines of waiting tankers and container ships in Gage Roads brought the scene abruptly up to date.

Then the wider Indian Ocean stretched to the horizon and to Rottnest Island and the panorama became timeless again.

18
THE ANCIENT MARINER

The night after my visit to the old nuclear observation post on Hermite Island we had another guest for dinner. The man from the pristine white yacht paddled a kayak to the island and turned up at our camp. His name was Don Drabble and he lived aboard his yacht, *Scarlett*. Such hospitality was expected and given in the north-west. He brought two coral trout, which he filleted for the barbecue, and a wine-cask bladder of Reisling slung over his shoulder. He was a salty old sea-dog.

Don was in his late fifties. He was bald, wiry and barefoot and his long ginger beard and sideburns were so tangled together with his copious chest curls that it wasn't clear whether the general hair flow was orange and downwards, or white and upwards. He resembled the castaway Ben Gunn in *Treasure Island*. But for an Ancient Mariner he was dapper. His long-sleeved pink shirt looked ironed for the evening's socialising, and his Hawaiian board-shorts rejoiced in a rakish hibiscus motif.

Don was proudly garrulous about the difficulties of maintaining a sea-vagabond lifestyle in the twenty-first century. As he drank from his Riesling bladder, he told of his running fights with the mining companies' 'security stooges', who tried to prevent him mooring off their islands. He mentioned hectoring radio calls from the Customs, navy and Fisheries Department planes.

'You'd be surprised how often the various authorities and I have a chat,' he said.

The swashbuckling outlook is not a rare viewpoint on Australia's north-west frontier, home to many daredevil dropouts and treasure hunters. The Pilbara has long championed the anti-establishment capitalist, the libertarian adventurer.

Don went on to talk of all the pirates, villains and unhanged murderers he'd known, and his close shaves with cyclones and official corruption in various lands. He interspersed these anecdotes with tales of his three African wives and daughters in Mombassa. Then there were his blood-curdling adventures while skippering a barge down the east coast of Africa, culminating in his doing time in a Somalian gaol.

This was not a standard dinner-party conversation. While we sat mesmerised in the sand outside Hurricane Hut and marsupials scampered over our feet, Don talked solidly for two hours. He had the habit of volunteering something dramatically off-the-wall, and the random statement, fascinating in its lubricity and brooking no answer, would hover defiantly in the air for some minutes.

'According to all my wives, the Ugandan marijuana made me perform like Superman,' he announced, out of the blue. He swigged from his wine bladder, stroked his beard, grabbed and twirled handfuls of chest hair. 'Unstoppable,' he chuckled.

We absorbed this information for a moment. Eventually I said, 'Somalia, whew. That must have been tough.'

'What a shit-hole Somalia is,' he enthused. 'Everyone carries a knife in order to stab their girlfriends in the buttocks during arguments.'

'Really?'

'Women squat down in front of their cooking fires with their legs apart so the smoke fumigates their vaginas.'

'I was referring to the gaol in Somalia.'

'It was no picnic,' he agreed, stroking his beard again. Or his chest hair.

'How did you survive?'

'Friends brought me food, and I paid people not to kill me.'

A couple of hours later, his wine and our day's beer rations all finished, he stood up and apologised for dominating the conversation. 'I don't get to speak to people very often,' he muttered. 'I miss the company.' Then he stumbled down the dark hill to his kayak and, in the face of a stiff westerly breeze, paddled off into the black lagoon. His white yacht was just a pale blur half a kilometre away.

Clouds clotted the moon and within seconds Don disappeared from sight. We couldn't see the yacht any longer. Paddling back to it in the dark, against the tide and wind, seemed a perilous prospect. Just to lose his paddle overboard would mean disaster. A school of panicked fish was jumping and flopping on the surface. Something big was chasing them. I thought how easy it would be for the kayak to tip over and for Don to disappear forever.

. . .

Next afternoon Brent and I were sightseeing in the dinghy when we came across Don in his kayak. For fun, we'd just gunned the dinghy through a narrow gap between islands called the Hole in the Wall. Even with outboard-motor power, the onrushing currents were stronger than we'd expected.

Don was heading that way. He saw us, grinned, and held up the coral trout and rock cod he'd just caught. Then, like an Olympic white-water canoeist, paddling frantically to avoid the rock walls pressing in on either side, he speared the kayak through the swirling tidal surge of the Hole in the Wall.

'He likes a risk,' I said.

'He treats every day like his last,' said Brent.

Perhaps Don's attitude to destiny had something to do with the purchase of his immaculate white yacht. As the only bidder in a government auction he was able to buy it very cheaply. Five tropical summers before, the yacht had been found drifting far out in the Indian Ocean. Its lone skipper was lying dead below deck.

The man had been dead for some time. It took months to get rid of the stench, which permeated the boat from sails to stern. Even five years later, people who ventured aboard, especially those who'd crawled into the cramped quarters below, said the fumigation efforts had not been wholly successful.

. . .

The luck of Don Drabble, the risk-taking raconteur that dark night on Hermite Island, continued to hold. But there was something ill-fated about the pristine white yacht the old sea-dog had bought cheaply at auction after it was found drifting at sea with a corpse lying below.

This previous skipper had died aboard her. Five years passed. Then, sailing at night between Dampier and the Montebello Islands twelve months after our dinner, Don Drabble felt the yacht strike something 'hard and heavy' in the darkness.

'I heard a bang and rushed below to find the rudder gone and the yacht taking water. I thought, "This is going to be a problem. I've lost my steering and there's too much water coming in." Then it sank.

Don had seen whales pass around the yacht earlier in the day and he wondered if he'd hit a humpback. Or perhaps it was a sea container fallen overboard from a ship. There were many navigation hazards here, natural and man-made, as evidenced by the scores of shipwrecks along the coast over centuries.

After seeing the damage to the rudder and hull of the *Scarlett* he realised the yacht couldn't be saved. 'Sometimes you can block holes temporarily with blankets and mattresses and all that sort of stuff, but it wasn't possible.'

His seafaring experience across the Indian Ocean, up and down the east African coast, paid off. Unlike the crews of all the other ships wrecked off the north-west coast since the seventeenth century, he was able to send off an emergency beacon before escaping in his dinghy.

As the dinghy drifted in the dark ocean, thirty kilometres from the wreck site and his original satellite detection point, he thought, 'I just have to sit through this. I don't really have much choice. You can't go into a state of panic. There's no good tiring yourself and freaking out.'

Fortunately the beacon's signal was received by the Australian Maritime Safety Authority in Canberra. They sent up a search plane from Perth which spotted him and alerted the North-West Water Police in Dampier. They set out in their vessel *Delphinus* and picked him up in the middle of the Indian Ocean five hours later.

According to the ABC's and *West Australian*'s reports, he remained in good spirits when brought ashore in Dampier. He was fortunate the weather was perfect for an emergency rescue. 'A flat sea, and the breeze was only ten or twelve knots, so I was really lucky. It's part of the life if you live on a boat.'

The *Scarlett* had been his thirteen-metre home and he'd lost everything. It was his closest call, but Don was happy to be alive.

19
TWO-AND-A-HALF

Eventually the surgical handiwork of Mr Stewart revealed itself to me. By the time I turned fourteen the number of testes facing me in the mirror had diminished from three to two-and-a-half.

Not only was Mr Stewart no mundane 'doctor', he wasn't even 'mister' for much longer. Avidly Anglophile West Australians still hankered after British titles and were dismayed when the Labor Prime Minister, Gough Whitlam, scrapped them and introduced an Australian honours system. In the nick of time, Mr Stewart was knighted and became Sir Hector.

I was almost able to deal with the excruciating embarrassment and necessity of always standing and shuffling right-side forward in change-room showers. But the elongated scrotum that the surgeon had created by nailing the left side to my thigh, and which now presented as two-and-a-bit (the extra, a subsidiary ball of gristle) hadn't quite finished causing me grief.

In case I burst Sir Hector's stitches, I'd had to forego rowing as a sport. But for some reason Australian Rules football was given the medical go-ahead. Within a minute of the ball being bounced in the first quarter of the first game, an ordinary house match, while leaping up to mark a pass on the wing, I was kicked in the balls. The two left ones, to be precise.

Walking painfully with my mother down the St George's Terrace hill to the surgery of Dr/Mr/Sir Hector (maybe Lord Stewart by now) for a testicle roundup, she said, 'You know what they're for, of course?'

What? Good grief. Of course I knew. Mothers. Testicles. Would the embarrassment never cease?

'*Umm,* yes,' I mumbled.

'So you can have babies when you're married,' she said.

20
PRISON DIARY

Even if I'm lucky enough to pick up a signal on Hermite from Barrow Island, the five-minute, top-of-the-dune opportunity for communication is insufficient for someone in a new romance. Without making the long and arduous trek up to the Observation Post, I missed being able to properly contact the woman in question. And I missed the children. No matter how pleasant the island, there's a point when it dawns on you that you're stuck there.

I know some women who won't attend parties on islands around Sydney Harbour and Pittwater for that reason. Usually they've had a bad experience on an island where they felt trapped and helpless. If the host was the person in charge of the boat, this put him in control of events. (I know a psychiatrist who tries this blunt sexual approach.)

Perhaps being driven to existential despair by an island is another form of islomania. It can cause deep anxiety being in a place you can't leave.

While dentists these days play films of tropical isles to get you to relax during drilling, and a psycho-therapist wanting a patient to sink into a dreamy trance encourages visions of an island's waving palms and translucent waters (maybe with added dolphins), islands are also traditionally evoked as places of punishment and misery. They're the devil's islands, at the furthest remove from the romantic coral atoll.

Throughout myth and history, islands have served as gaols. The actual Devil's Island, off the coast of French Guiana, is the prototype, and three other notorious examples immediately spring to mind: Robben Island, where Nelson Mandela spent eighteen of his twenty-seven years' imprisonment; Rikers Island, currently the world's largest penal colony, in New York; and, of course, Alcatraz, in San Francisco Bay.

A two-minute on-line search also produces Deer Island, in Massachusetts; Chateau d'If, in France; Imrali Island, in Turkey; Port Augusta in Jamaica; Port Blair, in India; and Prison Island in Ontario, Canada. Guantanamo Bay possibly qualifies, too. And the notorious Russian prison island with the bleak official name OE-256/5, supposedly 'the worst prison in the world' and known to prisoners as Petak.

It doesn't feature on the list of penal islands but the biggest example is of course Australia itself. This immense prison island then created little satellite island prisons to deal with extreme cases. For those convicts deemed especially criminal, dangerously political, or incorrigibly Aboriginal, Australia created spin-off versions in St Helena Island, Queensland; Port Arthur and Flinders Island, in Tasmania; Cockatoo Island and Fort Denison, in Sydney Harbour; and Norfolk Island out in the Pacific.

When I first set foot on my personal love-isle, Rottnest, I didn't know it had once been Western Australia's sad Aboriginal prison, where the inmates, like the Aborigines sent to Flinders Island, had sunk into pathos, subsisted on cooked marsupials and seaweed, gazed endlessly towards the mainland, and drowned when they tried to swim home. Aside from its Aboriginal-prison role, Rottnest was turned into an internment camp for German and Italian aliens during the world wars.

In recent times, with the prison-island ethos by now sunk deep into its psyche, Australia chose Nauru and Christmas Island as repositories for unwanted asylum seekers arriving by boat.

. . .

A prison is so isolated and isolating that it doesn't need to be surrounded by water to be an effective island. A place set apart from the normal world in every sense, it's as inaccessible, boring and perilous as the most remote desert island.

This occurred to me when I accepted an invitation from the Arts Council of England to teach creative writing to prisoners in London's Brixton Prison in 1994. I soon discovered that gaol fosters another variety of islomania. Some prisoners don't want to be rescued. They don't want to leave the island.

One of my keenest students was a prime example. Up to now, Peter Wayne has served the equivalent of two murder sentences, more than thirty years in prison, without ever committing an act of violence. He has never physically hurt anyone. All his crimes were fraud or robbery; or, if you count a pretend-gun – a pencil pointed at a bank teller from inside his shirt – armed robbery,

I mention his full name because by no means does he desire anonymity. Since our creative-writing class in Brixton he has become a celebrity prisoner, with a regular column in *Prospect* magazine. With very proper English erudition, his blackly humorous column reveals what it's like to be an habitual prisoner. It details prison life in intimate, mordant detail, as well as the increasingly depressing activities he gets up to on release from his gaol of the moment. Movingly, it then describes the mixed emotions – relief chiefly among them – that follow his inevitable return inside.

Although at first I thought he stood out merely because he was a middle-class chap with an education and a good line in bulldust,

Peter made an instant impression on me. In the diary of my Brixton stint in 1994, I noted, randomly:

> Peter, an architectural historian, has a journal a foot high, a thousand tiny spidery longhand words to a page. He loves to write but says he can't do it outside. He's too stunned by the beauty of the sky and trees and pubs. A classic recidivist, he's been out for only seven months in the last twelve years (he's thirty-eight). An intelligent, sensitive, ex-public schoolboy turned armed robber, he reads *Oliver Twist* to an illiterate gypsy boy every night and also corrects the spelling of a dyslexic Cockney boy.

. . .

Peter talks about his last time outside, of being a special guest speaker at a black-tie dinner-conference on prisoner rehabilitation at the Dorchester. His paper was on The Reformed Felon Point of View. He followed the Home Secretary to the lectern and successfully delivered his speech ('for myself, brutally hard-won self-knowledge would never allow me to offend again').

Then he got drunk in the Dorchester saloon bar, chatted to some American pilots and their girlfriends, was asked to watch the women's handbags and furs while they went to the powder room, and then disappeared with them. His departure with armloads of furs and bags was captured by a closed-circuit security camera. Because of his long time inside, the innovation of CCTV was unknown to him.

. . .

Peter arrives in the education cell complaining about his possessions not being sent on from his last prison in Oxfordshire. He says he 'absconded' from there disguised as a vicar, using a cut-up white plastic detergent bottle as a dog collar. Church of England dignitaries were visiting the prison, so he quietly joined the official church party and was pleased to accept a lift back into London in the ecclesiastical Bentley.

He's very indignant. 'When you abscond from prison they're supposed to send all your stuff on to you in the next prison. ('Abscond' sounds more acceptable than 'escape'.) My papers and some of my clothes haven't turned up from the prison before last, but today my tuxedo arrived from the Dorchester episode. The vicar stuff hasn't come back yet!' His manner is that of an irate hotel guest complaining that his dry-cleaning hasn't been delivered to his room.

To all this I say, 'Sure! ' I don't believe him. So he shows me his press cuttings.

. . .

Peter says he has a grant from the Arts Council of England to write a three-part musical dialogue on Henry Purcell, the eighteenth-century composer. 'Wren churches are the best places for Purcell performances,' he says.

'Really?' I say. He shows me his grant letter from the Arts Council.

. . .

Peter enters the class brushing his teeth and complaining that he's still waiting to get 'several volumes' of his journals back from Channel 4, for whom he recently wrote and fronted a series on the Victorian architecture of British prisons.

I don't question him this time. He's the Sir Kenneth Clark of the slammer.

. . .

Peter's in a state of high anxiety after being 'spun' and strip-searched five times in one afternoon. He says heroin foil has been planted in his cell and he's fighting the charge. He's complained to his lady gaol visitor, a Dame, and told the warders of his friendship with the architect of the new Royal Festival Hall, Sir Richard Rogers.

I imagine the warders' reaction to that. He said to one warder: 'Do you know who I am?' Not surprisingly, this didn't go down well. He keeps asking to take a blood test to prove he doesn't do heroin. 'I'll use cannabis if there's any around, but that's it.'

Obviously they're paying him back for being a smart-arse middle-class intellectual. Meanwhile, every day I enter the gaol carrying a big computer bag which could contain drugs – or weapons – and no-one's searched it once.

. . .

Peter's peeved about a Harvard Business School graduate in A-wing. 'He got six months for white-collar crime involving six million pounds while I got eight years for stealing thirty thousand.'

. . .

More 'possessions' of Peter's turn up from the other prison he left so rapidly: a brown paper parcel of human bones and a packet of condoms. In the last gaol he was allowed to go on supervised archeological digs outside, and he was keeping the bones in his cell. They're several centuries old.

'It was all right, I treated them with dignity. I used to put a Christian cross over them at night,' he says.

He likes the image of himself as a sort of zany Pimpernel figure.

His writing exercises are excellent. He always does the assignments.

.   .   .

Peter reads a story about his new cellmate, Dylan, a twenty-two-year-old blond boy with (Peter notes enthusiastically) aquamarine eyes. It looks like Peter's fallen for him. Dylan is the son of two British drug smugglers who operated out of Turkey. His earliest memory, aged four, is of watching his mother squat on the floor while his father pushed a sausage-skin of heroin up her vagina.

When they were arrested Dylan grew up on the streets of Istanbul, shining shoes and being intermittently looked after by the Turkish drug connection. Eventually his mother died of an overdose. His father was 'in prison somewhere'. Dylan's in Brixton for crack dealing.

From the excitable note of Peter's tale, it sounds like he's fallen pretty hard. Even though I've noticed the way he takes up young prisoners – skinny, street-rat types, I'd somehow thought he was hetero. Then again, he's been in gaol most of his adult life.

.   .   .

My class all read out their completed stories – understandably variable in quality and quantity.

I hoped this time I'd get something imaginative from Basil,

a sweet-faced, dignified old man from Ghana. In every class Basil nods and hums and agrees with everything I say. Then he goes his own way.

His story is the same as always. He writes in the first-person again even though I carefully explain I want third-person this time. His perfect copperplate stresses once more his full name, date of birth, parents' names, and his proud role as assistant treasurer for the Kumasi Engineering Bank's women's netball team. KEB were runners-up in the B-grade competition.

Though it would be the most interesting part of his autobiography, he doesn't mention he killed his son-in-law with an axe.

. . .

Peter's autobiographical story is publishable, even without editing. He adopts a broad Yorkshire accent to read it out. It's about growing up as a middle-class adopted child, of working in his father's slaughterhouse in his school holidays. He had to shovel the lungs and guts 'to show you a taste of the real world, lad'.

He would 'accidentally' cut himself with carving knives all the time to avoid dealing with the innards, and have to spend the day in the infirmary.

He started thieving early. An honour scout, he used to steal trinkets from his friends' mothers' mantelpieces and bedrooms. He'd get them out at night, spread them on his bed with his scout medals, and admire them.

. . .

A seagoing Australian has turned up in my writing class – Trent, a former submariner from a middle-class Queensland family. He's only attending the class because he's heard I'm Australian. He's homesick and out of place here, although being in the submarine service has at least given him a confident air among masses of men in confined spaces.

He gets me to bring him copies of *TNT* magazine, a publication for Aussie expats in London. I'm not sure whether this is allowed under prison regulations, but my bag is never checked and the mag is hardly a weapon. He wants to talk about surfing and football rather than writing. But it turns out he has a tale to tell.

On 3 August 1987 he was a communications officer in a submarine, *HMAS Otama*, undergoing equipment trials in the Pacific Ocean, off Sydney. Bad weather prevented the trials and two sailors were sent up into the fin to recover the hydrophone equipment. At 10.30 p.m. the submarine was preparing to dive, and it submerged four minutes later, with the two men still in the fin. Their absence wasn't noticed until 11 p.m., and not confirmed for another half hour.

The young sailors were washed away and drowned. Their bodies were never recovered. An inquest found that they had climbed to the fin's bridge and had unsuccessfully tried to contact the control room. Trent was a principal in the chain of orders to submerge. From that moment his life went wrong.

The navy went into cover-up mode. Trent says Defence Security kept him in custody until the media tired of the story, then he was discharged. He was paid off, but forbidden to talk to the Press. On being thrown out of the navy he bought a yacht and set off around the world. Now he's on remand in Brixton for what he says are 'tax matters'.

. . .

Trent finally opens up. The 'tax matters' turn out to be a charge of smuggling ecstasy into Britain, plus another charge of possession. Customs officers discovered (he says) one tab of E on deck when his yacht berthed at Dover. The ecstasy was left over from a party on the Riviera. He says it wasn't even his. Even if it had been, the charge should be simple possession not the serious one of drug smuggling.

'Why would anyone smuggle an ecstasy tab into Britain anyway? What's the point? Not only would it be a case of coals to Newcastle, eccies are available in quantity in every pub and club in the country.'

His girlfriend's on the same charge, on remand in Holloway Prison. They've already been in gaol for six months awaiting trial.

. . .

I note the tension of the men on remand like Trent the submariner, never knowing when their court appearances are coming up, or if their witnesses will be there, and having to queue to use the one phone in order to talk to their lawyers.

The remand prisoners stand out because they're allowed to wear their civvy T-shirts and jeans. They don't have to wear the prison uniform, which is actually smarter – a blue and white striped stockbroker-style shirt and cotton pants. Everything else is the same for them as the other prisoners. No privileges. They're still locked up all day like the convicted felons, except for the two hours 'free time' in the afternoon.

Considering his six months inside already, Trent's attitude is surprisingly confident. He's sure he'll get off the smuggling charge. He's always pleased to see me, to steer the class away from writing, and to chat about Australia – especially beaches and football.

The English crims treat him OK. They quite like Australians. It helps that we're classless by British standards and they think all Australians are fellow convicts anyway. Our paths have also been smoothed by the prison's favourite TV shows, *Home and Away* and *Neighbours*, which all the murderers, rapists and armed robbers watch avidly. They keep asking me what happens next in *Neighbours*. I say I don't want to spoil it for them. (I've never seen it.)

. . .

There's now a second Australian in the prison. He's been put in Trent's cell 'for companionship'. This only other Australian in Brixton is Darren, an Aboriginal public servant. He booked on an organised two-month European tour for his long-service leave but started drinking at Sydney airport, drank his way across the world, disrupted the flight and was arrested when he arrived at Heathrow.

Sadly, Darren won't make his already-paid-for European tour. Charged with his in-flight offences, he was sentenced to two months in prison, timed by the authorities so he'd have to leave Britain immediately his gaol-time was up.

I ask Trent to bring Darren along to class, for the 'Australianness' at least. But he's so depressed he just sleeps all day. He won't even leave the cell for 'free time'.

. . .

Trent isn't in class today. He's finally got his day in court. When I saw him yesterday, he confidently reckoned that even if – 'worst-case scenario' – he was convicted of both charges – possession and smuggling – taking into account the time already served, he'd get off.

. . .

It was a surprise to see Trent wearing the blue and white striped prison-uniform shirt today instead of his usual T-shirt. His eyes were red. His whole manner has changed and he could hardly talk to me. He left the class early. He'd been crying.

The court convicted him of drug smuggling as well as possession. He was given a 'menace to society' lecture and another nine months in prison.

21
THE SLIMY

For someone who grew up on the West Australian coast and has always loved the sea and the beach, I've come to associate it with death as much as pleasure. I know where this contradictory view comes from. As a teenager I was body-surfing on a reef off Cottesloe beach with four friends when one of them drowned.

We three others didn't realise Richie Male was having any greater difficulty in the ocean than we were. It was an overcast Saturday afternoon in November, not quite summer. On this limestone reef known locally as the Slimy, the surf was unpredictable, the waves high but choppy, and heaving with seaweed. But Richie was seventeen and a proficient swimmer, good enough to make his interschool team every year.

The Slimy got its name from its slippery carpet of sea-grass and mossy sea-lettuce. On a calm day it felt like soft matting and you could walk right out into the deep. On a day like this it was tricky keeping your footing in the undertow. You slithered and slipped and were easily knocked over. You had to dig your toes into rock crevices, or plunge head-first into the writhing kelp and try for a handhold.

There were five or six other boys out on the Slimy vying for waves, heading shore-wards and back throughout the afternoon. Then five fellows carrying heavy plywood surf-skis came out of the surf club, laughing and teasing each other, and paddled out to the back of the reef. Carelessly, with the arrogance of more years and strength, they began dropping-in on our waves.

Caught up in our individual contests with the waves, and trying to avoid the surf-skis and the swirling kelp, no-one noticed that Richie wasn't there.

In the late afternoon the wind strengthened and the waves grew more erratic and battering. Clouds the colour of pewter were massing in the west over Rottnest Island and the water began to darken.

Disgruntled and exhausted, we tired of dodging the wooden projectiles. One by one, we gave up and swam and stumbled over the reef to shore, then headed back home singly along the beach. I presumed Richie had wearied of the rough ocean and the competition of the heavy boards and left the beach before me.

. . .

Next day, still unaware of his disappearance, I missed another critical moment. I was a nineteen-year-old cub reporter on *The West Australian,* working in the paper's Fremantle bureau. My beat included events in and around the port, from the mundane daily shipping news to the occasional exciting Fremantle Prison breakout, as well as the fishing fleet and the local police, courts, ambulance and fire-brigade.

Fremantle was a busy working port, an Indian Ocean terminus whose waterside workers, fishermen and sailors had the usual seaman's penchant for drinking and trouble. While only four kilometres away and geographically part of our bureau's news catchment area, Cottesloe beach, site of the Slimy, was by comparison law-abiding and un-newsworthy.

Buzzing up the suburban coastline that Sunday morning in the office Ford Anglia, I drove through sleepy Cottesloe, oblivious to the quiet activity in the shallows. Three surf boats were slowly cruising the beach, but nothing appeared urgent in their rowing or in the solemn stance of their sweep oarsmen.

The previous day's bluster had cleared and the sky had the near-purple clarity that announces summer in Western Australia. A mild off-shore breeze levelled the sea and the horizon was geometrically sharp. I was keeping an eye out for the shark-spotter plane. The weather was perfect for me to scan the ocean for schools of sharks. I was primed for the perennial pre-summer 'Sharks Invade Beaches' story.

My life then was a coastal dichotomy: in my free time as a swimmer and surfer, I naturally feared sharks, but I weighed up the favourable odds and pushed them from my mind. When I was in the sea I didn't think of them. As a zealous young reporter on land, however, I hankered after 'man-eaters' and a grisly story for the front page.

Unaware of Richie's death, I not only missed the search for his body but its eventual discovery. Despite it happening just metres from me, I only learned of my friend's drowning when I read about it in Monday's paper, written by the reporter on the Sunday shift after mine. Richie's body had been found towards Sunday evening, shrouded in kelp and rolling in the waves ten metres from shore. There was a laceration on his head.

I was stupefied by the news, and remained so for more than thirty years. From the moment I read the story on page two, my mind blocked out his death. On my twenty-first birthday I moved from Western Australia to a bigger city, Melbourne, and to a broadsheet paper, *The Age*. Thereafter, I lived, worked and travelled in the eastern states and overseas. The boy who drowned near me on the reef retreated so far into my mind that I gave him not a second's conscious thought.

A decade after that November afternoon on the Slimy, however, as I left journalism in my late twenties to write fiction, the image of a person drowning, or in danger in the sea, began appearing in my novels and stories. Many more years passed before I realised how extensively drowning had become both theme and metaphor in my writing.

Although the coast featured prominently in some of my books, such as *The Bodysurfers* and *The Bay of Contented Men*, I'd somehow forgotten that the gaol-cell death of a protagonist in *Fortune*, a risk-taking underwater explorer, was a metaphorical drowning. Or that in my editorial introduction to *The Penguin Book of the Beach* I dwelt on the dramatic drowning of the poet Shelley in the Gulf of Spezia.

I'd entitled one book of stories, *The Rip*, inspired by the Tom Waits song 'The Ocean Doesn't Want Me' about a raging riptide. Two children drown at the start of my short story 'Radiant Heat' and an unknown man's body is washed ashore in another story, 'Stones Like Hearts'. A small boy fears a tsunami in 'Sea Level'. The young Ned Kelly heroically saves a boy from drowning in *Our Sunshine*.

I also had no knowledge of how the following newspaper clipping came to be among my cuttings file on *The Drowner*. It's from *The Age* and dated 22 February 1886. I have no memory of how it got there.

. . .

It is feared that another terrible tragedy has taken place in this community. A Mr George Greenwood, residing in Albert Street, East Melbourne, and his two children have been missing since Friday last, and it is thought that the father has destroyed his children and then put an end to his own life.

About one a.m. on Saturday the caretaker of the Corporation Baths on the Yarra River, opposite the Botanical Gardens bridge, heard the voices of children, and remarked to another man that it was strange that children should be out so late at night.

Mr Greenwood has been suffering from religious mania, and it is feared by his friends that he took his children to the Yarra at the place and hour named and drowned them, and that subsequently he made away with his own life.

. . .

If all this wasn't proof enough of my unconscious fixation, I'd titled one novel *The Drowner*. Within this book, unsurprisingly, there are several deaths, and other near-deaths, by drowning.

Whatever my subconscious continued to declare, I still didn't give Richie's drowning a mindful thought. Then, quite suddenly, I did. I was writing *The Shark Net,* a memoir of interconnected dramatic events in my family and the wider community, including multiple murders, in Perth's coastal suburbs in the 1960s. As I neared the end of the book, the memory of that afternoon on the reef rose from the seaweedy depths as clear as yesterday.

The milky light, the sky the colour of tin, the gusty south-westerly, the bile-tinted sandy froth of the breakers. Above all, the aggressive kelp, churning and rolling like a many-armed creature, snatching and scratching at our bodies. I couldn't get the episode out of my mind. I needed to write about that afternoon on the Slimy as well.

22
EUTHANASIA

When we woke each morning on the island there were dew-damp claw prints on the porch. At night, as they became used to us, the emigrant wallabies and bandicoots from Barrow Island, and their young Hermite Island offspring, had begun hovering shyly around our camp.

One night as we ate our barbecued meat and potatoes outdoors at the picnic table in the sand, our plates on our knees, two bandicoots crept from the spinifex, skirted around the dolphin and cat skulls, and lurked at the outskirts of our meal.

Sniffing spillage, they gradually lost their shyness and ventured into the light. As omnivores they were happy with whatever was on the menu. Every scrap and crumb that fell to the ground was acceptable. They'd sniff the air, race in and gobble down the morsel, then flee back into the bushes.

Next night there were six bandicoots around our legs. Soon they were emboldened enough to take their time and not dash back into hiding immediately after eating. From then on there were too many to count, although Kelly could pick out some individual animals by their chubbiness, and began giving them names.

Their boldness, cuteness and darting curiosity made them our evening entertainment. It was hard to resist them. They were like plump and nosy cartoon characters, always hungry and amusing to watch as they chased each other around the camp, twitching and sniffing and dashing about our feet, pausing only to eat or to unself-consciously mate in front of us.

What high-jinks will they be up to tonight? we'd wonder, as we flicked trail-mix and Jatz crackers in their direction.

Within a week the bigger bandicoots were jumping on to the veranda of Hurricane Hut and rustling around in the packaged and canned goods and garbage. Boxes had to be sealed or stacked out of reach. By standing on tiptoes the bigger bandicoots soon managed to make the final leap up the step into the kitchen. During meals they nibbled at our bare toes and ankles. Since they'd joined the Ark from Barrow Island they'd doubled their weight.

The nightly bandicoots were soon so blasé that they paid us no heed unless we were dishing out the snacks – and they had to be snacks that they preferred to other snacks. Top of the range. Tuna in olive oil was acceptable, and Turkish bread. No more Jatz crackers. And they were everywhere underfoot.

It occurred to me they were in danger of becoming the marsupial version of rats. They looked like the rats they'd displaced, and they were beginning to behave like rats. Fatter rats, with longer noses and pointier teeth. And no cats to eat them.

It had to happen: there were so many bandicoots underfoot that one evening Andy the scientist stood up suddenly and trod on one. It was a plump bandicoot and it squished and popped like a half-filled balloon. The expressions 'faces fell' and 'jaws dropped' don't begin to describe the scene around the dinner table. The silence was instant and deathly.

In the preceding few days, when he'd dropped a crate of cans and broken a plate into shards, Andy had remarked wryly, 'You can see why my wife won't let me wash up the good crockery at home.'

Like a man in a dream, he now bent down and picked up the flattened bandicoot. Ashen-faced, he held it in both hands like an offering, staring disbelievingly at it. The other four conservationists were still speechless. *What is it again that we do for a living? Oh, yes – saving endangered species. Of which there's now one less member. And, would you believe it, there's a writer present!*

No-one spoke, moved or ate. Time stood still. Poor Andy was immobilised. The others continued staring at him. They seemed in shock, too. Finally, he turned on his heel and strode off, announcing, 'I'll have to euthanase it.'

Still no-one spoke. Seconds later, Andy returned, still holding the bandicoot in his outstretched hands and looking dazed and bewildered. He said, 'It died.'

He could have been talking of a beloved family pet. Again he carried it off, and this time he got rid of it somewhere. He returned to his sausages and beans, his head down, saying, 'I don't want to talk about it while I'm eating.'

No-one else mentioned the flattened bandicoot either, not that night or for the rest of the fortnight on the island.

23
ON THE ROCKS

Sometimes by day the Montebello Islands seemed like the World's End. This was when you came across a dusty stretch as dead as a moonscape, or a burnt-out jeep with a wire-wood bush growing through it. And when the night sky was irradiated by Barrow Island and the flares of the oil and gas rigs, the islands became the post-nuclear New World.

In the lagoon below the camp lay a crusted slab of military-tank tracks, iridescent with orange rust and green weed. They were the habitat of crabs of the same vivid colour combination, and of the sting-rays that hunted them. Only by remembering there were no straight lines or perfect circles in nature could I recognise this underwater formation as man-made. And relatively modern, and European.

In the Old World, on 25 May 1622, the Montebello archipelago was the first piece of Australia sighted by Englishmen. They should have been paying better attention to their navigation. That day they ran their East Indiaman *Tryall* onto an uncharted reef off the Montebellos' north-west edge, causing the earliest known shipwreck in Australian waters.

On its maiden voyage from Plymouth, the *Tryall* was bound for

Batavia with a cargo of silver for trade in the East Indies and gifts for the King of Siam to encourage him to look favourably on the endeavours of the British East India Company.

The skipper, John Brooke, rescued a cache of silver from the cargo before fleeing in a skiff. Ninety-three seamen were left clinging helplessly to the wreckage, while forty-six survivors made it to Batavia in a longboat. Brooke was later accused by the first mate of incompetence and of abandoning the ship a day before it sank. The wrecked treasure ship and the Tryall Rocks named after it then became mired in confusion and controversy deep into the twentieth century.

For three centuries, Dutch and English sailors, including William Dampier and Matthew Flinders, searched unsuccessfully for the rocks and the treasure at their purported location. Described in 1820 by the explorer Phillip Parker King as 'the theme and dread of every voyager to the Eastern Islands for the last two centuries', the Tryall Rocks continued to be marked on charts, but gradually seamen began to doubt their existence.

Almost 350 years later, a team of West Australian scuba divers determined the true position of the Tryall Rocks and found the shipwreck. One of these gung-ho treasure hunters was a nuggety and confrontational former navy diver named Alan Robinson. For the next two decades he would become the country's most notorious underwater explorer, as well as the nemesis of the police, the bureaucracy and the legal system: a sort of sub-aquatic Ned Kelly.

Robinson simplified the salvage of the *Tryall*'s cargo by blasting the ship from the reef. But treasure-hunting with gelignite damaged the wreck site, scattered the valuables and attracted other scavenging divers. It cruelled his relations with the original diving team, which included several media personalities. There were big and offended egos all round; even today, any public mention of his name elicits angry letters-to-the-editor. In an extraordinary ricocheting effect, his action also made enemies of institutions as diverse as the Perth Museum and the Federal police, the West Australian Government and the police forces of four States.

Alan Robinson was already rocking the boat following his part in the discovery of the Dutch treasure ship *Vergulde Draeck (Gilt Dragon)* further south, in 1963 and his salvage attempts of the *Zuytdorp* in 1967. An approving television documentary entitled *The Gelignite Buccaneer* was made about him, but blowing up an historic shipwreck was seen as taking salvaging a step too far.

The *Gilt Dragon* and its cargo of bullion made Robinson famous in Western Australia. The public liked his knockabout winner-loser-winner image. He claimed to have found the wreck five years earlier, then lost the site, and now he (and others) had found it again. He salvaged many valuable artefacts and coins but the State Government passed retrospective legislation in 1964 which seized the wreck and passed its contents to the museum.

This niggardly decision set off a long and tortured passage of events. Robinson went to the High Court, determined to fight the government for salvage or compensation rights. Thirteen years later he eventually won his case, with the court declaring the State legislation invalid. Another seven years passed while he waited for the promised but unforthcoming compensation, amounting to millions of dollars, while his legal battles took him to the brink of bankruptcy and had him gaoled for failing to pay court costs.

By now his pugnacious legal defence and fiery temper were making him enemies everywhere, from the Supreme Court to north-west bar-rooms. He became persona non grata with the State and Federal police, who resented his cavalier media persona. The cops began a campaign of harassment, arresting him on one trivial charge after another: for minor traffic offences of the dust-on-the-tail-light variety and the possession of a single ship's ballast brick. He was forced to leave town.

. . .

In 1982 I was supporting my novel-writing with assignments for the *Bulletin* magazine when Alan Robinson contacted me unexpectedly in Sydney with 'a huge story to tell'. He was out on bail on a charge of conspiring to kill his ex-wife.

From the offhand way he mentioned this allegation it might have been a speeding charge. He feared 'certain people' were intending to 'remove' him and he was sure the law-enforcement brotherhood had passed on their negative opinion of him from State to State.

I went to meet him. He and his pregnant girlfriend were staying in a flat in Five Dock, by the harbour. As a former Perth boy, I was aware of his swashbuckling reputation. I was also intrigued by the relentless staying power of the national archetype, the working-class larrikin in the Ned Kelly mould. He fitted the bill.

These characters had by no means vanished from the north-west coast. While their impetuosity could make the news and win them plaudits for bravery, they were clearly temperamentally unsuited to the bureaucratic constraints and middle-class tedium of suburban life. I found it interesting that the discovery of a seventeenth-century treasure ship could make the life of a modern fortune-hunter tumble into disarray. It was like the Ion Idriess stories I'd devoured as a boy.

I thought Alan Robinson was entertaining and maybe paranoid. He was fifty-four, a short, muscular, weather-beaten man with a loquacious charm. He and his girlfriend Patricia Green, a freckled and bewildered-looking girl thirty years his junior, had been charged with conspiring to murder his former common-law wife, Lynette Hunter, and with having solicited two men to murder her.

Robinson insisted he'd only 'verbally abused her in anger' because she owed him $100,000. No attempt had actually been made on her life and he claimed the charges had been trumped up by his enemies. However, when he then disappeared, it appeared his fears of these unspecified enemies might have come true.

. . .

As it happened, Robinson had fled while on bail to a remote hut in the Dead Heart of the Northern Territory. Here, three months later, the fugitive was arrested in a dusty shack by a heavily armed eight-man team of the New South Wales police force: the CIB's notorious Special Breaking Squad.

Fighting extradition from Darwin to Sydney, Robinson told the territory's Supreme Court he'd fled because his life was being threatened. Police had told his daughters he would be 'found hanging from a tree or blown away.' The court decided that his fears of being harmed by the police were groundless.

In custody back in Sydney he found another retrospective legal decision awaited him. The Historic Shipwrecks Act had been passed, which nullified the earlier favourable High Court decision. A further six charges were then laid against him of possessing relics from the *Gilt Dragon*.

I wrote four stories for the *Bulletin* on Robinson's life and misadventures. As background material, he inundated me with copies of his legal papers, sheafs of notes, diaries, newspaper clippings and a roughly written, self-published and self-regarding autobiography, *In Australia Treasure Is Not For the Finder*.

After the articles were published I began receiving threatening anonymous phone calls, telling me to stop writing about Robinson 'or suffer the consequences.' Without giving a reason, a detective from the

Special Breaking Squad also warned me off writing about him. The next day he came to the *Bulletin* office to obtain back copies of my stories. Why all this drama? I couldn't understand why this skindiving rebel warranted such official scrutiny and nationwide enmity. It made me more, rather than less, interested in his activities.

I was subpoenaed to appear as a character witness at his conspiracy-to-murder trial in Sydney's District Court. I was called to the witness box, gave my name and occupation, had my presence noted and immediately negated by the prosecution, and was asked to stand down. The trial proceeded for another three days, enlivened by the court appearance, squawks and coos of Robinson's and Green's newborn baby.

At 6.25 a.m. on the day that Alan Robinson was to be acquitted of the conspiracy-to-murder charges, he was found hanged in his cell in Long Bay prison. A twisted bed sheet was tied to his cell window. He was dressed only in a singlet and underpants. There was no suicide note.

. . .

It can be said confidently that Robinson would have been acquitted. This is because Patricia Green was found not guilty, and the judge had directed the jury: 'It takes at least two people to conspire. If you acquit one defendant in a conspiracy charge you must acquit the other.'

While I digested this ricochet in the drama, I had a coffee outside the court with Robinson's stunned legal team and his daughter Sandra Bright. No-one thought for a moment that he'd committed suicide.

As his barrister said, 'He was a vain man, with a proper sense of drama. It's hard to imagine him going out in his underwear. At this optimistic moment, after all his drawn-out court battles had ended and he faced freedom, why top himself now?' The barrister went on, 'Alan also had verbal diarrhoea – he constantly expressed himself through the typewriter in his cell. It's totally unlike him not to leave a note.'

Libel laws prevented the publication of the defence team's suspicions about his death. I felt helpless and frustrated. At the inquest, the coroner, accepting the police version, said no evidence had been presented to suggest anything other than suicide. True enough, but who was it that had gathered the evidence?

Maybe fiction is a conduit to the truth. I began writing my next novel, *Fortune*, immediately. I set out to make one of the two lead characters an underwater explorer whose life falls apart after he finds a sunken treasure in a Dutch shipwreck. My character's name is Don Spargo. The final chapter features the death of Spargo at the hands of unnamed people in a Long Bay gaol cell.

. . .

It took thirty years for the *Tryall*/Alan Robinson ricochet to stop. My family and I had moved to a small New South Wales coastal village. Collecting the newspaper from the general store one morning, I noticed a florid, heavy-set, middle-aged man who looked familiar. He was buying his paper, too. He gave me a stare as we tried to place each other.

After a few days I remembered his flushed face glaring angrily from newspaper photographs. I also recalled him looking fixedly at me when I was in the District Court witness box at Robinson's trial. He was one of the detectives who'd arrested Robinson in the Northern Territory. Following a Royal Commission into the State's police service, the Special Breaking Squad had since been disbanded in disgrace and its leading members forced into early retirement.

One day we brushed elbows in the store's doorway. 'Morning,' said the ex-copper. He grinned and murmured something else as the shop door swung shut behind me. 'Pity about your mate.'

. . .

I was curious to find out what became of the man who had begun this chain of events off the Montebellos in 1622, the *Tryall*'s skipper, John Brooke.

It seems that despite making a navigational error of ten degrees of longitude and steering his ship on to the Tryall Rocks, he escaped censure. Notwithstanding his first mate's evidence to the contrary, Brooke blamed incorrect mapping, was given the benefit of the doubt and the command of another British East India Company vessel, the *Moone*.

Shortly afterwards, the *Moone* was deliberately wrecked off the coast of Dover. This time Brooke was held responsible and spent two years in prison before the case was suddenly dropped and he was released. Rumour spoke of quantities of silver changing hands.

24
THE WITNESS

In these days of the perpetual teenager, when people cling to adolescence until their thirties and beyond, it's instructive to consider the young adulthood of men like Pat Coverley, who spent five years in the vicinity and aftermath of nuclear bombs and war.

As a nineteen-year-old sailor with the occupying forces in Japan, Able Seaman Patrick Coverley saw the devastation in Hiroshima. Two years later, in 1952, he was sent to the Montebello Islands for eight months and observed the detonation of Britain's first nuclear bomb, then served a second term in Hiroshima, then two tours of duty in the Korean war. This was all by the time he turned twenty-four.

Pat Coverley, at time of writing a jovial eighty-three, lives in Mosman Park, Western Australia. During our first conversations he was recovering from having more than a litre of fluid drained from his lungs after surviving a quadruple heart bypass operation. He counts himself lucky. Most of his shipmates died young, of various cancers. That he is still alive makes him an exception among Montebello bomb veterans.

He's not given to overstatement. In the cheerfully taciturn tradition of teenage Australian servicemen, his nuclear experiences tend to be overshadowed by memorable events involving food, beer and sport.

'We weren't told anything officially about what was going on – only rumours that an atomic bomb was going to be exploded in the Montebellos. We had no idea what part we were to play until we actually arrived at Onslow (then the nearest mainland port),' he told me. 'Once we were in Onslow there was no secrecy about it. Everybody in town, all the locals, knew about the bomb.'

He had his twenty-second birthday on HMAS *Wareen*, a week before *Operation Hurricane*. 'We had a sweep on what time the bomb would actually explode. The eight a.m. blokes won the money.'

When he got there he was transferred to a refrigerated lighter, the prosaically named *MRL 252,* and another cargo barge, *MWL 251,* which supplied the British units and the Australian navy and air force personnel in the islands with their food and water supplies, and their mail from home.

'We didn't feel too many emotions – it was just a job we had to do. Most of us had spent time at Hiroshima and seen the destruction there. Even so, we weren't unduly worried. Being young, you didn't think of the consequences. We just went about our daily duties. We were up there for eight months and worked like navvies. One day I cut my foot on coral and had to have a tetanus injection in my bum in Onslow hospital. It was very hot but we were all too afraid to swim because the ocean was alive with sharks.'

He brings up the subjects of food and drink. 'We ate well but we didn't have a proper cook so we had to take turns at cooking and mess duties. No-one was any good at gravy or apple sauce. At one stage our fridge broke down so we had to throw all our perishable food overboard. Luckily fish were plentiful, so we did lots of fishing. All the sailors finally got so sick of eating fish we complained about it. Then we had kangaroo for a change. The Captain of *MWL 251* went across to the mainland and shot a couple of kangaroos and brought them back on board.

'We were issued with one bottle of Swan Lager every night. It cost us nine pence. The Poms opened a marquee on Hermite Island and sold cans of warm Tennents Lager. We Aussie sailors had never seen beer cans before, or drunk warm beer for that matter.

'At no stage were we aware it was a dangerous assignment or what the health repercussions might be. There were no safeguards in place. We weren't issued with any protective clothing or special gear. On the day the bomb was exploded we were wearing the usual shorts and toeless sandals – no shirts, hats, sunglasses, et cetera. No special allowances were made for us, before or after the bomb blast.

'They called us up on deck to watch. No cameras were allowed. We weren't told to turn our backs or take any safety precautions. We didn't shower after the explosion, or wash or destroy the clothes we'd been wearing. We weren't told anything about radioactivity and its physical effects. There were no lectures or any other information about the fallout.

'We were on the closest group of ships to the island, but the RAAF were even closer. They were actually sitting on the island before the bomb went off. Their toilets were on top of the sand hills and they saw the explosion from the lavatories – the best views on the island.

'At the moment of ignition there was a flash as though a match had been struck in the dark. Then it went up like a huge bundle of smoke, more like an enormous bushfire than a mushroom shape. It took minutes for the huge roar to reach us, and even longer for the sound to abate.

'After the bomb went off we carried on normal duties as though nothing had happened. The Poms went their way, we went ours. We took our orders from Bob Menzies and Australia, not the Poms. We sailed back to Onslow to load materials for Fremantle, and then returned to Fremantle a month later. No extra pay was involved. We even missed out on being in a tax-free zone by a couple of degrees of latitude, which didn't help morale.'

Asbestosis actually worried Pat Coverley more than nuclear fallout from *Operation Hurricane*. To insulate heat and muffle noise, the lagging around the pipes and tanks on his various vessels was made of packed asbestos fibres. 'I wondered how much of that stuff I breathed in over the years.'

'I've stayed in touch with other blokes present that day, not that there are many left. Over the years I've gone to lots of their funerals. Cancer related, from radiation. I've heard that the English marines and sailors who'd been sent to the Montebello Islands were dying like flies.'

'The first of us blokes to die from cancer was Phil Smith, a navy diver. Immediately after the blast he was ordered to dive on the *Plym* bomb site to retrieve the mooring cable. The navy wanted the cable back. He didn't live long after that.'

. . .

Private Sydney Baker was a young soldier at the time. His unit in Perth was paraded and asked whether any volunteers wanted to go 'somewhere warm'. Syd Baker stepped forward and found himself building barbed-wire fences around nuclear test sites on the Montebellos.

Radiation 'safety precautions' consisted of the soldiers being paraded on the beach each evening, ordered to strip off their clothes and discard them, being marched naked into the sea, and then re-kitted on the beach.

Nevertheless Syd Baker survived nuclear radiation. In March 2007 the elderly atomic bomb veteran was still living on the Pilbara coast, at the Indee Station camping ground, when tropical Cyclone George, a Category 5 cyclone, struck the coast with wind gusts of 285 kmh (180 mph), demolished his hut, crushed his spine, lungs and ribs, and killed him.

. . .

When Pat Coverley was a nineteen-year-old sailor in Hiroshima in 1950, he was taken to the target area by Australian soldiers. Their base was situated on a flattened area near where the bomb exploded. 'The place was devastated, completely crushed. I'd never seen anything like it.

'It poured with rain in Japan and we were very cold and uncomfortable because we had only our tropical uniforms. But we were all happy to be there and hadn't a thought about the bomb or radiation. The food was very good, mostly hot English food, not Asian. There was a bar called Hiro House where the boys played snooker and darts. We named a park Anzac Park and we sailors played footy against an army side.

'Everything was cheap. The goods on the ship had to be rationed though, due to the sailors' generosity to the Japs. Especially the women. The soldiers and sailors paid girls to dance with them, and to do everything and anything else. The women welcomed us with open arms but the Japanese men weren't very friendly.'

. . .

Atomic Fallout, official magazine of the Atomic Ex-Servicemen's Association, has a photograph in its June 2001 issue of sixteen of the eighteen members of the Australian Rules football team from the Occupation Force in Japan 'relaxing after the game' in 1947. The footballers look suitably muddy and exhausted.

The photo caption says: 'The game was played on a field within the contaminated region of Hiroshima. Thirteen of the sixteen players are now dead from cancers of radiogenic origin.'

. . .

In estimating the possible hazards of ionising radiation, it is clearly necessary to assess the effects of radioactive fallout from nuclear weapons, since this sort of general environmental contamination is of recent origin, has been of uncertain significance, and has led to concern in the minds of many people.

The physical characteristics of ionising radiation and the amounts of human exposure to it are at present more accurately known than its biological consequences. These exposures may involve the whole body uniformly, or may be greater for certain organs or tissues, as when radioactive material is selectively concentrated in them.

Tissues of the embryo, of the bone and bone marrow, and of the gonads are of particular importance. Irradiation of the embryo may lead to abnormalities of development or may prove fatal.

Irradiation of the gonads is able to bring about changes in the hereditary material; and these may be transmitted to subsequent generations if the irradiation is received before or during the years of reproductive activity.

Exposure of gonads to even the smallest doses of ionising radiation can give rise to mutant genes which accumulate, are transmissible to the progeny and are considered to be, in general, harmful to the human race. As the persons who will be affected will belong to future generations, it is important to minimise undue exposure of populations to such radiation and so to safeguard the well-being of those who are still unborn.

During my Montebello research I discovered the preceding extract from the Report of the United Nations Scientific Committee on 'The Effects of Atomic Radiation', presented to the 13th Session of the General Assembly in 1958.

It was one of the first warning shots across the bows of the new craze. This nuclear business was serious, it informed the world. Listen, you women: irradiation leads to abnormalities of your embryos. Listen, men and boys: you might think you've escaped, you're feeling hunky-dory, but radiation surreptitiously gets you in the balls. It messes with your genes, makes them mutant and harms future generations.

The world said *tsk tsk* and stocked up its nuclear larder.

25
HIROSHIMA MON AMOUR

I've never been sure whether the reputation of *Hiroshima Mon Amour*, the famous film directed by Alain Resnais, rests more on its originality, its politically sensitive backdrop or its evocative title. It's certainly a great title.

When I first saw it as an anti-bomb teenager I considered its images pretty gruesome. Viewing it again decades later as a *Sydney Morning Herald* film critic, I was struck by its graphic restraint. Of course the opening documentary-style footage of the bomb's effects on Hiroshima's citizens is still troubling. What is most disturbing is the matter-of-factness and ordinariness of the anonymous nuclear victims.

As Resnais and the screenwriter, Marguerite Duras, continually stress – and this is what is most disconcerting – is not the mutilated bodies you expect but the Japanese women's hair loss. Everywhere, even in women who appear otherwise unharmed by nuclear radiation, their hair is falling out in huge hanks and handfuls. Impassively, the women run their fingers through their hair, which comes away in loose clumps and waves.

Does the film's creativity still stand up? Back in 1959, international critics lauded its originality, especially the innovative flashbacks inter-cut into scenes to suggest flickers of memory. They named it as the most important offering of the French New Wave, quite an accolade in a year when France also presented Francois Truffaut's *The Four Hundred Blows.*

The year was a big one for important films, including Alfred Hitchcock's *North by North-West,* Billy Wilder's *Some Like It Hot,* Howard Hawks' *Rio Bravo,* and Otto Preminger's *Anatomy of a Murder. Ben-Hur,* William Wyler's chariot-race epic with Charlton Heston, won the Best Picture Academy Award (and ten other Oscars as well). Oh, and *Pillow Talk* put Rock Hudson and Doris Day in bed together.

Politically? Even though it was fourteen years since President Truman had dropped the bomb, *Hiroshima Mon Amour* was excluded from official selection at the 1959 Cannes film festival to avoid upsetting the US Government.

It's set in the partially rebuilt Hiroshima a decade after the war. Most of the film is a series of disjointed conversations on memory, forgetfulness and leave-takings during and after the tastefully erotic one-and-a-half-night stand of a French actress (Emmanuelle Riva) and a Japanese architect (Eiji Okada).

Referred to only as She and Him, the lovers, both married to others, move between silent and stylised sex, naked shoulder-stroking and intense, jerky and repetitive dialogue. The woman talks over and over about the effects of memory. Though smitten by her beauty and anxious to continue the relationship, the man constantly interrupts her to say she's wrong, lying or confused.

Resnais has the lovers meet for the last time at a bar called the *Casablanca,* an obvious reference to the classic 1942 movie. As the bar's location is one of the film's rare establishing shots, you presume the *Casablanca* allusion must have been important to him. Tapping into *Casablanca*'s reputation does come as brief sentimental relief. Although if he's suggesting their post-nuclear troubles amount to a hill of beans, and that we should care for his elegant, angst-ridden lovers like we do for those earthier romantic souls, Bogart and Bergman, it doesn't work.

The woman almost loses the viewer with her incessant talking. The man doesn't have much to say (and thankfully not 'Here's looking at you, kid') except he does have the film's most repeated line: 'You are not endowed with memory.'

As far as she's concerned, he's definitely wrong there. She's over-endowed with memory. And these scenes suddenly work well: flashbacks to her younger days in Occupied France show her head being shaved in the classic war-time shaming punishment for an inappropriate love affair with a German soldier (who is later killed by an unseen Resistance sniper). Though she's now a beautiful and successful actress, the disgrace and sadness of forcibly losing her hair (not to mention her lover) still weigh on her.

And now for her, if not for Him, of whom we learn nothing, we have a moving back-story. The film comes alive at last, it turns into the woman's story alone, she becomes real for the first time and we begin to care for her. She identifies with the plight of the Japanese women and compares her shaven-headed shame to the widespread loss of hair 'which the women of Hiroshima find has fallen out in the morning.'

It's a very womanly consideration, one the film clearly owes to the feminine sensibility of Marguerite Duras. Apparently Resnais had insisted the film couldn't be made unless Duras wrote the screenplay. She certainly brought a personal emotional response to the script: her own childhood and adolescence in Asia, and a French-Asian love affair. Her youthful romance with a Chinese man was the theme of her prize-winning novel *L'Amant* (The Lover).

As for *Hiroshima Mon Amour,* a film which contained far more pillow talk than Rock's and Doris's *Pillow Talk,* it earned her an Oscar nomination. Perhaps the Americans weren't so upset after all.

26
OUTSIDE OUR IMAGINATION

There's a strange phenomenon that occurs when I'm writing a book. It doesn't matter whether it's fiction or non-fiction, as the book progresses, more and more coincidental and pertinent real-life events begin to intrude.

The normally discarded nutty religious pamphlet found in the mailbox suddenly assumes relevance. A family argument, an overheard conversation in a coffee shop, an item buried in the back of a country newspaper, can seem extraordinarily applicable to the work in progress. So, too, can a particular person.

This time, while I was writing the chapter about *Hiroshima Mon Amour,* a coincidence occurred that was more direct and frightening than usual. Having long planned and saved, and given up her job in publishing, for an extensive stay in Japan, my daughter Laura arrived there two hours before Japan's most severe earthquake on record – magnitude 9 – struck on 11 March 2011.

She'd just checked into her Tokyo hotel room and was resting on her bed after the flight from Sydney when the building rocked and shook, the TV set sprang from the wall and the toilet exploded. Then the tsunami struck.

As radiation spread from the damaged reactors at the Fukushima Dai-ichi nuclear plant over the next week, her mother and I worked and worried to get her home. Every day brought more news of explosions and fires at the plant, and rising radiation levels. Each day the situation seemed more dire.

Bland official statements did little to allay our anxiety. As if he were announcing news about the US dollar's parity to the yen, the Prime Minister, Naoto Kan, deadpanned, 'The level seems very high, and there is still a very high risk of more radiation coming out.'

Laura managed to get through to us occasionally by phone text messages. At our urging – she wanted to continue her Japanese tour – and amid the chaos, she also bravely managed to battle her way to Narita airport and to her parents' great relief eventually catch a plane home.

. . .

TOKYO: Japan's response to the nuclear crisis that followed the March 11 tsunami was confused and riddled with problems, a report into the events revealed yesterday. The response included an erroneous assumption that an emergency cooling system was working and a delay in disclosing dangerous radiation leaks.

The disturbing picture of harried and bumbling workers and government officials scrambling to respond to the problems at Fukushima Dai-ichi nuclear power plant was depicted in the report detailing a government investigation.

The 507-page interim report, compiled by interviewing more than 400 people, including utility workers and government officials, found authorities had grossly underestimated tsunami risks, assuming the highest wave would be six metres. The tsunami hit at more than double those levels.

The report criticised the use of the term *soteigai*, meaning 'outside our imagination', which it said implied authorities were shirking responsibility for what had happened. By labelling the events as beyond what could have been expected, officials had invited public distrust.

The report found workers at Tokyo Electric Power Company, the utility that ran Fukushima Dai-ichi, were untrained to handle emergencies like the power shutdown that struck when the tsunami destroyed backup generators – setting off the world's worst nuclear disaster since Chernobyl.

A better response might have reduced the core damage, radiation leaks and the hydrogen explosions that followed at two reactors and sent plumes of radiation into the air.

The report said the government dallied in relaying information to the public and used evasive language to avoid admitting serious meltdowns at the reactors. The government also delayed disclosure of radiation data, unnecessarily exposing entire towns to radiation when they could have evacuated.

The report recommended separating the nuclear regulators from the unit that promotes nuclear energy, echoing frequent criticism since the disaster, which left 20,000 people dead or missing. The report acknowledged that people were still living in fear of radiation spewed into the air and water, as well as radiation in the food they eat.

'The nuclear disaster is far from over,' the report said. 'This accident has taught us an important lesson on how we must be ready for *soteigai*.'

– From the *New York Times, Reuters, Associated Press, Guardian, Hindu News, Sydney Morning Herald*, etc. (27 December 2011)

27
WINDY HARBOUR

When he came back from serving in the Montebellos and Hiroshima and Korea, the nuclear veteran Pat Coverley liked to unwind in the beach shack his family had built at Windy Harbour, on the shores of the Southern Ocean, around the corner from the Indian Ocean in the D'Entrecasteaux National Park.

Windy Harbour is still a well-kept secret. Its coastline of rugged limestone cliffs where the two oceans meet is the sort you imagine could harbour smugglers. Though the fishing is good it's not the sort of place to encourage regular tourists. The dramatic ocean views and pounding surf appeal to the more intrepid holidaymaker. With no electricity or mobile-phone reception, it's somewhere to get away from it all. It would be a fine place for writers to work, or for anyone wanting peace and solitude.

I wrote appreciatively about beach shacks in *The Bodysurfers;* I've always loved them. Not slick modern ones, but the salty, weather-beaten coastal shacks of the old Australia – unsophisticated comfy huts with lino floors, decorated with driftwood and shells and unmatched furniture, stocked with board games and decks of cards and dart boards and swimming gear. I was pleased to be invited to visit the Coverleys' shack at Windy Harbour.

It's four hours by road from Perth. On the way we drove through the karri forests to the timber town of Pemberton where Pat grew up, raised by 'Little Nanna', in a small wooden house a block from the timber yards.

At the village coffee shop I read in the *Pemberton Community News* an interview with a family who said they recently saw a panther padding along the South West Highway at night. Darren, Jessica and Leona Harding said it was 'a large black feline with reflective eyes and the swagger of a cat.'

Fifty-seven kilometres on, we arrived at Windy Harbour to be met by a sign on the settlement's Information Board: 'If you have any unusual stock losses, or sightings of a cougar or black panther, contact Sharon. I have a huge data base of sightings of these mysterious big cats.'

Sharon left an email address which I couldn't wait to contact when I returned to Perth a few days later. Alas, the mail dispatch system announced brusquely that my email couldn't be delivered. I can only hope Sharon's avid panther interest didn't end gruesomely.

As we strolled down to the shore, a male kangaroo as tall as a man stood in the dunes and eyed us suspiciously over the spinifex and pigface. It made no attempt to bound away so we detoured around it. Its eyes followed our progress. It looked more than a match for any panther.

Pat enjoyed recalling Windy Harbour's folklore, especially the wreck of the steamship *Michael J. Goulandris* on its reefs in December 1944. In the lives of the local population, this was the most exciting and lucrative happening of the twentieth century, strewing two thousand tons of general cargo, a month's wartime supplies for Perth, along Windy Harbour's beaches.

Everything from American canned meats, baby food, cocoa and soft drinks to fur coats, tyres, benzol in 44-gallon drums, medical supplies, tanned leather and half a hectare of lead pencils floated ashore. There were automotive parts, crates of typewriters, axe handles, soap, cosmetics, timber, torpedoes and trousers bobbing in the surf.

As the salvage mania grew, people from the nearby inland town of Northcliffe began hiding their spoils in the sand dunes so they could return to the shoreline for more goods. Pat said you could judge the IQ of the scavengers on the booty they coveted. Those folk who hankered after free axe handles and lead pencils, and their descendents two generations later, are still mocked today.

Similarly ridiculed were those who blew up their car engines with salvaged benzol, or hid drums of benzol in the bush just before the countryside's worst summer bushfires raced through.

And then there were those greedier scavengers, requiring instant energy for their endeavours but too busy acquiring luxury goods to stop to eat meals (or to read labels), who scoffed packet after packet of these unfamiliar chocolate bars they found. Laxettes, they were called. Soon men and women of all ages were squatting and moaning as a mass laxative overdose swept across the dunes.

. . .

Windy Harbour was the childhood holiday spot of Pat Coverley's daughter, Tracy. She loved it, and was pleased to have the rare opportunity to visit. She was at heart an outdoor girl, at ease with cold surf and generators and chip bath-heaters and wood stoves.

Her eyes lit up as she pointed out overhanging limestone outcrops on which her father and uncle had precariously balanced to fish for groper and herring, and the ocean pool where she and her sister Kim had learned to swim while her parents kept watch for great-whites from a nearby dinghy. 'As if they could have done anything about the sharks,' she laughed. 'Shooed them away?'

For years I'd heard Tracy's fond tales of Windy Harbour. She always spoke of it wistfully. For twenty years she'd visited only rarely because her husband shunned the coast and the rudimentary nature of the place. Early in their marriage he'd visited once and never again.

She would become the woman I thought of on those hot days trudging through the spinifex, animal grids and dusty bomb sites of the Montebello Islands. I would imagine her not in her home in Perth but in the shack at Windy Harbour.

I pictured her in this different climate on the country's far southern edge, next stop Antarctica. I imagined her walking alone on the beach, rugged up in a jumper and coat against the spray blustering in from two oceans. Her sea-mist coloured eyes. The Scandinavian hair blowing across her eyes.

I envisioned her pale hair whipping in the wind as I lay in Hurricane Hut at night under the shelves of Mortein and Nescafé and Four Bean Mix, the generator turned off till morning and migrant animals thudding outside in the humid dark.

28
DEATH BY TURF

In contrast to Pat Coverley's apparent resistance to nuclear fallout was the effect of war on my own ex-serviceman father, Roy, who ten years earlier had served Australia further north, in New Guinea. A bomber pilot, he survived Japanese anti-aircraft fire and flying and landing in dangerous mountain terrain but was officially war-wounded by another carcinogen: Turf cigarettes.

Cigarettes killed him, aged fifty-seven, in 1971. For years he smoked sixty unfiltered Turf a day – occasionally diverging to Ardath or State Express or Craven A, and in busy periods upping to seventy – although in latter years he cut down to thirty daily Benson and Hedges.

His morning coughing spells are fixed in my memory: the first ten-minute chest-clearing bathroom bout of coughing, hawking and spitting, followed by the second-stage phlegm dispersal out the car window as he drove me to school on his way to work. His lungs thus freed of overnight congestion, he'd light his first cigarette of the day.

In the RAAF in World War II, Roy piloted Boston bombers as a Flight-Lieutenant. In 2001, thirty years after his death, my stepmother Marie called up his wartime medical records at the Veterans' Affairs Department.

The young pilot, upset that two friends' aircraft had just been shot down in the jungle between Lae and Wau, had asked the squadron doctor for something to quell his nerves before he flew again the next day.

'Don't you smoke?' the doctor enquired, wonderingly, and prescribed him Turf cigarettes.

Amazingly, the doctor's notes and the 'prescription' remained in the official veterans' records. On that basis, the parlous state of his heart and lungs was considered a fatal war wound and my step-mother was granted a full war widow's pension.

Roy's last decade was emotionally and physically hectic. When my mother Dorothy, a twenty-a-day smoker – hardly a smoker at all by comparison – died suddenly of a cerebral haemorrhage, aged forty-seven, Roy was forty-eight and bereft. He absorbed himself in work and almost immediately was promoted by the Dunlop Rubber Company from West Australian manager to New South Wales manager. Two years later, on his first holiday as a widower, he met a thirty-eight-year-old holidaying nursing sister, Marie Keating, over gin slings at Singapore's Raffles Hotel, and fell for her.

In many ways they complemented each other. They both liked a laugh, a drink and a cigarette or sixty. They even shared the same birthday, 30 April. But in other ways Marie was from another world, one with a huge potential for disagreement. She'd been a hospital matron, had experienced life in the raw, and deaths aplenty, and stood no nonsense from him.

Unlike our mother, who would retreat from his drink-induced verbal blasts into hurt silences that went on for days, Marie fought fire with fire. Their ordinary kitchen conversations became a form of extended bickering that adult listeners found embarrassing and his children found strange and threatening.

To his Protestant, business-oriented, Liberal Party conservatism she brought strong Catholic beliefs and membership of a prominent right-wing Labor family, which included two MPs, Kevin and Frank Stewart, who would become ministers under Neville Wran and Bob Hawke respectively in the New South Wales and Federal Parliaments.

Within six months they were married. A week later they had to cut short their Gold Coast honeymoon when the wife of Roy's best man at his wedding, died suddenly. The timing was terrible. For Roy it abruptly brought back his own loss and grief and his post-honeymoon behaviour became aggressive and irrational.

Once he and I almost came to blows when he insulted my young wife for having two nuns as sisters. Yes, Ruth was Catholic. This was crazy stuff. What was his problem? As I pointed out, he'd now married *two* Catholic women himself.

Logic was no deterrent that summer morning in the front hallway of his house in St Ives, on Sydney's North Shore. Since our mother's death he'd stepped up his whisky and brandy drinking and his tempers took on a new ferocity. This wild-eyed stranger was begging to be hit, pushing his face into mine, his fists clenched and raised, daring me to hit him.

How I wanted to! But a tiny, fraying strand of familial regard held me back. *Hitting my father!* And just before the strand snapped and I swung my first punch at anyone since I was sixteen, his tearful wife of seven days grabbed him by the sleeve of his honeymoon casual wear and dragged him away.

Within a year Marie became pregnant. During the pregnancy Roy had a mild heart attack and was hospitalised for two days' observation. Dunlop seemed vaguely affronted at this inconvenient occurrence and promoted him sideways to national factories' manager, based in Melbourne. The couple moved cities with the new baby. My father was not chuffed with his new appointment and, accurately, saw the writing on the wall.

When my half-brother John was three, Roy had a second heart

attack (no routine bypasses in those days), upon which Dunlop brusquely put the loyal company man out to pasture. He was devastated by his forced retirement; the company had been his life ever since leaving school. As a young man, for experience, he'd even worked on its rubber plantations in Malaya, and on the grimy factory floor in Fort Dunlop, in Birmingham, England. As he liked to regale dinner-table guests during my childhood, 'I told Dorothy when we married, "You've married Dunlop as well as me."' And, worse, to her, 'You know Dunlop will always come first.'

And it did. Only a world war could interfere with his devoted service to rubber. I have a draft of a letter he wrote to Dunlop headquarters while he was piloting bombers in New Guinea: the young pilot beseeches the company (unnecessarily, the government insisted on it) to keep his job for him until he came home from the war.

Now a grumpy middle-aged man with health problems and surprisingly inadequate superannuation, he was rattling around all day in a boring suburban house in Glen Waverley with a deep grievance, a wife who was an inexperienced mother, a fractious baby, few outside interests, no office to escape to – and no (or hardly any) calming cigarettes,

At his relatively young age, he had no retirement plan, or any pursuits or amusements beyond selling tyres, tennis racquets, sandshoes, mattresses and fan belts: all those admirable rubber products and sporting goods that – cruelly, bewilderingly – were still blithely entering the market-place without the benefit of his forty years' know-how.

On doctors' orders, Roy had 'stopped smoking' and cut back on beer and the nightly Dewar's that so inflamed him. He began inhaling cigarillos instead, which he claimed didn't count as smoking. For 'medicinal purposes' he brought forward by ten hours his first brandy of the day. The Remy Martin was taken in his morning coffee 'to make it more interesting'. As the day's coffees mounted, his behaviour became more interesting, too. In mid-afternoon he dropped the coffee part of the equation, and by dinner-time the entire domestic environment was too interesting for words.

He was only in his mid-fifties, but in the mode of the times, apart from fathering a child at his age, he'd been acting elderly and becoming increasingly crusty since his early forties. Even before his heart attacks he'd begun finding cardigans surprisingly comfortable, given up golf for lawn bowls, and started wearing those tweed hats that Professor Henry Higgins had drawn to his attention on the album jacket of *My Fair Lady*.

Always a standard conservative Liberal voter, his views became cantankerous. Watching TV, on his umpteenth brandy and second pack of cigarillos, he'd shout down the pugnacious young union leader, Bob Hawke: 'Who does that commo think he is?' When my sister Jan was awarded an American Field Service student scholarship to live with an American family for a year, in her case a middle-class African-American family, he put his foot down. She was made to switch to a wealthy white brewing family in Milwaukee, whose lifestyle and attitudes she disliked so much that she soon left them.

The last time I ever saw him, however, on the shore of Sydney Harbour, he looked calm and happy. He was on his way home to Melbourne from a health-boosting Pacific cruise. He was eating lobster, drinking Sauvignon Blanc and winking at a young Canadian waitress in Doyle's restaurant in Rose Bay. The waitress had just tickled his chin while tying a bib shaped like a mud crab around his neck.

'You can do that again,' he said.

He had colour in his cheeks and suddenly seemed his younger and more amusing self. Remarkably, he had no complaints about the meal. Everything was delicious and compliments were sent to the chef. In front of my step-mother, he exchanged phone numbers and addresses with the waitress. 'Listen, Kelly, you must look us up in Melbourne. Our house is yours. I insist.'

Eating in restaurants with him had previously always been risky.

He was inclined to send things back: food and wine and cutlery with apparent smudges on it. His tables were presented with more apparently corked wine than any I've ever known. 'Sommelier, this dud bottle must have slipped past you.'

Unfortunately, he also regarded himself as an expert on the Waldorf salad. He would pick suspiciously through each one, itemising the ingredients. Apples, walnuts, celery, mayonnaise, raisins . . . 'Waiter!' he'd call. 'I don't wish to nitpick' – yes, he did – 'but the chef has left out the chopped lettuce!'

Invariably the waiter would return from the kitchen, saying, 'Chef says there is no lettuce *in* a Waldorf salad. The classic Waldorf salad is served *on* a bed of lettuce.'

To my sister's and my horror, at the Chelsea in Kings Cross one night he stood up and said, 'I'd better show him then,' and marched out to the kitchen. To our astonishment he escaped unscathed. A little later he returned, his tie speckled with mayonnaise, followed by a waiter bearing a bowl of green mush.

'Your *lettuce* salad, sir,' said the waiter.

'Thank you,' my father beamed. 'A proper Waldorf for once.'

The last time I ever saw him he was twinkling goodbye to his new favourite waitress as he left Doyle's, donning his Henry Higgins hat to face the breeze off the harbour. He died four weeks later.

Six months after his death, however, I heard from him again. His handwriting on the postcard gave me a start. He'd posted it in some sleepy Polynesian port while on the Pacific cruise. 'Dear Son,' he wrote. 'Having an enjoyable time. It's done me the world of good.'

. . .

He died in his bed at 8.30 a.m. on 10 August 1971. Marie found him when she returned home from taking young John to school. Being a nurse, and used to final procedures, she laid out the body of her dead husband herself.

The day of his funeral was wintry and the Uniting Church service was conducted by a minister who'd never met him. Nor had my father ever been to his church. The ruddy-faced minister focused on his Masonic Lodge membership, which had been a passing phase thirty years before. Dunlop was mentioned in one sentence. This alone would have made my father turn in his coffin.

In the church I was searching my childhood memories of him for something fond and tender. I remembered him once playing table-tennis with me, and once a game of squash, both of which he easily won. I recalled that in the early Perth days when I was six he would come home straight from work and let me sit on his knees and steer the car into the garage, and in summer he'd sometimes take us to the beach of an evening after work, and on those days he would eat dinner at the same time as the rest of us, not hours later after he'd been drinking.

I saw him standing on the shore at North Cottesloe wearing an embarrassing beach hat and unfashionable swimming trunks and beckoning us out of the water, his gestures becoming more impatient as we dived under waves and pretended not to see him. Our pretence couldn't go on for ever though, and we still got our after-swim ice-creams.

I remembered him mentioning the pet glider possum that flew with him in his cockpit in New Guinea. It sat in his shirt pocket as he dropped bombs from his Boston on Japanese fuel depots in the jungle. Then that rare war-time anecdote segued into a memory of him playing the ukelele once, and the mouth-organ once as well, and him singing *Bye Bye Blackbird,* which he'd learned in the airmen's wet canteen – that song only – during the war. That worked, too. And there was another good memory of him once doing amusing Hitler impressions at the dinner table. There were quite a few good things to remember, but all of them he only did once.

And then for some reason I recalled his colourful tale of his navigator friend Laurie Jackson in New Guinea who went swimming in the Solomon Sea despite warnings and got coral polyps in his ears. For the rest of his life, Laurie Jackson's ears seeped a seaweedy liquid and sprouted coral outcrops which had to be constantly cut out.

As a child I imagined ornate orange, green and purple Barrier Reef profusions fanning out from Laurie Jackson's head like moose antlers, but the coral actually grew inwards into his inner ears, and his brain as well, and Laurie Jackson went stone deaf and then died.

And in the church my memories became confused and strange again as the red-cheeked minister droned on about this stranger the ardent Freemason, and outside it was raining over Melbourne's outer suburbs of hardware barns and supermarkets, and we mumbled our way through an unfamiliar final hymn. And shortly afterwards my father went into the oven.

29
MOREAU'S ISLAND

The days on Hermite Island assumed a regular rhythm. We were up at five, everyone shuffling half-asleep onto the hut's porch, and staring out at the shadowy tidal flats that all of a sudden connected us to Buttercup Island across the bay.

As the birds began their chattering ablutions on the roof, we put on our boots and shuffled one-by-one down the dune to the toilet. Then we started the generator, boiled a kettle of Indian Ocean, drank our teas and instant coffees, ate cereal mixed with long-life milk, and watched the dawn come up.

The tides arrived and departed so swiftly the lagoon was never still for long. One minute it was deep and roiling with sharks' dorsal fins and stingray wings; the next time you looked it was a pearly expanse of sand criss-crossed by tidal streams.

Mainland Australia was far to the east over the sea. With no radio news, television, newspapers or computer reception on our desert island we had no knowledge of events in the wider world. No Middle East. No information on wars, earthquakes, politics or crime. Suicide bombings, oil spills and book reviews came and went without me knowing of them. Celebrities were out of rehab before I knew they'd been admitted. Despite being a three-newspaper-a-day man at home, I missed only the crosswords.

Squatting sleepily on the porch eating cornflakes for the first time since childhood (and enjoying them), it was hard to appreciate that the focus of the Western world was once directed on this speck in the ocean. And that all the destructive power that military science could marshal in the mid-twentieth century was concentrated here. Or, for that matter, all the force that nature, too, could muster – those cyclonic winds of 410 kilometres per hour.

No-one felt like speaking this early, and by five-thirty we were out on the track to check the overnight traps for bandicoots and wallabies. Another day on Hermite: just the five of us and the marsupials and birds and the Bushes of Doom. After several days of my acquaintance with them, of bursting heedlessly into and through the spinifex mounds countless times, I'd just discovered they could also house creatures other than spinifex birds.

'How lucky are these little bandicoots?' I'd remarked to Brent. 'Transported to an island with no predators to worry about.'

'Yeah, pretty lucky,' he said. 'Their only worries are the various raptors that fly over here from the mainland – eagles, kites, harriers. There are some big goannas. And pythons, of course.'

Pythons? Yes, the Stimson's python. Also known as the large-blotched python, for the patterns of its skin. Named in honour of A.F. Stimson, doyen of the reptile section of the British Museum.

There were no trees on the island. So where did the pythons live? But I already knew. As I was crashing through their prickly habitat, it was probably best that I didn't know until I returned home that Hermite Island's Bushes of Doom also housed not only the 'mildly venomous' orange-naped snake but the 'quite venomous' whip snake.

. . .

A simple routine soon has its daily highlights. Mine were the first coffee of the morning and the first beer of the evening. The coffee was instant Nescafé from a can as big as a peanut-butter bucket, but for the pleasure it provided it could have been ground and crafted by a prize-winning barista.

As for the first beer of a two-can daily ration: after a day spent trudging up and down the spiky dunes in the heat, and the knowledge that there was only one more beer to follow, the initial six o'clock mouthful of Victoria Bitter had a special significance. By this hour the generator had been going all day and the beer was properly chilled. The phrase 'nectar of the gods' never seemed more apt.

Pleasurable, too, were the chats at dinner around the tiny barbecue table and the gradual discovery of common ground. In Brent's and my case it was Bob Dylan, troublesome lower backs, and the East Fremantle football team of the 1960s. It was entertaining hearing of the adventurous wildlife experiences of Andy, the scientist, in east Africa. Here on the island a bandicoot had caused him extreme anxiety. In Africa, it was being bailed up by a hyena on his way home from the tavern.

Before the generator was turned off each night, I wrote a bit more and dipped into two books I'd brought with me. *The Island of Dr Moreau* was the first. It was a favourite of my adolescence and I wanted to see if it still gripped me.

It did, more than ever. It was hard to believe it was first published in 1896, a century before genetic engineering. *The Island of Dr Moreau* wore its years and H.G. Wells's bizarre imaginings very lightly. I'm no science fiction fan but I like a good thriller, and its plot – a deluded surgeon on a remote island conducts experiments on a wide range of animals in an attempt to turn them into humans – was still a page-turner.

Although Wells was only thirty when it was published, he already had two novels under his belt and an ethical opinion formed by Charles Darwin's theories. His Dr Moreau is a clearly drawn character, subtly and realistically introduced into the story. As matter-of-fact as he's misguided, he's the personification of science's continual attempt to control the natural world.

While migrant animals who owed their existence to political-ecological conscience scrabbled and thumped outside, I wondered whether reading *The Island of Dr Moreau* on a desert island turned Ark, the perpetual glow from Barrow Island – the Ark preceding this one – lighting my storeroom-bedroom window, would enable me to see Wells's ethical questions in a new light.

However, the premise was not the same. Even if some Darwinists in Wells's day did envision the life of a bandicoot or a spinifex-bird being of value, this was a different question: the Economy versus the Environment, pragmatic power and technology steering their way through a more subtle moral dilemma. Animals weren't being sliced up and sewn together in order to become Man; they were being shifted and saved.

We have taken your habitat from you in order to make trillions of dollars. But we understand that conservation is a sensitive issue and your survival is politically important. In order that you don't become extinct we are going to a lot of trouble and expense to resettle you in a secure environment. True, it used to be a nuclear test site, but that unpleasant-ness is all in the past.

Wearing my film critic's hat, my interest in the book had led me to compare it with the three movie versions. The 1932 and 1996 efforts were over-the-top, with the latter version, starring a primped, pow-dered and out-of-control Marlon Brando, so ludicrous that it warrants cult status. (The second version, in 1977, with Burt Lancaster as the doctor, is the most serious.)

Much of the Brando film's curiosity value comes from grotesque conduct not in the script. Once again it looked as if Brando the actor had found the ethos of islands irresistible. As an obese and oddly feminised Moreau, he seems not so much to be playing the doctor as the Balance of Nature. Or, as Hollywood wisecracked, the island itself. An extreme case of islomania? But the once-great actor is only partly responsible for the film's weirdness. Compared to his colleagues on this shoot, Brando was a pussycat.

Shot in far north Queensland, the film tested many people's careers, bankrolls, egos and grasps on reality. Not only do the beast-people seem to take over the movie as well as Dr Moreau's island, this was a film where the original director, Richard Stanley, literally went to the dogs.

Sacked by the film's backers only four days into filming, Stanley ran off to live with his pet dingo pups in the rainforest, only to sneak back on the set in disguise. Heavily made-up as Dog-Man, he secretly appeared in the film directed by his replacement, the veteran John Frankenheimer.

As for the star, considering his voluminous kaftans and calcimined cheeks have filled the screen for two-thirds of the film, Moreau/Brando's eventual murder, despite all the clawing, snorting and squealing that accompany it, turns out to be anticlimactic.

Predictably, the beast-people revolt, and even those with gentlemanly table manners and vertical postures soon revert. They aren't the only ones. This *Island of Dr Moreau* is so histrionic that you soon forget the worrying clash between nature and science and find yourself regressing with everyone on screen and behind the camera.

The first version also had a chequered passage. *Island of Lost Souls,* with Charles Laughton as Dr Moreau, was outlawed in many countries because of the ethical and religious issues it raised. Misinterpreting Wells's point, the American fundamentalist Right (as usual, not bothering to read the book) attacked both the book and the film for proposing the idea that Man could create Man by splicing and grafting the flesh of living animals. In fact, the author's whole point was to deplore this idea.

The Press mauled the film, it was a box-office flop and pulled from release. Wells himself denounced it. Laughton, an animal lover, was said to be so upset by the notion of vivisection that he would never again visit a zoo.

. . .

The second book I'd brought with me to the Montebellos was Gerald Durrell's *My Family and Other Animals*. A strange choice. Another island book, it was a prize awarded to me at age seventeen for editing my school magazine, *The Cygnet*. Maybe at last this was the appropriate time to read it.

After flipping through a couple of chapters back then, I'd tossed it aside as too quaintly effusive for my taste. At the time I was moving from the entertaining sex and violence of James Bond to Ernest Hemingway, Scott Fitzgerald and William Faulkner, via James Jones's *From Here to Eternity* and Norman Mailer's *The Naked and the Dead*. It's fair to say that all of them were at the opposite end of the literary spectrum to Gerald Durrell's cheery roundup of insects, siblings and tortoises.

Perhaps because it was a prize, the Durrell book held a strange power over me. In spite of it remaining relentlessly unread, *My Family and Other Animals* was ever-present in my life. More than any other book I owned, it had followed me from home to home, State to State, bookcase to bookcase, surviving the division of books, record albums and CDs that followed relationship break-ups, the school crest embossed on its green cloth cover forever announcing the motto *Duty*.

A memoir about the Durrell family's life on the island of Corfu, it featured a lot of interesting animals, as well as a character who would become the noted writer and islomaniac Lawrence Durrell. As I hurriedly stuffed the book into my bag, my thinking went that I, too, was heading for an island whose whole point nowadays was its interesting animals. I was also writing a memoir, and I was mildly curious to learn what Lawrence Durrell had been like as a young writer. Wouldn't it be a good idea to bring the ubiquitous *My Family and Other Animals* along, and finally read it? Maybe it was my *duty*.

After a couple of chapters I gave up again. My setting was wrong. Perhaps it needed to be read with a gin and tonic in a deckchair in an English country garden with bumblebees buzzing in the hollyhocks and the sounds of mixed-doubles coming over the hedge.

At any time I'm fascinated by the fauna in my surroundings, but in the prickly, marsupial-enlivened world of sand dunes and nuclear debris, Durrell's adjectival relish of ant-lions, mantids and fireflies was too jolly-hockey-sticks for me.

Apparently the author took a few liberties with his family in *My Family*. Elder brother Larry is depicted as an unmarried and constant grumpy presence in the household whereas I recently read that Lawrence hadn't lived in the family house on Corfu at all, but on another part of the island with his wife Nancy. The book's chronology of events is said to change the facts, and in order to keep the hearty atmosphere rollicking along, Gerald Durrell says that the family finally left Corfu for the sake of his education. The real reason was World War II, a more understandable reason in my view.

Not that it mattered. A raging best-seller, *My Family and Other Animals*, adapted for TV, film and the stage, has never been out of print since 1956. Even Lawrence Durrell gave it a favourable plug. Meanwhile, my copy, the bookmark intact at page 56, remains securely back on my bookshelves – *Duty* again unrequited.

. . .

On Hermite Island there was also a two-hour rest-period after mid-day that I valued. It was a luxury to be out of the sun. Each afternoon I carried a plastic deckchair and the small barbecue table into the storeroom-bedroom and read and wrote some more, took notes, and leafed through a sheaf of nuclear background reports and environment-news items I'd brought with me.

The news stories, especially those from the finance pages, were confusing for their contradictory information. They always had a bet each way. On concerns for Barrow Island, environmentalists made serious and definite statements, and then immediately acted counter to the opinions they'd just expressed.

In the news items you could sense an air of weary resignation, as if the environmentalists had put up a token resistance before succumbing to the sheer overwhelming pressure of the word 'trillions'. Trillions of tonnes, trillions of cubic feet, trillions of dollars. What hope did a turtle, a dugong, a bandicoot, a spinifex-wren, a conservationist, ever have against 'trillions'?

. . .

Gorgon Gas Expansion Approved
(*Sydney Morning Herald,* 30 April 2009)
The Environmental Protection Authority has approved Chevron's multi-billion dollar Gorgon liquefied natural gas project expansion on Barrow Island, despite highlighting serious environmental concerns.

In a statement that had been much anticipated by resource industry watchers, Environment Protection Authority chairman Paul Vogel today said he opposed more industry on Barrow island.

'Given the very high environmental and unique conservation values of Barrow island, which are reflected in its status as a Class-A Nature Reserve, it is the view of the EPA that, as a matter of principle, industry should not be located on a nature reserve, and specifically not on Barrow Island,' Dr Vogel said.

However, the EPA concluded that the expanded proposal could go ahead provided 'stringent conditions' were imposed.

Chevron said today it welcomed the recommendation that the expanded Chevron-operated Gorgon project could meet environmental standards. Chevron Australia managing director Roy Krzywosinski said the EPA's decision was an important step in the regulatory process for the project, which is forecast to create up to 6000 jobs.

In 2007 the WA Government approved construction of a gas processing plant on Barrow Island despite advice from the EPA that it should be built on the mainland. Chevron later applied to expand the proposal from 5 million to 10 million and now to 15 million metric tonnes a year in response to rising industry cost pressures.

Chevron, in partnership with Shell and Mobil, plans to develop the Greater Gorgon gas fields, located off the north-west coast of WA. The fields contain resources of about 40 trillion cubic feet of gas, Australia's largest-known gas resource.

Chevron's proposal includes a gas processing plant on Barrow Island; tapping the Greater Gorgon gas fields via sub-sea pipelines to Barrow Island; liquid natural gas shipping facilities to transport products to offshore markets; and greenhouse gas management, by injecting carbon dioxide into deep formations beneath the island.

. . .

Anger Over Turtle Death at Barrow Island Gorgon Project
(*Sunday Times*, 5 June 2010)
The death of an endangered-species turtle at Chevron's controversial Gorgon gas site on Barrow Island has sparked a major investigation.

The juvenile hawksbill turtle was sucked into equipment during dredging to deepen the port for shipping access to the Class-A nature reserve for construction of the $43 billion liquefied natural gas project.

The Department of Environment and Conservation has confirmed the turtle death is under investigation.

The turtle was discovered on Thursday in a dredging overflow tank three kilometres off Barrow Island. The island is home to a host of rare, endangered and endemic species and is surrounded by gardens of unique coral. Conservation Council marine expert Tim Nicol said dredging was also destroying pristine coral reef.

'It's hard to understand how a critically endangered animal can be sucked up and spat out by dredging machinery,' Mr Nicol said. 'It would have suffered a cruel death.'

Chevron said in a statement it did not know what had killed the turtle. 'Dredging activities started last month. We are not aware of any other turtle incidents in that period.'

· · ·

When the death of one turtle becomes a news story, clearly times have changed dramatically in the Dampier Archipelago. Considering the nineteenth and twentieth-century gourmets' fondness for turtle soup, it's a wonder there are any turtles left at all. Until 1973 the administrative body in charge of the turtle industry was the State Fisheries Department in its various incarnations, including a period when it was sensitively named the Department of Aborigines and Fisheries.

According to its records, 55,125 green turtles alone were officially killed for human consumption in the north-west between 1837 and 1973, when they were finally protected. These figures don't take into account those constantly killed outside the industry as lobster bait and as traditional food by Aborigines. In one year alone, 1960–61, five tons of green turtle eggs were commercially gathered from the beaches of the Dampier Archipelago as soon as they were laid.

Unfortunately for thousands of loggerhead turtles, 'fishers' often mistakenly killed them instead of the desirable green turtles, the loggerheads' body count not featuring in the official catch or export records. Their resemblance, and the suspicion that they ate the eggs of green turtles, led to them being referred to as 'rogue' turtles. (How dare they masquerade as tasty green turtles and confuse the turtle-fishing economy!)

A 1927 newspaper article was most unsympathetic to the rogues. 'They are of a very coarse nature and the flavour if converted into soup is easily detected by the ordinary epicure.' There was another variety which did not appeal to turtle-soup lovers either. The now more rare hawksbill turtles had an equally desirable attribute, however, and 77,513 of them were officially killed for their decorative shells.

. . .

Turtle fatalities of another origin were observed by Max Kimber, then a young seaman aboard HMAS *Mildura*, which backed up the *Operation Hurricane* nuclear taskforce in October 1952. Twelve months later, he was back on the Montebellos for a second tour of duty, this time two weeks aboard HMAS *Fremantle,* assisting British scientists monitoring the aftermath of the first British bomb test.

During a day off, Mr Kimber and a friend sailed around Trimouille Island in a small sailboat. Halfway around the island they were forced to land to repair their boat's rudder. On shore they found 'tens of thousands' of dead turtles.

'For the entire length of the island's two beaches, each about 500 metres long, dead turtles were piled three to four deep.' There were dead turtles of all sizes, some too big for a man to lift, others were hatchlings small enough to fit in one hand. 'The smell was very bad, and was still noticeable when we were offshore in the boat.'

After repairing the rudder, Max Kimber and his friend resumed their journey, taking a turtle carapace with them as a souvenir. They towed it behind the boat in an attempt to clean it. Once back aboard *Fremantle,* the shell was found to be radioactive, and was thrown overboard.

The incidence of hatchlings among the dead turtles indicated that these tiny animals had been born and died a year after the tests. Their presence one-and-a-half kilometres away from the *Plym* bomb site, and the radioactive condition of the turtle shell, also pointed to radiation rather than the direct bomb blast as the cause of death.

Trimouille Island's heavy turtle casualties aroused no official interest at the time. Discussing the presence of some live turtles on the island two years later, a British scientist offered the opinion that the nuclear tests might actually have advantaged the turtle population of the Montebellos, 'since the seabirds which would have preyed on the hatchlings all died with the bomb blasts.'

. . .

The discoverer of the turtle graveyard, Max Kimber, would later become president of the Ex-Service Atomic Survivors' Association, fighting for the rights of nuclear-test ex-servicemen and for full disclosure of information about the bomb projects. The association says British and Australian governments ever since have fobbed off claims that Australians were guinea-pigs exposed to high levels of radiation.

'The illnesses many Montebello servicemen received are testament to the fact we have been completely hoodwinked, and been used by these governments, who never recognised the service we gave.'

Recollecting for the ABC in 2001 what his tasks were on the Montebellos, Mr Kimber said he was sent with British scientists to the islands after the first atomic tests. 'I was part of the landing party and the boats' coxswain for the two-week stay. I transported the scientists to and from the island every day, and assisted them on the land. I followed the scientists around with a bag, and as they recovered samples they placed them in this bag I was carrying. I carted around all this collected material all day.

'They were dressed in protective white suits and boots and hoods, and I walked around just wearing navy-issue sandals, shorts and a T-shirt. At the end of each day I had to destroy their protective clothing and have a salt-water shower operating for them. No protective clothing was considered necessary for us in the ship's crew.

'One day when I returned to the ship I was found to be so radioactive that I had to remove all my clothing on the quarterdeck. My clothes were then burnt and I was hosed down with a fire hose. My sandals were soaked in a bucket of sea water overnight. This was interesting because the sea water for the fire hose and the bucket was pumped directly from the bay where the atomic bomb was exploded.

'After my discharge from the navy in 1958 I had already begun to develop skin cancers to all parts of my body.'

30
HIBISCUS

Occasionally I wonder how my father would react to the current Barrow Island trillions. Grumpily, I guess, and who could blame him? He held a swag of WAPET shares for years and sold them a month before oil was discovered.

Everything my father owned when he died went to my stepmother: his superannuation, house, money, his remaining shares and also what had been my mother's things: the possessions we'd always associated with her: the dining table and chairs we'd eaten at throughout our childhoods, the familiar crockery and cutlery and vases and pictures and motherly knick-knacks.

It was a peculiar feeling to visit my stepmother Marie's apartment over the years and see my mother's furniture in a central position and her trinkets randomly displayed on the dining-room dresser and side-tables of a woman who never knew her. Brother Bill and I told ourselves it was just *stuff*, what did it matter? But it did, a bit. And I know my sister, Jan, felt more strongly about it.

Marie lived another thirty-five years, the last five years on my father's Turf war-wound pension. I was fond of her and her death struck me with a ringing finality. It meant the end of my parents' generation and made me suddenly the elder of the family.

'Now you're the patriarch,' said Jan. That was a worrying image. I kept picturing a commercial for wine or pasta sauce: a white-stubbled old Mediterranean gent sitting at a long rustic table in a vineyard, eating spaghetti and drinking red wine with several generations of handsome patronising descendents wearing rumpled natural fibres.

'No more wine for Papa!' giggles one of his flashing-eyed daughters.
'Yes, fill it up. Ho, ho, ho!'
'But what about your gout, you naughty old fellow?'
'Let Papa have another glass (says the second flashing-eyed daughter) At his age, let him have some fun . . .'

After Marie's funeral I had an abrupt impulse to return to my childhood, or as near to it as I could manage. The urge couldn't wait. A school reunion gave me the excuse. So I phoned Bill, who now lived in southern Queensland, and we arranged, before we became even a month older, to make a boys' visit to Perth.

In thirty years this was the only occasion he and I had been in each other's company without partners or children around. I travelled on two flights from northern New South Wales; Bill caught the red-eye from Brisbane. It was our first time back home together since we were teenagers, since the family broke up and moved east when our mother died.

For the reunion we rented a flat in Fremantle, by the fishing boat harbour. Immediately the years fell away and for a week we were young bachelors again. We reminisced over wine every night. (We kept off politics and anything likely to ruin the mood.) Each morning we swam away our hangovers in the surf and then ate bacon and eggs and strong coffees at Italian cafés. We drank beer at the Ocean Beach and Esplanade hotels. We ate every meal out. The kitchen remained in a pristine state and the TV was never turned on.

In our rental car we drove to the house of our childhood, where everything had abruptly gone wrong that sunny March morning. Driving Bill to the school bus at eight a.m. in her eggshell blue Ford Prefect, she'd suffered a severe headache. Rarely ill, she'd played two sets of tennis the day before. The previous month she had turned forty-seven.

She managed to drive home though the morning traffic. Back in her kitchen, she uttered her last, commonplace, words on this earth. They were to me. 'Your baked beans are on the stove, dear.'

While my father, unaware, whistled tunes from *Oklahoma!* under his morning shower, my mother went back to bed, lapsed into unconsciousness, and died of a cerebral haemorrhage.

Our house had attracted neighbourhood criticism for its 'modern' design when it was built for $20,000 in 1955. Where the builders had soured the soil with their lime and cement heaps, the grass never meshed properly thereafter, but trailed across the lawn's sandy patches like a comb-over on a bald scalp.

Our back yard's main feature was a Davy Crockett cabin built by my father from pine off-cuts for Bill's tenth birthday. (He received a Davy Crockett 'coonskin' hat as well.) The house, now owned by a Chinese-Australian doctor with a young family, no longer stood out as more modern than its neighbours. An extra storey had been built. And some owner after us had given up on the patchy grass problem. The yard was paved over and where the Davy Crockett cabin had stood there was a swimming pool.

The most noticeable difference, however, was a high, all-enclosing limestone wall. All the houses in the street were similarly barricaded. In my childhood, Perth suburban fashion had spurned the front fence. The whole point of home ownership in that sandy, drought-ridden place was to provide the vista of an oasis. It was considered admirable to throw open your property's verdant, much-watered English lawn and compulsory rose garden to the admiring gaze of strangers motoring slowly by on that peculiarly West Australian phenomenon, the Sunday Drive.

The idea of deterring intruders was unthought of. By the 1970s that outlook had changed dramatically. The four-year prowling and killing rampage of Eric Edgar Cooke charted in *The Shark Net* had changed not only the suburb's psychological state but its architecture and landscaping.

The old middle-middle-class neighbourhood, most of its streets named after graceful racing yachts from yesteryear – *Viking, Curlew, Circe, Adelma, Melvista, Genesta* – had gone brashly and expensively upmarket since our childhood. Understated bungalows had become edifices. Our suburban streets now paid architectural homage to Los Angeles and Tuscany.

We passed the ivy-covered former home of Mrs Daphne B, an elegant brunette who allegedly 'went with' Americans in the war, and was still being ostracised by the local matrons twenty years later. There, too, was the formerly modest bungalow – now turned into a mansion – of Gillian C, an usherette at the Ambassadors Theatre, who was excitedly rumoured to receive house-calls from our local GP, a Gregory Peck look-alike, after cinema and medical hours

Our nostalgia cruise was becoming like a down-home version of a Hollywood bus tour. Here was the now stately home of Rex B, a schizophrenic albino larrikin who'd saddened his sedate parents by pioneering pink shirts and black stovepipe jeans in our region, and who eventually succumbed to his condition and hanged himself. And there was the bungalow of the beautiful Roberta A, the first girl I was crazy over, who would later be decapitated at twenty by the propeller of her husband's light aircraft.

One other house, five kilometres away, hadn't changed at all. This was the house of the cub reporter's too-young marriage, down the hill from Swanbourne beach. Back then it was the one-bedroom, lamb-smelling 'residence' attached to the butcher shop in North Street. We called it the House of Meat. Craving a meat-free home life, the butcher chose to live elsewhere. The rent was kept low by the fatty lamb smell and the blood and gut fragments he hosed every afternoon into the gully trap in the tiny cement back yard.

The House of Meat and its lone frangipani tree were surprisingly unaltered. The frangipani was exactly the same shape and size it was in 1964. I could easily recall our baby boy James splashing there in his paddle-pool, giggling at the frangipani blossoms floating in the water. The butcher shop was now a speech therapy centre.

Without discussing it, Bill and I knew the real purpose of our reunion was to visit our mother's grave. Nevertheless, we'd deliber- ately put off the visit until the day before we were to leave Perth. It was a hot Sunday in March, the same month of the year as her death, and inexplicably – I'd presumed Sunday would be its busiest visiting day – everything at the Karrakatta cemetery was closed. The office. The florist. The coffee shop. Most worryingly, the directory of grave sites.

A heat mirage shimmered over the hundreds of acres of pale deserted gravestones. There were no staff, no grave diggers, no other mourners. This was a needle-in-a-haystack dilemma. We'd come thou- sands of kilometres and there was no way of finding her grave.

In the scant shade of a spindly gum we wiped away sweat and tried to focus. Trying to recall the grave's whereabouts, I cast my mind back to the morning of the funeral. At eighteen, I was the youngest person there. At fourteen Bill was regarded as too young to attend. As for Jan, our nine-year-old sister, her presence was out of the question. For a whole week Dad couldn't even muster the courage to tell her Mum had died. Jan was told she was 'in hospital' somewhere. In my grief I was mystified at his restricting the funeral attendance, and by his veering away from emotion.

Apart from my father, my mother's brother Ian and myself, everyone present in that wasteland of grey sand was a business associate of my father's. None of her friends were present: no Jean or Pat or Joan or

Thelma or Molly. I don't know why my father permitted no women; perhaps in case they became emotional at the stern Presbyterian service. *She didn't even know most of these men!* I thought.

The funeral resembled an odd *al fresco* business meeting. Around the grave, the freshly dug deeper sand was a sour bile-yellow. Deadpan businessmen shook sand out of their trouser cuffs, chatted cryptically out of the sides of their mouths and dusted off their black shoes.

Now Bill and I set out to find the Presbyterian section. An hour passed as we roamed up and down the lines of graves, hatless, our shirts sticking to us in the heat. The Karrakatta landscape had changed. Catholics and Anglicans still prevailed, but straggly banksia trees and flowering gums had grown up everywhere.

Eventually we found the section. Dead Presbyterians stretched right up the hill, covering many acres, until they abutted the Muslims. But our mother didn't seem to be among them.

I recalled that she'd been buried near the grave of John Curtin. Religion and the alphabet had laid Australia's wartime Prime Minister and our little suburban mother close together. It wasn't difficult to find Curtin's plinth and column but the rest of the cemetery-scape was entirely and bewilderingly changed. Not only had hundreds of other Presbyterians crowded in, but Curtin's resting place was now surrounded by the graves of other dignitaries.

My mother's quiet nook had become the cemetery's VIP corner. The alphabet had been tossed aside as other important people such as the former Governor-General, Sir Paul Hasluck, and Dame Alexandra Hasluck, were laid down next to Curtin. Of her grave there was no sign.

By now we were emotionally wrung out. Had she been exhumed and moved? Been overlaid by another grave? Maybe her grave-space's allotted time was up. The idea was frightening and there was no-one to ask. Was the whole trip for nothing?

Then Bill had a brainwave. He mobile-phoned his wife Georgina in Queensland. She Googled the Karrakatta cemetery and found a map of the grave sites, all named and numbered. Ten minutes later, thanks to technology, we found the grave. It was small and plain and strewn with sun-faded sea-shells placed there by our sister Jan twenty years before.

Suddenly flowers were essential and the florist was closed. But we couldn't leave without placing flowers on her grave. In a near-frenzy of flower-seeking, I remembered some hibiscus bushes growing over the fence near the cemetery entrance. I hurried across the acres of tomb-stones, tore off two branches of scarlet blossoms, and trudged back.

'She used to like hibiscus,' I said, though I struggled to remember if this was so.

'Yes, she did,' Bill agreed. Then we each placed a branch on her grave.

'She was too young,' Bill murmured, and his voice broke. Then we two ageing men remembered her with intense affection and we became again teenage boys whose mother had just died. We wept a little and briefly clasped each other's shoulders – the lapsed-Presbyterian equiva-lent of a male hug – and went and had a quiet drink.

. . .

My clearest images of my mother are of her effortless swimming style and her fearlessly jack-knifing off the high diving tower like the Jantzen girl. There is also an everyday memory of her running up and down the back steps of our house with a cigarette in her mouth (she was always slim and tanned and vigorous right up to the day of her death) and another of her sitting quietly by his cage just before bed while she patiently taught Junior the budgerigar to talk.

In a budgerigar phase when I was eleven and twelve, I'd bred him and a dozen other birds. But he was the violet-coloured star, the only one to live by himself indoors, and he quickly became her pet. For half an hour each night she would cover his cage with a sheet, which had a hypnotic effect on him, and then she'd sit beside it, quietly repeating some slogan or jingle or song. Bill and Jan and I would fall asleep to her voice solemnly intoning calypso lyrics or a commercial for tyres.

This way, Junior learned to articulate in his squeaky voice a large repertoire including *Today You'll Use a Dunlop Product; Tie Me Kangaroo Down, Sport; Sha-Boom-Sha-Boom;* and *The Banana Boat Song*. And because his cage was by the telephone and it was my mother who usually answered it, he'd also say, 'Hello, Dorothy Drewe speaking.'

When excited, Junior was apt to run these melodies together in a tweety riff and warble jumbled things like, 'Today You'll Use a Banana' or 'Tie Dorothy Down, Sport'. Understandable, I guess, after some of his mishaps, like falling headfirst into a cup of coffee and a sink of hot washing-up water. On each occasion, however, his little eyes sparkled again when she resuscitated him with an eyedropper of Johnnie Walker.

When he was young, he soaked up my mother's teaching at the rate of a song a week. She'd cover his cage, sit by it and solemnly start the lesson. She usually finished with a repeat of the Dunlop jingle. Next morning, Junior would proudly begin the day's chirping with his commercial for rubber products just as my father, a fervent company man, with tyres and sandshoes on the brain, sat down for breakfast.

We dropped the nightly lessons when she died,. The mother-budgie association was too vivid in our minds and the light-hearted evening mood was gone. It made us sad to see him, but then everything was sad anyway, and in the new scheme of things Junior's discontinuing education didn't register.

He lived another five years. At fourteen he dropped off the perch. By the end, he was looking rough around the edges and his skull feathers had turned into a buzz-cut.

Occasionally he'd dredge up from the past a croaky 'Sha-Boom' or a 'Come mister tally man, tally me banana'. And for years a particular squawk would suddenly shock the room into silence: *'Dorothy Drewe speaking.'*

31
MANGROVE POINT

Raking over my mother's death and the series of neighbourhood murders, and the resulting high emotion on both a family and community level, had mentally exhausted me. After I finished writing *The Shark Net* I urgently needed a break from my material. I wanted to get as far away as possible.

Broome seemed a good choice. The old pearling town in the Kimberley was 3500 kilometres from my then home in Sydney and 2000 kilometres from Perth, where I grew up and where the book was set. Its nearest sizeable town was Denpasar in Bali. Broome was as far as I could travel and remain in Australia.

It used to be an exotic tropical settlement straight out of Somerset Maugham and Rudyard Kipling, a multi-racial outpost ruled by Anglo pearling masters in spotless whites and solar topees. Broome still clings, barely, to this old reputation. Over the years it suffered ferocious cyclones, racial battles and rioting pearl divers, maritime disasters and wartime strafing and bombing by the Japanese. Much blood was spilled on its translucent beaches and red pindan earth. It saw cycles of prosperity and depression. Pearls ruled its economy. Just as they did in Ion Idriess's novels, men lived, loved and died over pearls.

No longer. By the late twentieth century 'cultured' pearls were being farmed and harvested like a crop. Danger and romance had departed the industry and, anyway, the town had since become more dependent on tourism than pearls. And an even bigger step away from its romantic past, it was now becoming the hub of yet another massive offshore gas exploration project. Here was another threat to the environment, a new cultural battle: this one with the traditional – Aboriginal – owners of the land. One more mining venture worth 'trillions'.

Nevertheless, all the intensity of Broome's history still comes together at Mangrove Point at the south end of town. This small mangrove-fringed headland, which juts like a snub nose into the opalescent waters of Roebuck Bay, was where William Dampier careened the *Roebuck* in 1699.

What initially distinguishes Mangrove Point from similar tropical headlands around Australia's northern coastline are the signs warning of a recent saltwater crocodile-sighting in the area and the summer influx of a creature just as deadly, the box jellyfish ('Remove tentacles and seek urgent medical advice'). And especially the scattering of unfenced graves, headstones and unpretentious memorials known as Pioneer Cemetery.

The dead themselves also set it apart. Those remembered under Mangrove Point's whispering she-oaks aren't just the usual civic bigwigs. While several long-lived pearling masters and their families lie in the tiny cemetery, many people commemorated there didn't die of natural causes, nor were their remains ever found. Their memorials are without bodies because they were killed and lost in the ferocity of the sea: by cyclones or sharks or by war.

I arrived in Broome late one morning at the sweltering start of the monsoon season when the first cyclone warnings were being announced on the radio. Faced by that scourge of travellers, the

2 p.m. motel check-in, wearied by five hours in the air and a stopover in Alice Springs, and unable to shower or escape the heat until afternoon, I hired a car and headed for a cold drink at the Mangrove Point café.

Broome shimmered: the land and the bay merged and quivered in a heat mirage. Viewed from my café table, Mangrove Point's horizontal slashes of earth, mangroves, sand, sea and sky, all neatly framed by the rectangle of the café's veranda columns, suggested the red, green, white, turquoise and cobalt flag of some passionate tropical nation.

Just as foreign were the turbulent epitaphs in the cemetery, so far removed from the usual placid memorials of an outback churchyard. Here in the shade of the she-oaks lay Police Inspector Herbert Thomas 'whose joint effort with Captain Bardwell quelled the racial riots of 1920'. This was a three-day battle between two thousand Japanese pearl divers and four hundred Timorese. The battle over, Inspector Thomas 'collapsed and died after saving the town'.

Here, too, were remembered many seamen 'lost at sea' or 'missing in Roebuck Bay', and one hundred civilians, mostly women and children, refugees from the Dutch East Indies, machine-gunned in their flying-boat seats by strafing Japanese Zeroes while waiting to take off from the bay for the safety of Perth in 1942. The wounded who survived the bullets either drowned or were taken by sharks.

Fascinated by these highly charged memorials, I missed a simpler gravestone. Then it loomed before me: *In Loving Memory of Richard Cornelius Male. Son of Arthur Streeter Male and Phyllis. Brother of Kimberley. Passed Away 17 November, 1962. Aged 17 Years. Whom We Loved.*

For several minutes I stood stunned by this coincidence. I'd just finished writing about Richie's drowning on the Slimy at Cottesloe, so far away. His death and funeral service had taken place in Perth. I'd presumed he was buried there. No, he'd died in the sea and his father, the pearling master Sam Male, had brought him home and buried him by the sea.

A pearler's life was at risk from a multitude of maritime disasters, but who could have foreseen the drowning of the pearling industry's youngest son at a suburban beach down south?

With the seasons changing and the cyclones mounting and swelling out in the Timor Sea, a stiff breeze rippled across Roebuck Bay and raked through the half-submerged mangroves below the Point like a comb through wet hair. I cast my mind back to that afternoon on the reef and wondered again if I'd had any inkling he was in trouble and if I could have prevented it. The mind can play tricks after all that time.

The whispering she-oaks might have been graveyard trees in a film, except the sun shone defiantly through their restless branches and made a cheery play on the headstones. It was time to check in at the motel. I gathered my wits and focussed for a moment on the heroic view. I looked out on wild history and the timeless bay and considered what a fine position the headland was for the boy on the reef, eternally seventeen.

32
STINGRAY

After a morning's trudging through the dunes and spinifex in the heat of the Montebellos it was hugely frustrating not to be able to swim at the beach below our camp. From a distance our little lagoon was looking more and more desirable, like a Caribbean beach in a travel brochure.

The conservationists assured me the lagoon was 'reasonably safe' but I noticed they never went in the water. The sharks' dorsal fins weren't always visible – not that fin visibility means much – but the stingrays still massed wingtip-to-wingtip along the shoreline.

Normally, if you see a stingray nearby while swimming, you stamp your feet on the seabed and it flees. Here, there were so many rays always cruising the shore that I couldn't stamp for fear I'd tread on one half-hidden in the sand.

Until the death by stingray of Steve Irwin, television's Crocodile Man, this particular fish did not have a high or particularly savage wildlife profile. Of the nation's more dramatic creatures, the shark, the dingo, the snake, the crocodile, even the poor extinct thylacine, have a more prominent cultural image. Some of them – the snake and, increasingly, the thylacine – have crept into Australian literature. I've occasionally pondered this matter as I lie in bed, woken again by the sudden tingling numbness in my right hand, stung by a stingray twenty-five years ago.

I was body-surfing at Bondi late one afternoon, striking out through a patch of seaweed to catch a wave, when there was an explosion of pain in my right hand. I stood in the shallows, barely aware of a small brownish creature, not much bigger than my hand, brushing past me. We flailed away from each other. Immediately it seemed never to have existed, but my pinkie finger was bleeding and even as I stumbled ashore it had swelled to the size of a sausage.

The fingertip had a small jagged and bleeding hole. The pain was way out of proportion to the size of the wound, and worsening by the second. By the time I reached the first-aid room the 'little' finger was three fingers wide and bleeding all over the floor. I felt I was supporting a throbbing extra limb.

'Stingray?' muttered the laconic beach inspector, recommending hospital. 'Lots of them out there today.'

I barely managed to drive home with my left hand. The stung hand was pulsating with so much independent power it prevented me from sitting down. It dominated the entire flat. I circled the room, holding my own hand.

I later turned this experience into my first-ever short story, called, unsurprisingly, 'Stingray'. I didn't give it much imaginative embellishment. It was almost a straight anecdote. In real life, as in the story, I was 'between relationships' or 'in transition', as my daughters say. Hospital seemed warranted but I was unable to drive now and I wasn't sure who to call to take me there.

Phoning my ex-wife seemed inappropriate. I had an image of her new boyfriend, a would-be poet, rolling his eyes and saying, 'He's gone and done *what*?' Would it be presumptuous to call a young woman whose fondness for me had not yet proceeded much further than lunch, after-work drinks and a two-night stand?

I called Candida anyway. She arrived swiftly, and drove me to St Vincent's casualty ward, crowded with the usual inner-city victims of the Sydney summer night. Drug addicts, drunks and concussed fight victims were being asked to name the Prime Minister, guess what year it was, and to count backwards from one hundred. I was the only stingray patient in the hospital and the city that night, maybe that year, maybe ever. The bemused young interns and nurses had to send out for toxicology textbooks.

My pinkie was a medical curiosity. To cover all toxic bases they inoculated me against tetanus (chief causes: rusty nails, bacteria-filled soil, manure), and applied a tourniquet to my forearm (used for snake and spider bites, scorpion and centipede stings). They washed and dressed the finger, took my blood pressure, pulse and temperature, and blood and urine samples. They kept checking my chin for lockjaw.

In the universal manner of hospitals, in order to allow my little finger to heal they needed to expose my buttocks. They urgently removed my pants, as I couldn't do this myself, and dressed the rest of my body in a pale blue gown. Then they observed my finger overnight.

Unable to sleep, I sat on my bare bottom all night, holding my pounding hand aloft and observing drunks swearing and singing, and junkies swinging punches at orderlies, and an overdosed teenage girl having her stomach pumped. In the morning they permitted me to cover my buttocks again, zipped me back into my pants, bound up my finger and released me from the casualty ward. Candida collected me and drove me home.

How vulnerable and appreciative are men of acts of female kindness and attentiveness. Twenty-five years would then pass in her company. (And two special children would eventuate.) Over the next few days, the pain lessened, and although the finger remained numb it soon returned to its normal size. 'Stingray' became part of *The Bodysurfers* anthology.

About once a fortnight I'm woken by the pins-and-needles tingle of the punctured finger tip, as if the stingray poison is trying to reassert itself, or the damaged nerve is still fighting back. I try to find a comfortable position for my hand under the pillow so I can get back to sleep. C and the sting are no longer there, but the numbness is apt to return.

33
LION DREAMS

In the Montebello Islands the stingray finger woke me a couple of times as usual, but then so did the heat, the mosquitoes, the squeaking bed, my Bushes of Doom itches, people snoring nearby, and my embarrassment at the possibility that I was snoring, too. And, of course, my bladder, which wakes me in direct proportion to the difficulty involved in relieving it.

If I'm sleeping in a hotel, or a bedroom with *en suite* bathroom, I don't need to go. But if I'm sleeping in a shed on top of a dune in the pitch darkness (with women asleep on the veranda preventing a surreptitious urination over the side), and the stinking open toilet is fifty metres away in the sandy gloom at the bottom of the dune – or if I'm at sea on a barge with no safety rail, and I have to piss into the wind – I desperately need to go.

Similarly, if I'm in a tent in the African bush and lions are roaming around the camp, can I hold on till morning? Not a chance.

If the lions are roaring outside the tent, and the safari leader has offhandedly mentioned that the night before his African helpers had to chase them away from the camp by throwing chairs at them, there's a good chance my partner and I will nervously drink all the whisky and brandy miniatures gathered in the British Airways flight from London to Harare. This ensures that while she falls instantly and soundly asleep, I'll need to go outside the tent and join the lions.

When I was young, not unreasonably, I was scared of lions. But I took it further. I was even troubled by the *image* of lions. This fear extended to shutting my eyes or ducking under the seat at the start of MGM films, including Tom and Jerry cartoons, to avoid the roaring trademark at the beginning of the credits.

I dreamt of lions once or twice a week, always in a 'normal' domestic situation. They'd be lying on our lawn, climbing through our dining-room window, sauntering down our hall. Sometimes I'd hear their heavy breathing before I spotted them. Their visits were unfussed but purposeful. The lions were right at home. With their thin-hipped, calm diligence, they'd pad into our house and search every room until they found me.

I was always the only person home when the lions came. After a few unsuccessful attempts, I didn't bother hiding. I knew they'd find me. In the dream, I'd often be lying on my bed in the sleep-out, as I was in real life at that moment, so I wasn't sure whether I was awake, or dreaming of having a dream, or in some half-conscious state in between.

In any case, as soon as they saw me they always padded across and loomed over me in their leonine fashion so I felt their meaty hot breath on my face. There was no ferocity in their manner, no slavering jaws or roaring and clawing, just calm and absolute intent.

Before they took the next step and devoured me, I took control of the situation. The lions never prevailed but there wasn't a second to lose. I played possum. No matter where I was – in bed, in the kitchen or the laundry or playing outside in the garden – I'd flop down, close my eyes and keep very still. And in my dream, as the lions sniffed me in surprise (*What's going on here?*), I'd send myself instantly to sleep.

This dream-hypnosis procedure between the ages of seven and twelve meant I'd immediately wake up in real, conscious life, lying in my actual bed in the sleep-out. *I'd beaten them again.* And somehow this became the point. Even though I was in danger, I knew how to defeat them.

Usually when I forced myself awake it was dawn and a real lion was roaring on the opposite bank of the Swan River. The first thin rays were coming through the branches of the mulberry tree outside and my heart was thudding. At this early hour, in certain weather conditions and before the commuter traffic began, the easterly wind carried the roars over the estuary to my sleep-out and into my dreams.

Now I was awake, the real lion sounded not frightening but rather old and unhappy, its noise more an obsessive complaint than a threat. I imagined it pacing around its cage in the South Perth Zoo, stir-crazy and moth-eaten, its rhythmic coughing roar becoming weaker and weaker until it faded into the waking morning hum.

. . .

Although by the time I was twelve I could sit through the opening of MGM films without closing my eyes, the dreams didn't disappear entirely. By adulthood, though dreaming of lions less often, I was still aware of their significance and interested in why my subconscious had created them so frequently and vividly.

Why did the lion symbol still resonate with me? As Jung and others noted, the proudly maned lion when simplified looked like a bright yellow sun. Candida had a lot of emotion invested in Jung at one stage, so I looked up lion dreams in her arsenal of Carl Jung, dream-interpretation and self-help books. As is usually the case, Jung had both good and worrying news.

A lion in your dreams shows propitious circumstances and strength and porousness in your life: Sounds good to begin with, but not sure about 'porousness'?

A lion dream signifies a great force is driving you. If you subdue the lion, you will be victorious in any engagement: Is outwitting the lion by playing possum and self-hypnosis the same as subduing?

If the lion is in a domestic situation, you feel some predestined guilt: Hmm. Could be right.

A threatening lion to a male dreamer represents a person in waking life who poses a threat, most commonly the father: OK, now Freud as well.

You are a spiritual leader but someone is abusing their power over you and this is distorting your view of authority: Yes. Looking back, the lion dreams began when I was in the Grade Two class of Miss Doris Langridge. It was she who distorted a seven-year-old's obvious spiritual leadership.

Like the first love, the sadistic school teacher is a memoirist's cliché. That doesn't deny its importance. I've just realised that it was while I was in her class, aged seven, that I became a fat boy. This was the first of five overweight, daily teased, hopeless-at-sport, last-person-picked-for-the-team, fingernails-bitten-to-the-quick, bloody-cuticled, and intermittently bullied years.

I couldn't understand why I was fat. I didn't seem to be eating any more than in my non-fat days. I was always outdoors, playing and swimming and climbing trees. There were two other fat boys in my class. They were fatter than me, and they said their problem was this condition called *glands*. They were the helpless victims of glands and I supposed I had glands, too. I didn't want glands or anything to do with glands, especially during swimming classes or when trying on new school uniforms at David Jones. I'd sit in class, my pants tight on my thighs, my sleeves gripping my arms, and my body was mysterious to me. All I knew for sure was that the word *fat* exploded in my head whenever I heard it, or read it, and made my heart race, and that thin boys relished saying it to me.

Not all the aggravation came from other children. In the middle of my fat period, aged ten, my two closest school mates were Rodney Locke and David Ferguson. Our Grade Five teacher, Mr Longley, a tall, heavy-set, English polio victim who walked with two sticks and whose shirts had year-round sweat stains in the armpits, noticed our friendship. His infirmity ensured no nicknames were ever given to *him* (we were gallant ten-year-olds) but he felt bound to inform the class, with a smirk, that from now on David Ferguson should be called 'Stock'.

Why, sir?

'Because then the trio will be complete – Lock, Stock and Barrel!'

Aged seven, however, Barrel-to-be's nemesis was still the crimson-faced turtle, Miss Langridge. Following her latest anti-slumping knuckle-whack ('Do you want to end up looking like me?') I retaliated.

In the circumstances, my comeback was out of character and verging on suicidal. In Manual Crafts later that afternoon – as if, out of curiosity, observing a lunatic's antics from afar – I watched myself fashion a realistic facsimile of Miss Langridge out of plasticine and hold it up for the class's recognition and approval, which quickly came. As did the weapon-of-many-timbers, striking fast and hard. But judging by their shocked delight at my plasticine model, all boobs and bum, the jury of my peers was on-side.

But the enemy had more in her armoury. We had Library every Wednesday after school, and as an avid reader I always lingered there. My library bag full of *William* and *Famous Five* books, I was usually the last to leave, as I was one particular afternoon.

There was a rule forbidding riding your bike on school grounds, in case you struck someone. Seems sensible. But as there was no-one else left at school at this late hour, I hopped on the back of my bike (or rather trike – it was actually a more harmless tricycle) and scootered the last three or four metres off the empty playground. Just as Miss Langridge drove past with her equally fierce colleague, the principal, Miss Holland (a squat toad to Miss Langridge's turtle).

They leant out the window of the Austin A40, shaking their fists and shouting, 'You're going to be caned tomorrow, Robert Drewe!' Then passed a fitful night. I'm not sure if I told my parents. I felt guilty of a serious offence. Perhaps I knew there would be no sympathy for a child's position versus that of officialdom. Maybe they said I had to face the music. (Mother: *That's a shame, dear*; Father: *Rules are there to be obeyed, son*.)

At assembly next morning Miss Langridge informed the whole school of the heinous after-library crime that had been committed, and of the punishment the perpetrator (a seven-year-old on a tricycle on the edge of an empty playground) would face as an example to everyone.

The sadistic Misses Langridge and Holland weren't done yet. They intended to keep up the suspense. Punishment should not be limited to a caning. Let's draw it out. The school's equivalent of the medieval stocks was for a child to be made to sit under the school clock in front of the playground for the duration of mid-morning recess. There I sat.

Lunch time eventually came but the peanut butter sandwiches stuck in my throat. After twenty hours of anxiety I was led into the craft room for my punishment. The light glinted on Miss Holland's rimless glasses. My head swam as she closed the door behind us; I was dizzy with the smell of the hessian squares intended for Mother's Day pot-holders and the cold metal bin of modelling clay. Then I was caned by Miss Holland, once on my right palm, and then on my left.

I've had an extremely low threshold for senseless rules, bureaucracy and institutional injustice ever since. Maybe the Misses Langridge and Holland even turned me into an outsider. Perhaps it's stretching a point, but they're at least partly responsible for my view of the world. The powerless and misunderstood individual strikes a loud chord.

Maybe being caned for losing myself in books lent a defiant aspect to my character, and to my loving books and eventually writing them as well.

. . .

The weight, the bullying, and the tri-testicular anxiety abruptly fell away when at thirteen I caught meningitis. It was misdiagnosed as flu by the family doctor. Saved at the eleventh hour by a second doctor with the actual surname of Fortune, I came out of quarantine extremely thin, with a bright-light intolerance, oddly improved hand-eye coordination, and three inches more height.

This first teenage year was an eventful one, much of it spent in hospitals, starting with the Mount Hospital summer of the embarrassing sewed-on-mid-thigh scrotum and third testicle, and followed by an autumn of high pelvic anxiety and change-room mortification. Winter was occupied by my anti-bomb concern-for-all-peoples and endeavouring to learn the trumpet. I was emotionally and physically weakened by the time spring came.

I was bodysurfing in heavy surf at North Cottesloe one Saturday afternoon in late winter when a sudden sensation of such ebbing strength almost overwhelmed me. I barely made it to shore through the surf dump and undertow, and then weakly hitchhiked home.

Within a day, deep fatigue led to blinding headaches that caused a strange moaning wail that seemed to issue from some banshee in a far-off room, also an inability to raise my head, and then the onset of paralysis. Flu? Luckily, my parents obtained a second medical opinion. A half-conscious lumbar tap revealed the meningitis, and sulfa drugs were successfully administered.

The rest of August and the month of September was spent quarantined in Lucknow Hospital in Claremont. I spent much of it sleeping.

Then one day my parents were allowed into my room and cheered me up with fish and chips and a punnet of strawberries.

I felt well enough to read *Pix* and *People* and *Australasian Post*. *Pix* had interesting candid pictures of film stars at nightclubs smoking and looking drunk, with their eyes heavy-lidded, their bra straps showing and their bow ties undone. A nurse gave me a *Screen* magazine with Rock Hudson on the cover and said he was her dreamboat. 'A pity he's married,' she sighed.

As I convalesced at home, late spring and summer came as a magical relief. The daylight was different and amiable. The smell of boronia filled the air and rays and shadows filtered through the gumtree branches on to our lawn in a way that seemed novel and optimistic.

To get rid of my hospital pallor I sat on a step in the sun with our dog Shandy, crushing leaves between my fingers and drinking Fanta. Neighbours who'd previously ignored me now waved as they drove past; grownups called out hello as they watered their lawns. Meningitis had made me popular. School was a distant memory. Shandy and I chewed on eucalyptus twigs and every day dawned like a Saturday morning.

Here was an irony: once I was allowed to swim again I was teased for being so thin, my ribs and collarbones arousing skeleton jokes at the beach and the Claremont baths. But I didn't mind at all. Skinny-teasing was like adulation.

Thanks to Dr Cyril Fortune, head of the cardiology department at Royal Perth Hospital, and obviously good at fixing brains as well, life was looking good. For some months the bright-light intolerance of photophobia could make me dizzy and vomit at the white glare of a noonday beach or the sun shining on a field of pale daisies, but I was alive, I could move my head freely up and down and I was thin and taller. My parents treated me with greater favour than before.

I had a moustache to shave off. And I'd gradually dropped down to two-and-a-half balls.

. . .

Although in adulthood my lion dreams had faded away, the memory of individual dreams stayed vivid for decades and I could conjure them up as easily as if they had happened only the night before.

I remained fascinated by lions as symbols. Lions were of course a potent sign of Africa, so when after six months in England researching *The Drowner* and teaching creative writing to criminals at Brixton Prison, and to East End high-schoolers in Whitechapel and middle-class students at Royal Festival Hall, the chance came to return to Australia via Zimbabwe, I jumped at it.

There we were, Candida and I, out in the bush in Hwange National Park, the only guests at a small camp run by a melancholy white ex-Rhodesian, who'd had his farm confiscated by Robert Mugabe and of necessity was now a safari guide. He was a pleasant man, unlucky in his life, and with that white-African speech affectation whereby all plural animals – not just the usual grass-eaters like sheep, deer, antelope and buffalo – were referred to in the singular.

'Look over there,' he'd point out. 'Five elephant! And there's three cheetah!'

Round the waterhole at night he'd indicate miscellaneous baboon, ten or twelve warthog and five or six hyena. And of course the trees overhead were full of bloody dozens of monkey. I joked that I couldn't wait to get home to our two dog, but he just looked at me blankly.

Our first night under canvas passed sleeplessly for me. First of all, its shadow encompassing and darkening the tent, an elephant silently strolled in, delicately picked up our toothbrushes and toothpaste from the wash-stand outside, sniffed them, and soundlessly put them back. Then at least one lion wandered and roared near the camp. As a precaution, the two teenage African helpers proceeded to beat on saucepans for a while.

With all the roaring and the clanging, despite all the airline whisky and brandy miniatures, sleep was impossible. Nature was urgently calling, but as the camp lavatory was fifty metres away in the dark bush, and the lion was about, I was forced to defy the camp's hygiene regulations and lift up the back tent flap.

Wild animals were already front and centre in my mind next afternoon when the African youths reported that a giraffe had been killed three kilometres away during the night. Probably by our saucepan-irritated lions. The safari guide, who doubled as a park ranger, sighed heavily, put on his bush hat, strapped on his gaiters, picked up his rifle, and said he'd have to investigate. Did we wish to accompany him to the scene of the kill?

I didn't call him *bwana* but the key moment had arrived. 'Yes,' I heard myself say. The time had finally arrived.

In *King Solomon's Mines* style we set off in single file, through a plain of two-metre-tall adrenaline grass, to the giraffe. The *adrenaline* name appropriately refers to its effect on the nervous system. It pressed in on us and prevented us seeing to the left or right or, as I discovered as the grass instantly closed with a *swoosh* at my companion's back, behind us. The effect was of marching through the African bush alone.

The guide was in the lead, in the Stewart Granger role. He was followed by the two local boys stomping along in their unlaced army boots, then Candida (as Deborah Kerr) in her riding boots, with me (an anonymous equipment-bearer) bringing up the rear in my Dunlop Volleys.

From my position I couldn't see the guide or the African boys, only occasional glimpses of Candida's heels and shoulder blades through the grass in front of me. As I tramped along, my heart beating out the words *lion, lion, lion,* I thought, 'At least I'm protecting her back.'

Another part of me considered my own unprotected back and wished I was further up the line, nearer the rifle.

In a forest clearing surrounded by thick monkey-thorn trees we found the dead giraffe. It was so fresh it hadn't yet attracted hyenas or vultures. Its killers must have been still around. Everything was silent. Not a bird, monkey or insect chattered or rustled. Even the breeze had stilled and in the clearing the air hung oppressively close.

Giraffes are extremely tall when they're standing up; when they're lying down, stretched out and lifeless, they seem even bigger. We stood around the huge body. It didn't smell yet. It was scarcely nibbled around the stomach, much less devoured. The vegetation was shadowy and soundless. The silence was total and the afternoon was suddenly like nightfall.

'We interrupted them. They're watching us,' said the guide.

With one of the boys' machetes, he hacked out the giraffe's jawbone, to take to town for analysis. There followed a tense march back to camp, this time carrying a giraffe's dripping lower jaw. We'd just taken the lions' bloody kill and I was in the rear again. Visibility was close to zero. Any disgruntled carnivore could pick me off. The adrenaline grass *swooshed* in front of me and behind me. *We'd just stolen the lions' kill.* The trek back seemed to take twice as long.

. . .

How stalwartly our little camp defied danger and squatted bravely on the plain. How welcoming it was to arrive back to the tent and see our toilet utensils all set neatly on the wooden stand outside. The thermos of safe-to-drink boiled water, the enamel cup containing the toothbrush and Colgate toothpaste, filled me with a joyful contentment. The fresh cake of Pears soap reflected the African sunset in its triumphant ruby glow.

Enveloping the camp, dramatising the whole plain and the dark forest beyond and all the animals now gathering at the waterhole, this red sunset was an African cliché that retained all its power. As a baboon tribe squabbled in the sycamore-fig trees, I downed the offered gin and tonic in a matter of seconds.

34
MONSTERS OF GOD

More chilling than the discovery of Richie Male's relocated grave, another dramatic coincidence now surfaced. This coincidence occurred at the same small suburban beach, North Cottesloe, where the keen teenage reporter of *The Shark Net* had imagined witnessing a great-white shark attack. This disquiet was another one left over from adolescence, but one with a greater basis of probability than being devoured by lions.

I'd written of my journalistically ambitious younger self spending much of his life on the same strip of seashore between Cottesloe and North Cottesloe without sighting any fish bigger than a herring, but nevertheless fantasising about an attack there by a great-white.

This nineteen-year-old cadet reporter spent hours patrolling the suburban coastline, seeking dorsal fins in the rise of each breaking wave and willing some swimmer to be attacked. A deserving case, of course: no-one young or female. Preferably a leathery old politician or greedy businessman.

My fantasy front-page lead was a 'man-eater' story where I was the reporter-hero. My dream scoop required me to save a life and, importantly, risk my own. Then, dripping water and possibly blood over the Anglia's dashboard, shrugging off medical attention, and modestly keeping news of my heroic role until the fourth or fifth paragraph, I'd dictate the story over the two-way radio for the first edition.

I didn't dream how prophetic the naïve ambitions and anxieties of that adolescent would be. Immediately after the book's publication, on 6 November 2000, a forty-nine-year-old local businessman named Ken Crew was finishing his daily early-morning swim at North Cottesloe when a five-metre great-white sped south along the beach from Swanbourne, surged past surf-craft and through a throng of other swimmers and made straight for him.

Witnesses said it targeted him from a long way off. The shark tore off his left leg and he died within seconds. The shark then went for his swimming partner, Dirk Avery.

The attack occurred where and how I'd envisaged it. My first reaction was disbelief. Then another sensation intervened. In order to absorb the shock, my brain took the event back a stage and turned it into retrospective premonition. It was the same sensation I'd had about the earlier Cottesloe death – when Richie drowned near me.

The attack on Ken Crew had a curious effect on me. I didn't know him, but I couldn't stop thinking about his death. While I felt great sympathy for him and his family, I also took the shark episode personally. From the moment I heard of it, this attack, and great-white sharks generally, could truly be said to have lodged in my 'sub-microscopic moments' – the thoughts and feelings of my 'true life'.

Though crazily self-centred, this subjective response would turn out be a widespread community reaction.

· · ·

The main ocean pool at North Cottesloe is a placid little beach about fifty metres wide, nestled between limestone reefs to the north and south. The beach's swimming area was made quieter, narrower and rockier a generation ago by the misjudged construction of a stone groyne at the main beach at Cottesloe, five hundred metres south. The altered tidal effect swept away much of North Cottesloe's white sands, uncovered rocks and diminished its surf.

Once or twice over the years I'd heard lifesavers sound the shark alarm. People would nonchalantly leave the water until the all-clear siren sounded a few minutes later. Inevitably the shark would turn out to be a lone dolphin.

For generations, North Cott, as it's locally known, was a favoured beach of the middle-class western suburbs. It was where teenagers went through their summer rites of passage. We'd ride our bikes to Stirling Highway, leave them leaning against the Christ Church fence (no locking devices were then necessary), and, barefoot, oblivious to the hot road surface, hitchhike down the highway to the beach.

Skin cancer was yet to enter beachgoers' consciousness. Once at the beach, minus sunscreen, sunglasses, hats or shirts, teenagers would lie in circles in the sand or sprawl against the boardwalk, cigarettes ostentatiously ablaze, gossiping, flirting and adjusting their nutties. 'Nutties' were the local trend in boys' surf-wear. We shunned the boring shop-bought swimming costumes, preferring the colourful – and tight – bathers run up by our mothers on their sewing machines.

The tastefully named nutties were merely one local beach idiosyncrasy. Another peculiarity was our word for anything to do with the surf or an ocean beach: 'looms'. As in, 'Did you see that bloody big loom I caught?' Or, 'See you at the looms on Saturday.' A loom that carried you all the way into shore was a 'beacher'. If you weren't careful a beacher tossing you on to the shoreline's sand and shells would graze your chest – not to mention your nutties.

At lunchtime, eating our ham and salad rolls, drinking our Cokes and Fantas, we'd sit against the wall of the Ocean Beach Hotel across the road, enviously eyeing the hyper-tanned off-duty lifesavers, hairy superior beings who made a loud noise about repairing to the pub for noontime beers.

Male body hair – chest, shoulders, back, the works – was worth having back then, and was everywhere evident. In Teenage Boy World, hairiness was fostered and nurtured – individual chest hairs counted, logged and encouraged – as desirable evidence of masculinity. Even that line of hair that extended south from the navel (the 'flea track') was worthy of notice and credit. The power and appeal of body hair was unarguable. Those woolly brown heroes, the surf club men, had skeins of it and girls flocked after them. Case proved.

Hairless, too young to legally drink alcohol, we moped against the hotel wall, doomed to fizzy soft drinks until the age of twenty-one. But by the time we reached that magical age almost every boy I knew had a police record, having been caught by the ever-vigilant Under-Age Liquor Squad, summonsed to Perth Police Court and fined eight dollars.

Thus arose a peculiar local newspaper phenomenon whereby young police-court reporters, working on a paper with a policy of listing all court proceedings, often had to record their own misdeeds for publication.

These health-conscious days, North Cott is where State Governors jog before breakfast, where judges, doctors and business executives democratically join tradesmen, footballers and lean sportswomen to face the dawn's first rays in the ocean. By seven a.m. it's a busy place. Before work they hone their fitness with swimming, running, power-walking, paddling kayaks and surf-skis before the strong sea breeze, the 'Fremantle Doctor', arrives to whip up the sand and churn the waves to froth.

Seven a.m. would also seem to be the feeding time for great-white sharks.

. . .

I found it unusual, probably mentally twisted, that I was so upset by the North Cottesloe shark attack. I hadn't swum there for two decades. I was now middle-aged, living on the other side of the continent and swimming in a different ocean. But that November morning instantly made me a more wary swimmer. Swimming over rocks and patches of seaweed now quickened my pulse. No matter if it was the Pacific, Southern or Indian Ocean, I was no longer totally at ease being the farthest person out to sea, over my depth, blithely beyond the breakers.

The attack not only shook me up, it changed the order of things. As if I was still young, I felt my secure world knocked askew. It was a similar feeling to the time I described in *The Shark Net*: a period of community vulnerability when a serial killer roamed this same shore and murdered people we knew; and it turned out we knew the killer, too.

There was also the matter of coincidence heaped on coincidence. The attack on Ken Crew happened on the other edge of the reef where Richie had drowned.

Fiction disapproves of coincidence. As a plot device it's too neat and contrived. In real life, however, coincidence intrudes more often than the odds would suggest. While I was at my desk on 10 October 2011, writing the preceding paragraphs on the Cottesloe shark attack, another man suddenly vanished from view while taking his daily seven a.m. swim at Cottesloe beach. One minute he was seen swimming towards a buoy three hundred metres from the shore, the next he was gone, snatched from the surface.

A friend phoned from the beach to tell me of this. As he was speaking I could hear on the line the police search helicopters clattering overhead.

The victim's wife and son waited for him on the beach but Bryn Martin, a sixty-four-year-old business executive, was never seen again. Police divers found his Speedo swimming costume on the ocean floor, torn to shreds. Fisheries experts said the rips indicated an attack by a great-white shark.

As it was, the spate of fatal great-white shark incidents over that six-month period didn't always require coincidence. Only the month before, on 4 September Kyle Burden, a twenty-one-year-old body-boarder, had been taken by a great-white, which bit him in halves at Bunker Bay, south-west of Perth. Peter Kurmann, a thirty-three-year-old skindiver, was soon taken off Stratham Beach, not far away. And twelve days after the Cottesloe attack on Bryn Martin, a thirty-two-year-old Texan named George Thomas Wainwright, was killed by a great-white while skindiving in Little Armstrong Bay on Rottnest Island.

His two diving mates aboard their boat watched in horror as 'a flurry of bubbles' appeared in the water. Then their friend's body floated to the surface a short time later with 'obvious traumatic fatal injuries'.

First Cottesloe, then Rottnest. My favourite spots. The whole chosen environment of my coastal youth, the two places that had meant most to me and my sense of my adolescent self, were changed in my mind forever. And I was changed, too.

. . .

However, the onslaught of shark attacks didn't end there. Just as I was finishing this book, another five-metre great-white killed another surfer, 24-year-old Ben Linden, off Lancelin, north of Perth. This made five fatal great-white attacks on this coast in the past ten months. Was I alone in being rattled by the frequency of these occurences? Seeking some sort of explanation, I wondered whether the shark was imprinted on our collective unconscious. Soon after these attacks I read a book by the American natural-historian David Quammen titled *Monster of God*, sub-titled *The Man-Eating Predator in the Jungles of History and the Mind,* which put an interesting viewpoint.

Quammen asks us to consider a group of disparate creatures he calls *alpha predators,* made up of some mammals, some fish, and some reptiles. 'In scientific terms the grouping is artificial . . . its reality is psychological, as registered in the human mind.' Its main representatives are the lion, tiger, leopard, great-white shark, brown bear, polar bear and saltwater crocodile.

He wants us to contemplate 'the psychological, mythic and spiritual dimensions, as well as the ecological implications, of the one-on-one relationship between a particular dangerous flesh-eating animal and a human victim.' From the beginning of mankind that relationship had played a crucial role in religions, beliefs, symbolism and traditions in every society, and shaped the way humans construed their place in the natural world.

'It reminded us of where we'd stood for tens of thousands of years on the food chain of power and glory.' That is, when the occasional member of our species is relegated to the status of mere protein, we aren't always and indisputably on the top. We're just another flavour of edible meat.

'Have lions, tigers and bears made the dark forest scary?' Quammen asks. 'They have indeed, and in some ways it has been a good thing. Have crocodiles and sharks committed ugly, horrific acts of homicide and anthropophagy? Yes, and by doing so they've offered us a certain perspective. While we humans may be the most reflective members of the natural world, we're not its divinely appointed proprietors. Nor are we the culmination of evolution, except in the sense that there has never been another species so bizarrely ingenious that it could create both iambic pentameter and plutonium.

'Throughout the course of the human story, one reminder of our earthly status has been that at some times, in some landscapes, we have served as an intermediate link in the food chain. I mean the literal food chain – who eats whom.'

His view makes sense to me. This is the reason I find specious the common argument that our fear of sharks is stupid and unrealistic given that more people are killed by bees, or horses, or lightning, and of course by motor vehicles.

Yes, but these things haven't been imprinted on our psyches as horrifying since Day One on earth. Have some imagination, please. It's not just a matter of numbers. Fords and BMWs might kill many more people, but they don't carry a mythical threat to us. A great-white is more scary than a Toyota Corolla.

Similarly, I'm not scared of bees because I'm not allergic to bee stings and I seriously doubt that a bee will kill me. However, I am – and so is everyone else – highly allergic to shark bites.

Incidentally, I find it intriguing – and always quite moving – how the relatives of shark victims, when interviewed later, ease their grief by invariably searching for meaning in the frightful death of their spear-fishing father or surfing brother. Or are they numbly repeating the quotes they've heard from the family members of earlier shark victims, and thought similar words were required of them?

Without fail they say, 'Dad loved the sea. He would have wanted to go that way.'

Seriously? Torn in halves before his time by a great-white shark?

My guess is that Dad, whether a great lover of the sea or a mere shoreline paddler, would rather have opted to die peacefully in his sleep, in bed, aged ninety-six.

· · ·

Shark attacks were preying on my mind. Was it just me? Over the years this unlikely threat was looming larger and larger. Was it because I'd always been a keen body-surfer? One of life's main pleasures was surfing with my sons Jack, Sam, Ben and Jim. And when Amy, Laura and

Anna were little they'd ride my back like a surfboard. But wherever I turned now, sharks were in the news. People were being regularly killed by great-whites off the lower coast of Western Australia (overnight the south-west had become the world's primary area for shark attacks). And in South Australian and Queensland waters as well, and where I lived on the New South Wales north coast. They'd begun attacking humans in waters where sharks hadn't been prevalent before.

Abruptly, there were days like the following one at Byron Bay, the final day of the school holidays: the sort of warm, verdant morning the rest of the world believes Australia endlessly experiences. A balmy breeze riffled the casually dishevelled native flora around our house in the hinterland, while the fauna – water-dragons and brush-turkeys – reclined on the septic tank and scratched up the tomato plants and relished the sunshine.

As in countless sentimental paintings on the walls of coastal cafés, dentists and real-estate offices, dolphins gambolled off Cape Byron and tourists sighed at the mother-and-calf humpbacks rolling home to the Antarctic.

I'd dropped off Sam, my teenage son, and his three friends at The Pass, the most popular surf break on the north coast. Two boys and two girls, they'd taken much rousing after a sleepover. I'd been willing them to wake and finish their interminable breakfast routines so I could start work.

They woke in staggered intervals. The first boy tottered out into the kitchen at nine, the last girl exited the bathroom at eleven-thirty. Sixteen pieces of toast and two cartons of fruit juice later, they emerged, holding their surfboards and blinking like possums in the sunlight. Urging them to 'make the most of your last day', I'd deposited them at the beach and headed back to the desk.

An hour later a local radio news flash said a great-white shark was attacking surfers at The Pass. It had already shaken a woman out of her kayak. Although she'd escaped with scratches after bravely beating it off with her paddle, the shark was still patrolling the area. The woman described the huge head rising up out of the ocean. 'It was straight out of *Jaws*, and staring at me. I saw that look in its eye.'

The roads into Byron Bay have a 50 kmh speed limit. Despite the holiday double-demerit points, I broke the limit by a big margin. I visualised Sam and his friends in the ocean, propped on their boards, their legs dangling down in the water. I imagined them skylarking and paying no attention to the dark shape beneath them. I saw the boys competing for waves in front of the girls, oblivious to their surroundings. You didn't see a great-white until it hit you like a Mack truck on the highway.

When I arrived at The Pass the sea was serene and empty. But so were the beaches in *Jaws*. My son and his friends weren't in the water. Nor were any other swimmers. I recognised their towels lying on the beach but there was no sign of them as I stood helplessly on the sand.

Minutes later I heard Sam's stern voice. 'What are you doing here?' The boys were reclining languidly in the shade of a pandanus tree like young sultans. They were eating hot chips and the girls were sitting cross-legged behind them, combing the boys' hair.

To see if you are all right. If necessary, to try to save you. 'To warn you to get out of the water.'

'Why would we be in the water?' he said, obviously dealing with an idiot. 'There's a great-white in there!'

Driving home through the sugarcane fields, I ran over a snake. A red-bellied black. They're venomous but timid and I usually swerve to avoid them if possible because they help keep down the brown snakes, which are venomous and aggressive. This time I didn't. I was in a daze and forgot I'm fairly Green about flattening snakes, as long as they're not inside the house.

Some days I feel like I'm living in a travel book and that Australia *is* the wildlife stereotype the rest of the world insists on.

35
SHARK REPORTS

I couldn't help it. On my way to the Montebellos I had to return to North Cottesloe and speak to the people who'd been present the morning the great-white killed Ken Crew. I was compelled to go there and, rather tentatively, to swim there, too.

So early one morning, with an old friend, Jack Harrison, a regular swimming companion when I'm in Perth, I went for a dip at the spot in the ocean where Ken Crew was attacked. I'd swum there hundreds of times in my life, never feeling the slightest fear. I was uneasy now and I didn't want to swim out too far.

Then we stood on the edge of the reef where Ken's swimming companion Dirk Avery fought off the shark when it turned on him as well. As I struggled to keep my balance in the waves, I imagined the mayhem that morning.

As teenagers, Jack and I had surfed off this reef edge countless times. As always, the reef seemed shallow and benign. The waves were as choppy as ever, never totally satisfactory, with the habit of catching you behind the legs and knocking you over. On this morning it was high tide, the undertow was strong and the water over the reef was chest deep.

The experience was too familiar to be really unnerving, but

I wouldn't have wanted to be fighting for my life there, as Dirk had, to be balancing on the reef and desperately trying not to topple, with my leg inside a shark's mouth.

Then we went up to the Blue Duck café with Robbie Burns, the journalist who had witnessed the events that November morning, and written the front-page lead in the *West Australian* as I had dreamed of doing long ago. We had a coffee and spoke to Marie the waitress who had seen the shark charging past the restaurant, and through the throng of early-morning swimmers, speeding like a missile along the coastline towards its moving target, the man just completing his enjoyable daily exercise. 'It was huge and speeding straight at him,' she said.

Over several days I spoke to other people who were at the beach that morning. Their stories were similar – and different. Their views were highly subjective, with everyone – understandably, I guess – seeing their own role as pivotal to the drama.

There was one constant. Everyone mentioned the bravery of Brian Farley, who had plunged into the froth of bloody water and brought out Ken Crew's body while the shark was still there. He was a modest person, something of a loner in the view of everyone I spoke to, and so deeply affected by the experience that he could no longer bring himself to talk about that morning.

I understood and respected his reticence. Several people told me that Brian Farley did make one remark that stuck in everyone's mind that day. When asked to explain his actions in retrieving Ken Crew, he said simply, 'His eyes beseeched me.'

. . .

Dirk Avery is a lawyer, a tall, solid man and a regular ocean bather who surf-swims with a group of like-minded early-morning risers who call themselves 'The Pod'. Back on 6 November 2000, he was fifty-two.

That morning I arrived at North Cott around six-thirty. The Pod had gathered at the beach as usual. Ken was with us. It had just started to drizzle and the day was overcast. I'd had a late night and I was feeling a bit seedy. Ken and I had a common interest in the hits of the 1950s and 60s. Motown stuff.

A few of us walked to the break in the reef called Peter's Pool, halfway to Cottesloe beach proper. Ken said he saw something in the water and was a bit reluctant to go in, but I insisted it was probably a seal. I urged him, 'Come on'. It was only a four-hundred or five-hundred metre swim from there to North Cott.

The first group of swimmers took off into the water. Ken dived in ahead of me. He was about fifty metres in front of me, and further out to sea. We swam north as usual. The water wasn't murky but there was a great deal of bait and burley floating by. I heard later that some fishermen were throwing out a lot of bait and burley from the Cottesloe groyne to attract fish. The whales were migrating then too, and the salmon were running.

We reached North Cott OK. Ken was right in the middle of the swimming area and I was on the edge of the reef when I saw a big shower of water – a red-brown shower of spray – burst high into the air. I saw this big mountain of water and instantly I knew what it was. The shark got Ken and was making its way to me. I saw this huge dorsal fin coming straight to me, in waist-deep water.

I'm partly on the reef when the shark latches on to my left leg with its mouth. It was so big it had to turn on its side to bite me. It was having trouble with its huge girth scraping on the shallow reef and it was trying to get a decent hold of me.

I'm trying to get away, kicking like mad. I lashed out with my right leg and kicked the shark and managed to get my left leg out of its mouth. I'm thrashing about with my hands too, trying to scramble onto the reef. The water's waist deep and it's coming at me again. I kicked it again and again – and suddenly it swam away.

I was in such great shock that I didn't feel any pain at that stage. I got assisted out of the water just as Brian Farley went in and pulled Ken out. Ken lost his leg and he bled very quickly. He was lying there on the beach and his leg was gone. There was a doctor swimming there that morning, and a priest, and they tried to tend to him but it was too late.

The shark had come south from Swanbourne and swum under a couple of surf skis. There were about another twenty people in the swimming area and it swam right through them to get Ken and me. Ken had said to me, 'I think there's something out there,' and I'd said not to worry. Sometimes I wonder if I could have done anything more. I don't think he knew what hit him. He was in three or four metres of water and it just came up from below.

I think the shark was in a killing mood and focused on Ken from a long distance away. Maybe Ken and I had a faster heart rate – we'd just swum four hundred metres – and it picked up on it. Ken was swimming in a black rashy vest and black bathers. Maybe he looked like a big seal. It's hard to know. Knowing it had the first one, it tried to get a second kill with me.

Great-whites don't like someone being aggressive to them. That's what saved me. As my leg was in its mouth and I was kicking it with the other one I was thinking, 'I've got to maintain my balance and get out of here.'

I was in hospital for nine days and the doctor suggested some counselling sessions. I found them very helpful for the guilt I was feeling. Because of my injuries I couldn't swim for two months. I needed plastic surgery for the eighty lacerations on my left foot. The bites were deep, but luckily not to the bone. Most of my injuries were caused by me yanking my leg out of the shark's mouth.

I had complete disbelief that something like this had happened. Prior to that day, if something needed doing, work or whatever, I did it immediately. I did it yesterday. Now I try to be calmer. Things have to work to my timetable.

After some urging I went in the ocean again two months later, in early January. Most mornings now I go down there to the beach, and I still swim. But I never swim to the far-out buoys now. And every day I think about whether I'll go in or not.

I reflect on Ken and what his wife was going through. His wife Robin and his daughter were on the beach that morning. You count your blessings. I dream about it all the time.

. . .

Robbie Burns, a journalist and an ex-Australian Rules footballer with the Subiaco league team, was paddling a surf ski on the southern edge of the reef when he heard the shark siren sounding.

His was the role I'd marked out for myself as a cub reporter all those years ago: the journalist as eyewitness. The story he wrote was a fine effort which led the *West Australian*, and filled two inside pages. When he spoke to me, ten years after the incident, he was still animated about that morning.

The hairs on the back of my neck stood up. There was an intangible atmosphere and I sensed something really bad was happening. People were running to the shore and waving their arms at us and shouting. Three Swanbourne lifesavers, John Verity, Alex Harrison and Gary Whyatt, were out on surf-skis when they saw a massive shark speed past them. They were shouting, 'Get out of the water!'

When we got closer to the beach we saw people milling around.

A brave guy on the beach swam out into the pool of blood, a bloody great circle of blood, and got hold of Ken and dragged him in. This was Brian Farley, a tanker driver – a shy, modest guy. He dived in and pulled Ken out and quietly walked away.

I knew Ken. I changed in the dressing shed alongside him every morning. I saw his body brought ashore. His leg was chopped off with surgical precision. His femur bled very quickly. Dr Murray Jacobs was on the beach and if Ken could've been saved, he would have been.

Ken was obviously dead and we covered him. We put him in a body bag. We carried him up the steps and put him in an ambulance. It was incredible: forty minutes before, he and I had been chatting as we got changed. Next time I saw him, I'm putting him in a body bag.

The shark went for Dirk next. When it attacked Dirk, he climbed on the reef and the shark was so deep in the belly, a great-white five metres long, the reef was too shallow for it. Dirk risked his life and was able to kick it away.

The shark was only interested in Ken and Dirk. Anne Vincent was standing chest deep in the water when it swept past her, having targeted Ken. The force of the shark pushed her aside. She was an absolute mess, in shock.

I guess I got the demons out, writing the story for the *West Australian*. I never wrote a story with so much impact. I wrote it as I felt it. I guess it was therapeutic.

I went back in the ocean a couple of days later. We paddle every morning for exercise, banter and camaraderie. I wouldn't miss my paddle for quids. But I realise we took this little strip of water for granted. In that brief moment we lost our innocence. I won't ever again take for granted our right to be in the ocean.

. . .

Chris Mews, a marine broker, was also deeply affected by the attack. He described the particular ethos of the early-morning North Cottesloe swimmer, at least until that morning.

We would walk from North Cott along the water's edge until we got to the groyne at Cottesloe. The idea was to touch the granite rocks on the groyne with your foot and this symbolic gesture meant that the swim back to North Cott was about to start. If we didn't do this and touch the rocks it wasn't a full and proper swim.

Then we waded out into the water and swam past the pylon towards North Cott. Twenty years ago this used to take me eighteen minutes. If the waves were bigger, it took a bit longer.

Sometimes our group got into the water at Peter's Pool, a small gap in the reef about half the way to the groyne. If we did this, we felt like we'd slacked off somewhat. Walking out on the reef here, we had to be careful we didn't tread on a bloody cobbler. They say you should piss on a cobbler sting and that helps the agony. I don't know, I've never trodden on one.

We did this every day, rain, hail or shine – even through the winter. Over a long period the swimmers in our group slowly changed, with people coming and going, but every day there was always someone to swim with. There were lots of swimmers who had their own little groups. But everyone knew everyone on the beach, either just by a first name, or only a nod, but the people there at dawn every day were familiar faces.

After the swim, it was up to the public change rooms for a cold shower. There were captains of industry, judges, lawyers, truck drivers, jewellers, not to mention homeless folk sleeping on the benches overnight, with their cigarette butts and empty beer bottles on the floor. We didn't care – we just liked the swim and the camaraderie.

After the shower and a few jokes, lots of folk went to the old North Cott café or Blue Duck, always to their special tables. These tables were by invitation only. Swimmers stick together, like fish in a school. Everyone knew who was having an affair, and who was paying. Ken and Dirk were there every day.

It all changed just after dawn on 6 November 2000. I was ten minutes late to the beach. I'd had a quarrel with Pauline, my partner, and didn't want to swim with her that day.

I was in the change rooms and had just put my bathers on, when I heard the most blood-curdling scream coming from the beach below. 'Shark!' I jumped up on the bench and peered over the change room wall. The sight in the water below was surreal. The sea was all red, scarlet, with blood.

In the middle of the huge billowing bloody pool were two enormous fins racing through the water at great speed. A person's head was visible just above the water. It wasn't moving, it wasn't moving. I immediately thought the head was Pauline's, as she never missed a day, and I panicked.

I raced to the water's edge to see what I could do, but the huge shark was now chasing Dirk, who seemed a lot closer to shore than the head of the person in the water.

The shark came in so shallow – about knee or waist height – that the top half of its body was out of the water. Dirk kicked at it and climbed away out of the water. The shark then raced off north.

By this time I saw Brian Farley dragging a man towards the beach. I could see it was Ken. I hopped into the water and Brian and I grabbed Ken to try to carry him out. Ken was a strong, burly guy, very heavy, and the two of us couldn't lift him. People just stared in horror and shock. I shouted at a chap and he came and helped us lift Ken on to the beach.

Ken was totally white. His right leg had gone. Someone wrapped a towel around the wound. A nurse called Jo started giving Ken mouth-to-mouth and I began pumping his chest with both hands. I don't know how long we did this – it could have been fifteen or twenty minutes. I was in a frenzy trying to do something. Someone grabbed my arm and said something. A doctor. We kept going.

An ambulance woman came and tried to take a pulse. There wasn't one. About this time, Ken's wife, Robin, who had been for a walk along the beach, came and knelt down next to the three of us and said, 'Ken, don't go. Please don't go, Ken!'

Jo and I kept trying to give Ken life, pushing his big chest and blowing air into him. The ambulance woman said, 'I think we should put him in the bag now.'

People gathered at Robbie Burns's place for tea and hugs. I stayed a while and then thought I should go and see Dirk in Fremantle Hospital. I'd seen him staggering up the beach with blood everywhere. I went into the emergency department and Dirk was in a cubicle with the curtains drawn. Dirk had lots of lacerations to his legs. This guy still swims every day, sometimes on his own. This bloke is tough.

I still swim nearly every day at North Cott, and enjoy the friendship and coffee afterwards. But I can't swim more than three or four metres from the water's edge now. My mates laugh at me, call me the Reef Crawler, because I slide over the reef in a metre of water. I figure that if a shark turns up, it won't be able to get me on the reef. If it does, I can stand up on the reef and defend myself.

I can't stop thinking about it.

. . .

Brian Sierakowski, a well-known Perth lawyer and former league footballer with the St Kilda and Subiaco Australian Rules teams, was also present the morning of Ken Crew's death. He'd already survived his own great-white attack off Cottesloe three years earlier. His shark-damaged surf-ski 'Extract of Poland' now adorns the ceiling of Cicerello's landmark fish restaurant on Fremantle harbour.

It's still vivid fifteen years later. We used to paddle from North Cott to a little break three kilometres south called Dutch Inn. It's a reef one hundred and fifty metres offshore where the waves build up. Most mornings you can get a nice ride of about sixty or seventy metres.

On this day it was very overcast and a bit choppy. I was on a double ski with Barney Hanrahan the surgeon. Malcolm McCusker (the Queens Counsel, now Governor of Western Australia) and his wife Di were on another ski, and a friend, Milton Barker, was on a single ski. The five of us paddled south.

Our ski was two hundred metres off shore. I was looking out to sea in the direction of Rottnest for a swell. Milton and the McCuskers had caught a wave and I was waiting and being patient. Next thing, there was this massive thump on the ski from the beach side, like being hit by a truck.

My brain was setting off alarm bells. One side of my brain was screaming 'shark', the other side was saying it must be a volcanic eruption.

Then this huge shark – a five-metre white pointer – raised its head out of the water and its jaws completely engulfed the ski, and the jaws slammed down. The ski was a metre wide, but the shark held the ski in its mouth as if it was a pencil.

I could see the whole head and eye looking at me, and the jaw more than a metre wide was protruding over the other side of the ski. Then it started a thrashing motion, holding the ski and shaking it. Its whole body contorted as it swung the ski back and forth, and the dorsal fin hit me in the face and threw me in the water.

So both of us are now in the water, the shark and me, and the shark's still there with its jaw wrapped around the ski.

Barney screamed, 'Shark, help us!'. The others had paddled into shore. They thought it had taken my legs. Diana McCusker kept screaming, 'We've got to get them! Now!'

The shark backed off from the ski and sank down under me like a submarine. And I'm in the water, thinking, 'Here I go, this is it!' And I lay partly on the back of the broken ski, screaming for help, and they came out to get us.

I weigh 108 kilos and I grabbed the back of their ski, and they were paddling so hard my body was fish-tailing out the back. My mind started laughing as we went over the reef, 'Yes, you've beaten this thing!'

And as I was being towed into shore the shark passed me, and attacked my ski again.

This good-luck scenario changed dramatically when Ken Crew was attacked. I was there that morning, too. We got changed next to each other at North Cott. He said, 'Have a good paddle,' and I said, 'Have a good swim.' A bit later I saw all the commotion on the beach and we got involved in that. It's astonishing the great-white should come into that little water pool at North Cott. I carried his wife up to the surf club.

It took us a good week to get back in the water. Now I'm in there every morning again. Last year I was paddling out in the swell and I felt a huge whack on the side of the ski, and someone said, 'Did you see that? It was a shark.'

There have been many sightings lately. Some say they're after the whale calves, or that the fish stocks they feed on have been depleted down south, forcing them to come further up the coast.

I believe the same shark killed Ken that had attacked us. It's too great a coincidence – both great-whites, both five metres long and in the same area. Obviously this one had set up territory.

I have this huge feeling of lost innocence now. When the shark attacked us, I talked about it and got it out of my system. But after Ken was killed the situation changed.

My house in Cottesloe overlooks the spot where we were attacked. I remember standing on the veranda looking at the ocean. I could feel the shark's eyes looking at me. 'Come in, I'm waiting for you!' I stood there and I was openly crying.

36
BUTTERCUP ISLAND

For days I'd been wanting to explore Buttercup Island, across the lagoon from our Montebello camp. From the hut it resembled a classic desert island; not a single-palm-tree cartoon island, but one a castaway like Robinson Crusoe or Tom Hanks might wash up on. It appeared an easy walk at low tide from Hermite but the tides never seemed to coincide with my free time. Seeing the tide receding fast one morning, I determined to do it when we got back from the dawn animal-trap releases.

The thing about an island – if you're an islomaniac and a sailor – is that you feel bound to circumnavigate it. If you're on foot you're compelled to hike completely around the shoreline at sea-level.

It took only fifteen minutes to plod across to the island over the bare sand that only a couple of hours before had been a sea-bed five or six metres down. Remembering this sweeping white expanse recently seething with dorsal fins and stingray wings, I cast the first of numerous wary glances towards the wide channel that led from the open ocean.

When I climbed up the steep dune to the island's main level, following the scraped flipper-prints of a turtle, I thought how difficult it must have been for the ungainly animal to patiently haul itself up this forty-degree slope. Buttercup Island, of course, was ridiculously named. Its only vegetation was prickly spinifex: the dreaded Bushes of Doom, a plant at the farthest botanical and symbolic remove from English buttercups, and so thickly and spikily clustered as to be impenetrable without a machete.

Crusoe and Hanks would have been in trouble. The cliffs themselves, jagged black limestone teeth at sea-level, rose from the high-tide line into smooth and bosomy pink formations like Henry Moore sculptures. A pair of hawks nested in the cliff's serrations. The legacy of the cats and rats was a comparative absence of Australia's most common shore birds: seagulls and crested terns. The only seabirds I saw all morning were a pair of pied oyster catchers on the vast sandbank and a scattering of cormorants resting on the islets far offshore.

I stepped up onto the tidal platform and set off anticlockwise around the island. The flat rock ledge was still in shadow and the footing was slippery with many different algae formations – replicas of hair and lettuce and sausages and grapes and bubbles and necklaces and babies' brains – all interlaced with rock pools and each presided over by a single fat sea-slug as black as patent leather.

I became conscious of the total silence. Apart from my squelching footsteps, there were no sounds. No waves broke and no boats were on the sea. There was no litter on the shoreline, no trace of human activity, past or present. Back on Hermite the hut was now out of sight and the only sign that people existed in the post-nuclear world were my footprints, already somehow eerie and foreign, in the sand behind me, and the dark outline of the bomb observation post, on top of Hermite's highest dune and always starkly visible.

I reached the eastern end of Buttercup and followed the shore ledge around the corner to its seaward side. Immediately the sun was beating down and the open Indian Ocean stretched west to Madagascar, rippling and glistening over the reef. The shore ledge was drier and the walking easier, and everywhere I looked the rocks were swarming with vivid red and green crabs. Like liveried sentries, they emerged from caves and crevices to investigate the intrusion, advanced threateningly, rattled their weapons in a show of aggression, paused to reconsider the situation, thought better of it, and scuttled away.

I kept on around the seaward shore but I seemed to be making little progress. I'd wade around one more jagged headland, thinking I'd reached the end of what, after all, had appeared to be a very small island, only to find another stretch of rock ledge, more rock pools, more inky sea-slugs, scores more red and green crabs spidering up the cave walls, and yet another jagged promontory obstructing me and forcing me to step off the ledge and wade around it.

The water here reached my shins, and then my knees and thighs, and as I ever-warily glanced at the open sea, I noticed, bobbing gently over the reefs towards Buttercup Island, what looked like a human head.

It couldn't be. I tried to imagine what a water-logged, decapitated head would look like. Dark or pale? Bloated, certainly; its features nibbled off by fish and crustaceans. From what I could see of it, this floating 'head' was discoloured: sallow, blotchy and bloated, its 'features' blurry. It didn't look like a buoy or a fishing float or a bobbing coconut though; it was round but not perfectly round. It looked quite weighty and had a dark patch of what could have been short cropped hair. From where I stood it looked disturbingly like an Asian man's head (an Indonesian fisherman, an asylum seeker?) that had been in the ocean for a while.

Yes? No? Scattering panicky crabs, I hurried along the rocks to the nearest point for a closer look. The shore ledge was too high and serrated here, and the water too deep – and full of sharks. If I swam out to it, it would turn out to be a *beche-de-mer* or something similarly mundane and squashy. Even if it really was a human head from a fishing-boat accident or a would-be asylum seeker fallen overboard (after the sharks had fed) I'd be risking myself for a lump of dead person.

It reminded me of a recent experience at home. I was strolling along the beach at Broken Head, south of Byron Bay, one Saturday morning, mulling over life at low tide, when something caught my eye on that flat expanse of firm clean sand unmarred by shell, pebble or jellyfish. A piece of pure white bone had washed ashore.

I stopped and picked it up. It hadn't been long in the sea; it had no marine growth and wasn't pitted or eroded. It didn't look like picnic or barbecue rubbish and it was unlike any animal bone I could recall: thick, quite heavy and about twenty centimetres long.

As I turned it over in my hand it occurred to me, with that well-known icy sensation of hairs rising on the back of the neck, that it looked like a human femur. I was holding a section of thigh bone in my hand. The sides were smooth and one end of the bone was cleanly snapped. At its widest end the bone was jagged, with a zigzag edge of sharp points, as if it had been severed with a pair of pinking shears.

The discovery was a shock, for good reason. Three weeks before, a prawning trawler, the *Sea Rogue,* had overturned at night in rough seas off the north coast. The skipper and his two deckhands were believed lost. Then one of the deckhands, exhausted and dehydrated, crawled up on to New Brighton beach late the following afternoon. Guided at first by the light of Cape Byron lighthouse then, after dawn, by the misty blue peaks of Mt Warning and the Nightcap Range, he'd swum thirteen kilometres in fourteen hours to shore.

He was able to tell the rescue services approximately where the boat sank, and that he'd left his two companions clinging to floating debris. Sea and air searchers concentrated their hunt and, amazingly, after another twelve hours, they found the second deckhand alive, badly sunburnt and clinging to a styrofoam drinks cooler. Of the *Sea Rogue's* skipper, however, there was no sign.

I held the white bone with the jagged, severed edge, recalling the intense search for the skipper: the patrolling coastguard craft, the helicopters and surf lifesavers and water police. For another week they combed the coastline and river mouths in a thorough but fruitless search for the missing man.

What should I do with the bone? Take it to the police station? The cops would probably laugh it off as bait from a lobster pot. But many different and difficult questions arose. If it was indeed the skipper's thigh bone, would his next-of-kin even appreciate its discovery? Wouldn't the evidence of the bone – that sharp, zigzag pattern – be too brutal a realisation? Shouldn't there be a DNA test? Could you hold a funeral service for a piece of femur? What quantity of remains, what percentage of flesh or bone, was necessary in order for a vestige of a human to be counted as a body? Would a leg bone count? Did it have traces of a soul?

The white bone in my hand had assumed immense significance. It had emotional weight. In the harsh beach sunlight it had a pale aura and I didn't want to hold it any longer.

I decided to continue my walk while I thought about what to do. I had no pockets and the bone was too cumbersome to carry. I placed it on a patch of dry sand securely far from the water, and jammed a branch of driftwood into the ground to mark the spot. I'd pick it up on my way back.

I was free of it. Suddenly I was tense and needed to jog. I jogged a couple of kilometres along the shore, all the time thinking about the bone, and at Tallow Beach I turned back. I decided I'd take it to the Byron Bay police station and leave any further assessments to them.

But a decision had already been made. I reached the spot I'd marked with the driftwood branch but it was gone. The tide was still fairly low but the patch of sand had been inundated by an errant wave, swamped so recently that air bubbles were still popping on its soggy surface. The bone was washed away too, returned to the sea.

· · ·

On Buttercup Island, while I kept watching the head shape floating in the sea and tussled with questions of common-sense versus curiosity, with a touch of ethics thrown in, the decision was again made for me.

When the head – or the 'head' – was in line with the end of the island, it bobbed to a standstill for a moment, becalmed in the com-mingling tides. Then it met a faster receding current which swept it up, rotated it, bounced it around for a moment, and bore it away.

37
A WOULD-BE WRITER

How many important *either-or* decisions in a lifetime? My first fork in the road appeared at seventeen, in my last year at school. One signpost said *Would-be Writers This Way*. The other said *Cartoonists Over Here (We Have More Fun)*.

I was torn. I wanted to be a writer, as soon as I worked out where Writing Headquarters was, and who was the Person In Charge. The *West Australian* and its editor seemed the nearest thing to it. However, I'd loved comic books when I was younger and I was a keen would-be cartoonist. I was a slavish imitator of Paul Rigby, whose cartoons in the evening *Daily News* and gregarious personality had made him a local cult figure. I was also a fan of the English cartoonist Ronald Searle, and of Chester Gould who drew *Dick Tracy*, and the *Phantom's* creator, Lee Falk.

I admired the different way these fellows drew noses. I drew noses for hours. My school books were covered in noses – in left and right profile, front-on, and as other nose-sketchers or possibly Freudians will appreciate, three-quarters on. My big-nosed, Rigby-influenced cartoons were prominent features in the *Cygnet,* as were my 'poems' and precise recording of sports results. Owing to a dearth of contributors, the editor gave my work a good run. I was the editor.

The *West Australian* took its journalism cadetships seriously. While still at school I was assigned to write trial editorials for the paper and invited to show them my cartoon portfolio. My 'editorial' on the Collie coal strike was heart-wrenching in its concern for the miners' families – not an angle canvassed by the paper's real leader writers. Nevertheless, I was eventually offered two cadetships for the next year: in the art department and on the reporting staff. The first-year salaries were the same, $23.80. Which should I accept?

Before I leave my schooldays behind, I should address a lack in *The Shark Net*: the absence of any mention of schooling after the age of eight. I managed to steer the memoir's narrative away from my having attended school for all my high-school years.

I welshed on this matter for a very Australian reason, one recognised by Australian writers, and Labor politicians, too. I went to a *private school*. Those two words are often freighted with vehemence and envy. To make this transgression public supposedly alienates your readership (or voters). An eight-year-old child is hardly in charge of their educational future, but for the rest of your life you're resented as an elitist.

Writers are keenly aware of the reverse social-climb. In the world's most middle-class country, the middle-class is an unpopular backdrop for both life and art. The reading public and media are sentimentalists who prefer the Log Cabin to White House cliché for their writers. Keep the private-school education under wraps.

I know chip-on-the-shoulder 'working-class' writers with expensive boats and holiday houses. Sensibly, they're never photographed anywhere near them. It's safest to scowl into the camera on a moody windswept beach. Many is the shoreline I've been snapped on myself, frowning knee-deep in the ocean.

The alternative is to stand in a khaki work-shirt (sleeves rolled up) by the bookshelves in your publisher's office. This is having a dollar each way: salt-of-the-earth but scholarly. You might never have actually 'worked' beyond writing, but in pictorial interviews you're only a small step removed from a tiller of soil. (A grim city-alley backdrop is compulsory for younger writers. And no smiling.)

A small example of the ethos: my father sold rubber goods in a remote provincial city for a living. His mother used to sell hats in Myer's millinery department. After the publication of *The Shark Net,* a memoir which outlined this family background, the first question I was asked by the chairman of a panel on *The Memoir* at the Melbourne Writers' Festival was, 'How was it growing up as part of the Establishment's power structure?'

Before I leave the subject of my private schooling, I should say that the eight-year-old State-school boy received the news of the private-school years to come with some apprehension. The main reason was the motto emblazoned on the crest of my new cap and jacket: *Duty.*

As it happened, *duty* was the euphemism that generations of bowel-obsessed Drewe parents had used for defecation. As in (to five-year-old Robert) 'Have you done your duty today?' Or, too often: 'Oh, no! The dog's gone and done its duty on the carpet again!'

. . .

I should add (has he no shame?) that not only did I go to a private school, and take *Duty* as my daily maxim, but that in my last year I was school captain.

The school was an Anglican boys' college, Hale School, the first private school in the State, a century-old limestone institution in West Perth that had indeed produced many notable characters, from explorers to State Premiers. But by my term it had fallen on hard times.

My final year was the school's last on that campus and the student numbers, the staff morale, the crumbling buildings and the already rudimentary sporting facilities had been allowed to run down. For more than a decade the school's funds had been channelled into the state-of-the-art Hale School which the following year would rise grandly from the grassy paddocks of Wembley Downs.

Our old headmaster, Vernon 'Spud' Murphy, had been invalided out against his will, and as a stop-gap measure the school was run by the deputy head, an enigmatic and often ferocious man who resembled a rhesus monkey. A.C. 'Monkey' Marshall was the Chief Punisher, a lean, wiry man whose abrupt rages, from standing start to foam-flecked apoplexy in a matter of seconds, and subsequent savage cane-wielding, sparked fear in hundred-kilogram farm boys and football heroes alike.

For an apt pen-picture of my year in command, imagine a particular sepia-tinted autumn afternoon. Twenty years after the German occupation of his country, and fifteen years after the formation of Tito's republic, Ex-King Peter of Yugoslavia has let it be known he would be paying us bemused West Australian schoolboys a visit.

He was on a tour of the State to make contact with Yugoslav émigrés and to bolster anti-Communist morale. There was a growing Yugoslav community in Perth, mainly vegetable growers in Osborne Park. It included our teacher of Italian, a tall, saturnine gentleman named Dr P.V. Pusenjak, who favoured lemon-coloured, double-breasted, middle-European suits and pointy tan shoes, and looked and sounded like the suavely menacing actor Vincent Price. Dr Pusenjak had loyally invited his ex-King to address the school.

The school was slightly confused about where Europe's continental monarchies stood at that moment. Naturally, we had turned out en masse for the Queen Mother's two laps of Subiaco Oval in an open Land-Rover two years before. Now a (former) King wanted to visit us. As a Royal, he could hardly be knocked back.

After all the orange peels and lolly wrappers had been hastily picked up, everyone lined up on the asphalt in front of the assembly hall and awaited the visitor. Eventually Ex-King Peter arrived. He too was a tall, saturnine figure resembling the actor Vincent Price, although this wasn't obvious at first. He was crammed, knees to chin, into the back seat of Dr Pusenjak's green Morris, and when he extracted himself it was my duty to welcome him.

As school captain, I'd been instructed to stand on the marked spot on the threadbare school lawn where the Morris would come to a halt, and open the rear door with my left hand. As he emerged, I was to make a sweeping motion with my right arm – a gesture welcoming but suitably subservient – somewhere between a medieval courtier's bow and Sir Walter Raleigh laying down his cloak. Then I had to snap to attention and shout, 'School! Three cheers for *King* Peter of Yugoslavia!'

My instructions from Monkey Marshall were explicit. I had to call him *King* Peter, not *Ex*-King Peter. Diplomacy was very important, as was our respect for European monarchies, even dead ones.

He'd been in exile half his life, and was reduced to driving in a Morris around Perth's sandy outer-suburban market gardens, looking up his big-boned expatriates in the onion and rhubarb trades. But apparently he was very sensitive about his position in European history. I was under strict orders not to call him *Ex*-King Peter. This was seriously preying on my mind.

Somewhat mystified, the boys stood and watched the Morris slowly approach the school. Dr Pusenjak successfully brought it to a standstill. My bow was rather stiff and self-conscious but the car-door opening, and the shout, and the three-cheers went off successfully.

The official visitor, the welcoming party, and all the teachers and students filed into the assembly hall. Dr Pusenjak's stocks had never been higher. In the hierarchical conga line of teachers he had suddenly jumped from his usual second-last in the pecking order (between biology and art) to second. He was walking on air.

After *Ex*-but-not-*Ex*-King Peter had addressed us in the stuffy, crammed assembly hall for forty or fifty minutes in what seemed to be his own language, and I was pretty sure he'd finished – although this was difficult to tell – my job, after silently signalling the other prefects to remove the fainters, was again to lead the school in three grateful cheers.

I was so intent on waiting for my cue, and concentrating so deeply on not calling him *Ex*-King, that when at last he drew breath, and Monkey Marshall quickly caught my eye and nodded, I shouted out, 'School! Three cheers for King Peter of Czechoslovakia!'

Monkey Marshall shot me a frown. Dr Pusenjak looked as if he'd like to see me instantly and painfully despatched. The former King had a stunned expression on his grimly handsome face, his gaze fixed somewhere beyond this peculiar sandy country, the Balkans perhaps.

'Yugoslavia!' hissed Monkey Marshall.

Desperately rattled now, I shouted again: 'School! Three more cheers for Ex-King Peter of Yugoslavia!'

. . .

By today's media standards, the newspaper company was extraordinarily thoughtful. First, it showed its potential junior reporters around the building. We went down to the composing room. We saw the presses rolling. We poked tentative fingers on hot metal. We inhaled the ink. We saw compositors and sub-editors reading metal words upside down.

On the editorial floor, we got to individually meet and converse with the editor and assistant editor. We were even presented for appraisal to the board of directors, who checked out our haircuts, suits and ties for extremism and questioned us about newsy local topics. They wanted to see if we were on the ball and worthy representatives of the Perth Press. They asked me the subject of Rigby's cartoon the previous day. Whew, I knew that.

The art-department tour was low key by comparison. The younger press artists were all morosely air-brushing out net-ballers' underarm hair or painting in missing teeth and depilating women's moustaches in social photographs. No-one looked the least bohemian. Their most creative task appeared to be drawing isobars on weather maps. And they never left the office. That was the crunch. It made journalism an easy choice.

I began work as a cadet reporter on my eighteenth birthday. The job seemed to offer everything I wanted. I would be paid to write, to travel and to have adventures, and although initially the job was actually to peck out weather details and radio and TV programs on giant Siemens typewriters, one level above copyboy, that eventually became the case. This was the real world, and I loved it.

We had an excellent taskmaster as cadet counsellor, a dour ex-Fleet Street man named Jim Dunbar. When we'd written something idiotic he would gaze at the ceiling, then grimace into the mid-distance – filled with tweed-jacketed men busily smoking pipes – and suck his snaggled Scottish-looking teeth and sigh, and patiently explain the error.

He gave us current-affairs and observation tests, and went over our copy with us when it came up from the composing room with the sub-editors' corrections on it. He'd point out our factual mistakes, clichés, potential libels and unacceptable grammar. He'd say, 'Where's your lead paragraph? That's too woolly. You've got to speak directly to the reader.' I think I owe him plenty.

Only recently I've realised that the frightening Monkey Marshall was also a literary influence. He wasn't the mentor type, not by a long way. But as well as being Chief Punisher he also taught English and French. As an actual teacher he dropped the menacing executioner role, assumed a cynical, seen-it-all stance and became a sort of marmoset boulevardier, an intimate of Lord Byron, Noel Coward, Samuel Taylor Coleridge and Alexander Pope. As he aired his knowledge of these mainstays of our English course he implied that he'd be strolling down Hay Street with them as usual on Saturday night.

Thankfully, he'd never paid me any special attention. Then in my second-last year he began reading out my creative-writing stories to the class. He read them without his usual sarcasm, and forty six-teen and seventeen-year-olds actually sat still and listened. I found their sudden quiet attention a strangely pleasing sensation. When I got over the embarrassment of being momentarily approved of by Monkey, a possibility began to dawn on me. Writing for a living.

Journalism took a naïve adolescent from the suburbs of a conserva-tive provincial city and shoved his nose into human drama: courts, crime, politics and the Claremont-Cottesloe ladies' croquet competi-tion. While still a teenager I saw murderers and corpses and corrupt policemen and drunken politicians. I spoke to sad crime and accident victims and victorious sportsmen and dumbstruck lottery winners. I saw how the State's power structure operated, and its lower reaches as well.

Especially the lower reaches. I can still conjure up the carbolic-acid smell of the holding cells at the old Perth police headquarters where my father's former employee, the serial killer Eric Cooke, was taken when he was finally captured. The daily procession of human-ity in the dock, the dust motes in the afternoon rays coming through the west-facing windows of the police court, even the varnished dock rail, are as clear to me as yesterday.

That period of my adolescence would colour my fiction. A chaotic time of mingled community and family crises showed me that life could go haywire without any warning. Your mother could complain of a headache, cook your breakfast and immediately die. Friends could be murdered in their beds by total strangers, or drowned while surfing beside you, or decapitated in light-aircraft accidents. It gave me a lasting expectation of sudden inexplicable drama.

After three years, however, I felt I'd squeezed every drop of newsworthy drama out of Perth. During a flat news period, the night chief-of-staff had begun sending me to the airport to interview people getting off the nightly plane from the eastern States. I thought the time had come to move on when I had to confront travel-weary strangers and ask, 'Excuse me, are you interesting?' I knew I'd reached my nadir when I was sent to the railway station with the same instructions.

To be honest, there was another reason beyond ambition for leaving Perth: to leave behind the hypocritical, country-town, gossipy, ultra-conservative attitude of my parents' generation and, less understandably, some members of my own age group. After three years I was weary of the 'scandal' of me marrying at eighteen when my girlfriend became pregnant, and still confused at the disparagement of us for doing our *duty*.

The hypocrites included some girls who kept out of sight in the country or interstate during their own pregnancies, and who then gave up their covert babies for adoption. Their sad secrets intact, their inclination to gossip about a couple who, however naïvely, took what they thought was the ethical approach to the dilemma, was undiminished.

After the publication of *The Shark Net*, one of these secret babies, now a mature professional woman, contacted me unexpectedly. She'd been raised interstate by her adopted parents and was committed to uncovering the mystery of her natural parents. She'd tracked down her mother. She'd also read my book and urgently needed to know if I thought my friend John Sturkey, one of the eight victims of the murderer Eric Cooke, might have been her father.

I couldn't help. I didn't know if John had dated the woman she mentioned, whom, coincidentally, I also knew. Although my correspondent had successfully tracked her down, her mother wanted to maintain the secret and refused to have anything to do with her.

I saw a photo of my correspondent and she so resembled her unwilling mother that they could have been twins.

. . .

When the second fork in the road presented itself – to leave or to stay in Perth – I accepted an offer by *The Age* to move to the bigger journalistic pond of Melbourne. I left Western Australia on my twenty-first birthday. I look back on this time as a maturing process, a letting-go of the past. I also remember Melbourne for the Thursday night in Fitzroy Street, St Kilda, when I was hit from behind with a chain (I think) and kicked by muggers, whom I never saw.

My pay packet was stolen, of course. Uselessly for the muggers, it was a cheque rather than cash. The concussion required overnight observation in hospital, my right eyebrow needed stitching, and my danger-attracting left testicle was transformed, in colour and size, into an avocado.

I thought to myself, *The third time! Surely this is it. It's lucky I already have a child.*

38
JUNGLE BARS

At twenty-two I desperately wanted to bestride the world. I wanted to file scoops from exotic trouble-spots and sip gin and tonics under slowly whirring ceiling fans. I wanted to wear tropical seersucker suits by night. By day, of course, it would be dusty khaki bush-shirts with epaulettes and pockets on the sleeves to hold my pens and notebooks and Swiss army knife.

My travel urge was easily as strong and poignant as the most powerful of youth's other urges. It was made all the fiercer by the overwhelming obstacle in its path: supporting a young family. Four years after my marriage I was a vaguely melancholy young husband and father. I thought of myself as loving and mature but emotionally I was as green as the tropical foliage I lusted after.

Every noon, before my five p.m. night-shift in *The Age* Sydney bureau, I would catch a few waves at Freshwater beach, walk north around the point, and then sit on a particular rock that was curved like an armchair and overlooked the swells rolling on to Curl Curl beach, and daydream of travelling.

Like all my less hamstrung friends, I was desperate to go 'overseas', but not merely to join them on the lower decks of the *Stratheden* to

England, to serve the regulation eighteen months in Earl's Court and as a down-table sub-editor in Fleet Street. I wanted settings more exotic than the sub's table.

I wanted to be a working traveller, a foreign correspondent, not a tourist. The difference was important. A traveller was a young searcher for 'experience' whereas a tourist was middle-aged and passive. I was scornful of anyone addicted to visiting castles and old places of worship and buying crappy souvenirs.

I sat on my rock-chair overlooking Curl Curl's point-break and imagined the stories I would uncover, write and file for *The Age*. These imaginings would fade as I trudged back uphill to our flat in Soldiers Avenue. I had a wife and child and Ruth was pregnant again. I wasn't going anywhere fast, or anywhere exotic either. The bus to Manly, then the ferry to Circular Quay, were my limit.

Nevertheless, as *The Age*'s Sydney bureau chief I optimistically applied to be promoted to the paper's London bureau. The previous London man, perhaps mis-hearing the job description as *foreign co-respondent*, had dissipated a lot of *Age* expenses in Paris bistros, Hamburg brothels and Munich beer halls. He was twenty-eight, and an edict came out that no-one under thirty was to be sent overseas again. The editor, Graham Perkin, said to me, 'Jesus, chap. We're paying maintenance to frauleins all over Bavaria. Ask me again in seven years.'

He relented somewhat by allowing me to make my first naïve foray abroad: a travel freebie with Philippine Airlines to Manila which coincided with the election of Ferdinand Marcos. Like many young Westerners before and after me, I found the Third World an exotic and sensual experience. The Philippines was suffering from the disparaging reputation 'Four hundred years in the convent and forty years in Hollywood.' Amorality and poverty were new to me, and ostentatious wealth, for that matter. Not to mention the signs in the nightclubs insisting *All Handguns Must Be Left in Lobby*.

Filipino nightclubs and hotels in their infinite variety left such an impression that ten years later I used a combination of their images in my novel *A Cry in the Jungle Bar*. I conjured a fictional hotel from the lounge bar of a two-star hotel called the Paradise. The Paradise had narrowed its clientele down to adulterers and the disabled. It catered to the Manila businessmen's after-lunch sexual-liaison business and the foreign chronic-invalid trade: optimistic sick Westerners in the Philippines to visit the faith healers.

I can't remember now how much of the Jungle Bar I made up and how much was real. As I entered, rather tentatively, did I pass a sign announcing *Tonight Live in the Jungle Bar – Fantastic Bong-Bong Nick Diaz and The Emotionals (Patrons Must Check All Handguns)*? Did the bizarre ornamentation, a mock-tropical forest of creepers, palms and vines, actually exist? Did it seem to grow and throb before my eyes?

Let's say a mossy reptilian reek did hang over the bar. I was definitely 'overseas' now. I see myself peering through the Paradise's foliage, struck by a wall of sharks' jaws, various antlers, and the heads of a wild boar and a big feline of indeterminate species. Perhaps a rattling movement, an aggressive frisson, catches my attention. Two bitter-looking iguanas are mating spitefully behind glass, like a porn-show out of *Star Wars*. Nearby, sea snakes writhe in a cloudy tank; in another, a three-flippered turtle bumps unhappily against the glass.

Above the bar, I visualise a tree of taxidermised civet cats and bats, shrews and flying lemurs simulating life. A solitary stuffed pangolin stands stolidly on the bar top. I pull up a leopard-print bar stool near the pangolin and order my first seasoned-traveller-style gin and tonic.

The barman says, oddly, 'Sir is looking very well, not too sick at all.'

Indeed not. I'm overseas at last. I'm twenty-two. I've never felt better.

'We got the works for your health. Make you dangerous to be with.' He nods towards the turtle-amputee's tank. 'Real *appro-deezac* food!

Turtle soup, boss-male iguana, your choice of sea snake. Make your health better, put lead in your pencil.'

I stick to gin and tonic. I'm desperate to drink a gin and tonic in the tropics. I take my first sip as Bong-Bong Nick Diaz savagely kicks his snagged microphone cord from the iguana tank and strains to make himself heard above The Emotionals' piano-accordionist. Bong-Bong Nick Diaz begins sullenly crooning *Arrivederci Roma* as the first of the Paradise's favoured customers limp in.

Later that night, as I help lift fifteen boisterously drunk – and surprisingly heavy – American invalids from the bar into their taxi-van, bound for the faith-healers in the mountains, I wonder whether this evening counts as a travel 'experience'.

. . .

Many years later, Ian McEwan, in his book *A Move Abroad,* said something that rang loud bells for me. 'Choosing a new form in which to write bears some resemblance to travelling abroad. The sense of freedom is no less useful for being illusory or temporary. The new place has its own rules and conventions, but they are not really yours, not quite yet. What you notice first is the absence of the old familiar constraints, and (my italics) *you do things you would not do at home . . .'*

Apparently no-one actually said, 'When in Rome do as the Romans do.' The saying is believed to have originated in St Ambrose's *Letters to Augustine* in the fourth century. St Ambrose wrote, 'When I am here [at Milan], I do not fast on the Sabbath; when I am at Rome, I do fast on the Sabbath.'

. . .

The first travel 'experience' that counted was to come in the Philippines a few days later. My older journalistic colleagues disported themselves with the prostitutes supplied as a matter of course by the airline. As an ethical married man I refused to participate, though I was culpable in another way. I fell in love with the beautiful daughter of a Cebu pineapple millionaire.

Her name was Mina Estalilla. We went on one date, if you call sitting at a table in the company of eight chaperones a date. It was in Cebu City. This was where Ferdinand Magellan was killed by the Filipinos while trying to circumnavigate the world in 1521. To make amends, they'd named a flash hotel after him. I'd casually asked Mina if she wished to join me for a drink in the Magellan Hotel's discotheque.

She said yes and gave a little skip. So did my heart. And so, at eight p.m., through the door of the disco (resident fifteen-piece band: *The Moody Sheriff and His Bad Guy Posse*) filed Mina, her mother, two aunts, two teenage sisters and three female cousins.

The nine women all ordered Cokes. As an urbane foreign corre-spondent out with the local ladies, my quandary was whether I should drink gin or scotch. Maybe gin was for invalids. I chose scotch this time. 'On the rocks,' I ordered firmly.

Eventually I gathered the courage to ask Mina for a dance, to Petula Clark's *Downtown*, rendered by the moody sheriff and his sulky sidekicks. Meanwhile, the eight other Dole pineapple heiresses whispered and giggled and sipped their Cokes and marched back and forth like a sort of relay team to the powder room, always leaving three or four heiresses on guard duty.

Mina, admiring my savoir-faire, nevertheless asked my age. I put it up three years to twenty-five. Her breath smelled of Coke. Of course we didn't kiss: I was a married man and anyway she had eight chap-erones. Once, just before eleven p.m., my nose accidentally brushed the top of her cool ear. It was the closest I came to infidelity. At eleven

ne chaperones put down their glasses in one fluid movement
wept Mina away. I sat and finished my drink as I perused the
ill for three scotches and thirty-seven Cokes.

Past the pulsating rooms of my colleagues, I went upstairs then and
ooned around my lonely, humid room, writing Mina a love letter on
Magellan Hotel stationery. 'Although our lives take us along separate
paths . . .' I was still swooning from our nose-to-ear contact. Of her
Coca-Cola aroma, I wrote, 'Your fragrance lingers in my senses.'

I didn't post it. I was married. I knew I was too young to be married,
but I was. I wouldn't try to see Mina again. Like a character in a film, I
felt depressed, confused and world-weary. Decidedly Bogartish. *('Of all
the gin joints in all the world she had to walk into mine.')*

But there was something else, a feeling not entirely unsatisfactory.
I'd been right about the essence of travel. Travel was the most intense
experience. Travel was romance.

. . .

The next fork in the road was the big one. After five years and a second baby boy, and after living together in three States, my teenage
marriage to Ruth broke up in Sydney. It was chiefly my fault. I was
too young and ambitious to settle down in the outer suburbs. I'd only
ever had one real girlfriend and no adolescence. *Duty* could go awry.
I felt I was missing out on life.

Guilt-ridden and sad, I would spend three days a week for another
five years out in the suburbs anyway, trekking back and forth from
inner-city Sydney on the 190 bus to Avalon to see my adored little
boys, James and Ben.

However, running *The Age* bureau was interesting, and thanks to
the aid of my deputy, Joan Edison, not the least difficult. It was well-
paid enough for me to buy a hip suede jacket to wear to the premiere

of *Hair* with my new girlfriend Sandra, an attractive reporter on the *Sydney Morning Herald*.

This unchallenging journalistic side-road could have gone on forever. Indeed, with the help of a friendly switchboard girl, and sustained by cheap beer and free cheese and pepperoni, my capable assistant Andrew Clark and I managed a great deal of news dissemination from the billiards room of the Journalists' Club.

I'd work from five p.m. to midnight, until *The Age*'s first edition came out, with a dinner-time break for moussaka or stuffed capsicums at 'The Greeks', then meet Sandra at the club when she finished work on the *Herald*. After a couple of hours of drinks and stimulating conversation with colleagues, with maybe a detour for hamburgers at Binkie's, and to play *Jumping Jack Flash* and *Street Fighting Man* on the burger-bar jukebox, we'd be home in our old bed-sit in Milson's Point by three a.m.

The flat was so small we shared a single bed. The shadow of the Sydney Harbour Bridge fell on one side of us and the droppings from the fruit-bat-filled fig trees of Luna Park on the other. On Tuesdays, Thursdays and Saturdays I'd set the alarm to rise at eight a.m. and catch the double-decker bus to North Avalon, a fifty-minute trip, to spend the day with my boys. On the other days, it was eight whole hours sleep, followed by some laps in the North Sydney Olympic pool, only fifty metres away. At five p.m. I'd be back at work, ready for more news distribution, moussaka, beer and snooker.

The Age was good to me; I received rises and a Christmas bonus every year. There were many genial fellow travellers on a similar undemanding route but I felt a growing discomfort with myself and my occupation. My mind, my imagination, my sense of self was idling and dwindling. I was coasting.

One Saturday afternoon in my mid-twenties I was playing in the park with my sons when I went to retrieve a football Ben had kicked into the bushes. As I picked up the ball from the lantana, I had an epiphany. No divine beings or bursts of light were involved but this was a genuine blazing notion. In an intuitive burst of understanding, I thought, 'I'm going to leave journalism and write novels.' It was even more irresistible than my travel urge, and so strong it was almost sexual. On Monday morning I resigned from my job.

As it happened, it was a false start. I quickly ran out of money and my first attempt at a novel came to nothing. At twenty-five I was all reckless intention and no application. I was still too young. Although devastating things had already happened in my life, I lacked the emotional wherewithal to draw on them. The deaths, the tumult, were too recent and easily pushed aside. Worse, they were a block. They overlaid my whole existence but they were still a confused blur. My mind was numbed by them, and would remain so for several decades.

But I'd had enough of writing facts for a living. My urge was to write fiction. I saw it as a form of freedom. Two years later, when the compulsion again became overwhelming, I took the precaution of retaining my job – now on *The Australian* – and writing the novel before and after work.

This time I felt I had something to say. Sandy and I had a great relationship. She was beautiful and kind and liked books. She was a great support, I loved her deeply, and we decided to get married. At twenty-seven I was now mature. Or so I thought.

39
HITTING THE OLIVETTI

In my head I was calling this first novel, with ominous Robert Ludlum overtones, *The Genocide Thesis*. I worked at night on my little pea-green Olivetti portable on the kitchen table, and if I was unhappy with a sentence, with one word – if I made a single typing error – I screwed up the page, tossed it on the floor and started again.

Sandy's and my tiny sandstone terrace cottage in Euroka Street, North Sydney, was only three metres wide; by the time I gave up for the night almost the entire two and a half downstairs rooms would be carpeted in wads of A4, those small white cabbages of failure. The house already had a reputation for literary failure: in an unproductive, heavy-drinking, poverty-stricken period, Henry Lawson had once lived here. (Perhaps that explained all the broken beer bottles I turned up in the back yard.)

Nevertheless I'd speedily managed the first sixty or seventy pages of the book. What was so difficult about writing novels? Then one night an abrupt voice in my head informed me, the triumphal negativity of the thought bringing a frightening hot throbbing in the temples, that I had no idea what I was doing.

Even if I did know, the voice hectored me, who would want to read a big novel about history? Not an historical novel, but a novel *about* history. This was the mid-seventies; the local literary trend was for short stories and slender paperback novels about hard-drinking, work-shy libertarians and sexually cynical English Department lecturers.

All the hot young Sydney and Melbourne writers implied they were writing from Life: from shared inner-city households rife with booze, drugs, politics and brusque sexual experimentation (the men), or end-less cups of tea, hand-rolled cigarettes, faux working-class dialogue, world-weary conversations and melancholy sexual experimentation (the women). Lifestyle equalled literature. Lifestyle had no place for children. Lifestyle meant sex. English Department lecturers across the land were immensely flattered at the sexual attention, and remained so for the next twenty years.

And this humid Sydney night I was sitting at the table amid baby paraphernalia (we'd recently had our first child, a little girl, Amy), attempting to write about someone obsessed with the 1830s. What was I thinking?

Too agitated to work, or to give up for the night and try to sleep, I poured myself a Metaxa brandy, and I worried. (Influenced by our favourite restaurant, the New Hellas in Elizabeth Street, Sydney writ-ers regarded Greek food and drink as a literary mainstay.) As I sipped, I watched the slugs gliding across the kitchen linoleum towards the cat's bowl. Big slugs with leopard-like markings.

How in tune was I with the other end of the fiction process? If the tweed jackets, brogues and prim grey hair-buns at the annual general meeting of the Australian Society of Authors were anything to go by, not at all. I was the youngest member of the ASA committee by about thirty years. Though the childless, hard-drinking libertarians and randy English Department lecturers were coming up fast, the tweeds and buns still ruled.

Would readers of any age care about my big Australian themes:

racism and national identity, for example? Or my nineteenth-century Tasmanian characters? Or my twentieth-century West Australian ones? Or the genocide of the Tasmanian Aborigines, for that matter? I wouldn't bet on it. It wasn't that I'd run out of steam or story. I'd just run out of confidence and will. I saw myself pecking away at my amateurish little Olivetti and I felt unfashionable and raw.

Into this vacuum of anxiety flooded back all the cynicism and negativity nurtured by three newspapers and ten years of journalistic culture: all the cracks about Poofters' Corner (the arts pages) and Wankers' Weekly (the Saturday Review section). And that was just the editor's opinion.

The voice in my head could be an Ocker philistine too. This was News Limited. This was Surry Hills. This was the Invicta Hotel, where my editor – nicknamed the Romney Marsh for his woolly yellow hair and sheep-baa laugh – groped pretty young female journalists on their first day on the job and settled arguments by pouring beer on his reporters' heads. This was the Journalists' Club, where the distinguished foreign editor, having lunched on beers and polished off the bottle of gin in his briefcase during work hours, could phone in his brilliantly forensic editorials on Watergate or the Two Chinas Policy, then copulate in the library with a favourite barmaid. This was crass, afternoon-tabloid, rugby-league-loving Sydney. I was a morning-broadsheet, Australian Rules fan. What did I think I was doing?

For a start, I had a problem with territory. I sat somewhere in the demilitarised zone between Town and Gown. By day I was the books editor of *The Australian,* the national daily, not conservative in those days, and the paper's *Perspective* columnist as well. These jobs gave me an overview of the local writing scene and brought me droves of instant literary best friends. I upped the Australian content of the Saturday book review pages. I started a mid-week books page as well. Novelists I'd never met began inviting me to Sunday lunch parties filled with academics and ABC people. Even poets shouted me beers.

My introduction to writers *en masse* was Writers' Week at the Adelaide Festival, the country's first literary festival, always held in a picnic atmosphere in marquees in the city's Pioneer Women's Memorial Gardens.

Now that every town in the country seems to boast a writers' festival, it seems strange recalling that these heady events were once a novelty. In the plane to Adelaide I chatted with Frank Moorhouse, who'd been to Writers' Week before. 'What's it like?' I asked him.

'Oh, it's the best al fresco dating service in the country,' said Frank.

I was excited. Wasn't it fun, I thought, the Life of the Mind.

As a young, would-be novelist masquerading as a book-review editor, I hung on the words of the famous writers in attendance. The first to step up to the plate was Ted Hughes, the English poet. In the circumstances, this tall, dark, brooding figure, who was shadowed, heckled and even spat upon throughout his stay by local female supporters of his recently suicided wife, Sylvia Plath, impressed me with his dignity and restraint. As did his poetry.

Not everyone was as politely restrained as Ted Hughes. Literary animus and paranoia were more publicly expressed in the seventies than they are nowadays. Released from their garrets into an atmosphere of free Barossa valley wine and cheap Cooper's beer, without the restraining presence and civilising influence of publishers, agents and miscellaneous minders that is prevalent today, writers were soon apt to become tired and emotional.

The various poetry divisions were at each other's throats, of course: Melbourne versus Sydney, and Pastorals versus Urbans, and the 'performance' poets versus everyone, much to the astonishment of the ice-cool young Canadian poet, Margaret Atwood, not yet a celebrated novelist, whose eyebrows seemed permanently raised in polite disbelief.

But even the old social realists and outback yarn-spinners were pretty edgy. Apropos of another topic entirely, Frank Hardy leapt to his feet from the audience and, from left field, proclaimed hotly that Patrick White was over-rated, over-civilised, and knew nothing about the working class. Frank loudly insisted that he could write Patrick White under the table any day, and while it wasn't for him, Frank, to say who should have received the Nobel Prize instead, he could think of more deserving cases.

As soft-faced young women poets wandered the lawns in caftans and clouds of patchouli oil, the elderly outback novelist Donald Stuart took the microphone during a discussion on gender roles in fiction to announce that he was proud to be heterosexual.

Donald went on to state that while his room in the boarding house wasn't anything to write home about, it wasn't too far away from the festival, the landlady was a good sport, he was very fit for a bloke his age, and open to any fair offer.

If the amiable patrician Geoffrey Dutton, seen gracefully squiring the Russian superstar-poet Yevgeny Yevtushenko around the Adelaide lawns in a Hawaiian shirt, pointed to a certain sort of literary grandeur, it was Morris West who brought home to me what a certain sort of writer's life could be.

When I arrived for our interview at the Hotel Adelaide, the front desk informed me that Mr West was in the pool and would receive me poolside. Well, he wasn't exactly swimming laps. The international best-seller writer, Australia's most financially successful author, was standing at the shallow end – a large, pale, chesty figure, whose neatly parted and oiled hair showed no signs of immersion – importantly taking calls on a phone with a very long cord while a succession of bellboys brought him telex messages on silver trays.

That evening he would loudly proclaim his Christian humility in a long, mellifluous sermon at the town hall that deferred to God eventually, but only just.

The audience lapped it up. At the end of his speech an elderly male fan stood up, shaking his head in wonderment, and said, 'Mr West, I just want to thank you for *existing*. I could listen to your *vinaigrettes* all night.'

Writers' Week: A tasty time was had by all.

. . .

While there were local novelists I respected, it was because they had written novels, not because I saw the world in the same way. With the exception of Christina Stead's *The Man Who Loved Children*, David Ireland's *The Unknown Industrial Prisoner* and *The Glass Canoe,* Tom Keneally's *Bring Larks and Heroes,* and Peter Mathers' *Trap*, books I revered, no Australian novel spoke to me personally. Aust Lit and I were on different wavelengths.

They say you should never meet admired writers in person, that you're bound to be disappointed. In the book-review editor's job I managed to meet Stead, Ireland, Mathers and Keneally, and I liked them all. There were no poolside interviews, but in all but one case there was alcohol in abundance. I met David Ireland at the Sydney Journalists' Club, and Peter Mathers at Stewart's Hotel, in Melbourne's Carlton. Tom Keneally, then thin, clean-shaven and barely on the crest of fame, welcomed me to his small suburban house during the family's dinner. His wife Judy gave me an ice-cream cone.

On our first appointment, Christina Stead met me at her front gate at nine a.m. with a glass of bourbon in her hand and another glass balanced on the letter-box waiting for me. She was then seventy-four and living a melancholy recent widowhood back in Australia in the spare room of a young half-brother's house in the Sydney airport flight path. 'I feel like a stranger here,' she said wistfully. 'I'm happiest when I'm thirty thousand feet up in the air.'

Nevertheless she offered kind advice and I gained the impression she was lonely and liked the company of young writers. As planes roared overhead we talked books for five hours and drank the bottle of bourbon.

The next time I met her she was boarding at another brother's house on the North Shore. She was eighty-one: it was a few months before her death. We sat on the back veranda while she fed parakeets honey-water and we sipped white wine.

. . .

The rest of Australian literature had always left me unsatisfied. It seemed self-consciously rural and chaste. It was lugubrious and lacked zest and humour. It had yawning gaps: the cities, the coast, the professions, politics, Aborigines, migrants. In the most urban and middle-class nation on earth, it ignored the urban middle class, the very people who bought books.

Where was our Cheever, Updike, Mailer, Pynchon, Roth? Our Alice Munro and Joyce Carol Oates? Its landed gentry and school-teacher authors and poets romanticised salt-of-the-earth labourers, farmers, indeed anyone who lived in the country. At the same time they either feigned ignorance of, or abhorred, popular culture.

Not that this particular habit has changed completely. The scene is a recent breakfast in a rustic hotel in the Adelaide Hills where the guest writers have been quartered for a brief sojourn before performing at the Adelaide Festival Writers' Week. The hotel has provided the weekend Sydney and Melbourne broadsheets for the writers to read with their bacon and eggs. I pass a paper to one of Australia's more distinguished novelists. He waves it away scornfully. 'I never read newspapers,' he says.

I feel as if I'd offered him a porn magazine. 'Why not? Where do you get your news?'

'News isn't on my agenda,' he says, reaching for the quince jam.

This exquisite high-art pose reminds me of those English judges who were still professing ignorance of the Beatles in the 1970s. Throughout our three-day stay, his rarefied demeanour suggests confidence that the Nobel committee approves his attitude to newspapers, television and computers (against) and writing only with a fountain pen (for).

Christina Stead would never have said that. She was shunned by the literary establishment in her day for living much of her life overseas, and was never feted by the academics and prize-givers like the quince-jam man. News was definitely on her agenda. So, definitely, was politics, and passion, and life in general.

The old version of Aust Lit bewildered me with the way it skated over life in general: it evaded physical relationships and emotional confrontations. Oblique can be eloquent. Opaque? *Hmm*. You hardly knew whether their characters were having sex or not, or with which gender. Everyone mooned around under the jacarandas and donned crisp linen to go to town but it wasn't clear what their sexual preferences were.

If their characters had inner lives, they didn't let on. Females were usually plain, robust and sassy to the point of cliché, while any men who weren't labourers had the will and emotions of hydrangeas. At least you weren't in doubt about the younger writers' protagonists. Those English Department lecturers were at it like rattlesnakes.

· · ·

And then that night I snatched up a Penguin paperback of *Herzog,* by Saul Bellow (recommended to me in the pub by an English Department lecturer), which had lain unread on the table with little Amy's bath toys. I read, *If I am out of my mind, it's all right with me, thought Moses Herzog.*

First sentences are important and this one hit the spot. Over the page another sentence sealed it for me: *Late in spring, Herzog had been overcome by the need to explain, to have it out, to justify, to put in perspective, to clarify, to make amends.*

Not only Moses Herzog. Through my character Stephen Crisp, I was, too. I read a few chapters, and more bells rang. Bellow's hero was a wry, Canadian-born, Chicago Jewish intellectual (not a million miles from Bellow himself), whose wife had just left him for his best friend, and who was teetering on the verge of a breakdown. He could hardly have differed more from my character, a disgruntled agnostic journalist (not a million miles from myself) obsessed with recording the last days of the Tasmanian Aborigines.

Saul Bellow, his jacket biography told me, was thirty years older than I. His concerns were those of his era, background, religion, education, nationality . . . and yet I could identify with him. As a reader I was swept away by his universality. As a would-be novelist I saw how effective a literary device meditative or inner realism could be.

A decade later Bellow won the Nobel Prize; two decades later, he died. According to Martin Amis, who knew him, he wrote just as he spoke. Certainly, as Amis said, the reader has a real conversation with his characters. I read all his novels. I admired the way he aired his scholarship yet wore it lightly. I liked his range and depth – how he wrote about small-time criminals as well as professors, politicians and lawyers. No snob, he was equally at home in the street, the restaurant or the academy.

I thought this was how it should be. If the Americans could do it, why wasn't it being done here?

If, as Amis suggested, the best writers were made up of three ingredients: innocent, everyman and *litterateur,* Bellow had each component in equal measure. He relished and admired women, agonised over children, and knew about male friendship. Here we had a full and imaginative human being.

That night at the kitchen table his work was new to me but he already seemed a pretty good literary model. Forget what was expected of you, Bellow told me. It was OK to try to write about the whole human picture. *To explain, to have it out, to put into perspective, to clarify, to make amends.*

This was what Montaigne had advocated four centuries before: to look at everything in the world with curiosity, and try to make sense of it without worrying about being self-conscious, inappropriate or sentimental. Digress into anecdotes and personal ruminations, if you wanted. ('I am myself the matter of my book.') Freely express doubt. That was easy. ('What do I know?')

I'd been reading *Herzog* for three hours. By now it was two-thirty in the morning. I screwed up my title page with its Robert Ludlum overtones and tossed it on the floor with the other white cabbages. I changed the title to *The Savage Crows.*

On the kitchen lino, the leopard-print slugs were still grazing around the cat's bowl. I watched them for a while. They were quite interesting. (Why the necessity for spots for camouflage, I wondered, when they had the effect of making them more noticeable?) I was tired by then but I hit the Olivetti again and put the slugs on the first page.

. . .

Eventually I realised *The Savage Crows* was as finished as it would ever be. I'd written 120,000 words, I was becoming sidetracked by fascinating research and fictional tangents and realised I had to call a halt.

I submitted it to Ken Wilder, managing director of William Collins, on my birthday, 9 January. I thought this might be a good omen, seeing that I'd started work as a cadet journalist on my eighteenth birthday, and left Perth for the big-time on my twenty-first birthday. Ken sent it out to five readers for their opinions. Four liked it and one didn't.

Interestingly, the one who advised Collins against publication – not realising they would tell me – was a friend of mine, a book critic and would-be writer himself, with whom I'd discussed the book's progress over lunch on a weekly basis while writing it. He'd been enthusiastic. Furthermore, I'd given him work as my chief book reviewer, providing most of his income, when I was literary editor of *The Australian*.

Putting his action in the best light – a difficult thing to do – I guess you could say he'd behaved in a rigorous critical manner. Anyway, it was an eighty per cent approval rate: Collins told me they'd publish *The Savage Crows* if I cut 20,000 words from it. My razor worked with the speed of light.

On its publication, the novelist Tom Keneally, the poets Douglas Stewart and Rodney Hall, and the historian Manning Clark gave it favourable reviews. To my delight, the English papers were also enthusiastic, likening the novel's view of Australia to the work of the painters Arthur Boyd and Sidney Nolan. One astute local critic, the *Nation Review*'s D. R. Burns, obviously a *Herzog* fan, picked up the debt to Saul Bellow.

It was an odd period of changing attitudes and contradictions. On the basis of *The Savage Crows*, the fledgling Australia Council, recently set up by Prime Minister Gough Whitlam, awarded me one of the first twelve-month $9000 literary fellowships to write another novel. On one hand, I'd never been more proud and delighted. On the other, the journalists' pubs, my friendly old haunts, were suddenly no longer welcoming. Their atmosphere had cooled. A beer shower was a distinct possibility.

Earning many times that salary and never having given the arts a second thought, former colleagues were bitter at the government's largesse towards writers. Sanctimoniously, they sniffed that arts-grant recipients were stealing taxpayers' money. The same concern for tax-payers' earnings, of course, did not extend to sportspeople, or, indeed, to painters or sculptors or musicians or potters, or to the huge sums granted to opera and ballet.

It was the literary grants that got their goat. They could identify with those, of course, and were envious. My book's success made it even more galling. Two former friends found it difficult to talk to me, or to review my books in their pages, ever after.

It seems odd now, but young Australian writers were not celebrated in the seventies. There were no young-writer prizes or Saturday-magazine profiles, no helpful paragraphs in literary columns or moody rock-star photographs posed in gritty urban alleys. If anything, there was a vague and puzzled resentment in literary circles.

Stuart Sayers, literary editor of my old paper, *The Age,* who had regularly requested essays from me, took three months to send *The Savage Crows* out for review. Eventually it fetched up with the distinguished critic A. R. Chisholm to be reviewed in a single-column round-up of *Steam Trains of Great Britain, Recollections of the Raj,* and a book on mountain climbing.

But Chisholm was nearing the end of his long life and career. The ninety-two-year-old critic summed it up in one sentence: 'This novel is too erotic for my liking.' Sadly, he died shortly after.

. . .

Not only was the older generation of writers not keen on letting young-sters through the portals, there was little crossover between journalism and fiction writing, as was – and is – common in Britain and America.

While journalism secretly envied those rare birds seen to have escaped the cages of Rupert Murdoch and Kerry Packer, academic critics were sniffy about acknowledging the arrival of denizens of Grub Street, those untenured persons obviously unfit to share the life of the mind.

Australian writers traditionally came from teaching, private incomes or gentleman-farming. To the man in the street and most journalists, and indeed to me initially, there seemed something rarefied and elitist about the job. If you were a woman writer (an 'authoress') in my home state of Western Australia, for example, you would either have three names, like Katherine Susannah Prichard and Henrietta Drake-Brockman, or be made a dame like Dame Mary Durack and Dame Alexandra Hasluck.

In answer to a cab driver's or barber's question, 'What do you do for a crust?' it took me three or four books before I could bring myself to answer, 'writer'.

I'd say instead, 'I'm a reporter.'

That made for a less embarrassing cab ride or haircut. They were at ease with that job. It was unthreatening and somehow shrewdly Australian, and smacked of cops and robbers and bad politicians. Anyway, if you said 'writer' the next, unanswerable, question would be, 'Have I heard of you?' Closely followed by, 'Should I have heard of you?'

. . .

On the matter of writers' festivals: regardless of how festive they are and where they're held – and these days even the smallest rural or coastal hamlet can drum one up – they can be summed up in this question to me from a woman in the audience:

'My book club has been studying the works of the wonderful Jane Austen, and it seems to me that in the history of world literature there has never been a writer who understood the human condition as exquisitely and sensitively as Jane Austen.

'I recently borrowed from the library your book on Perth serial killers and I thought it must concern you that your writing in no way resembles the work of Jane Austen. Do you intend to rectify this?'

40
BIG DOG

It was while researching *The Savage Crows* that I travelled to an island called Big Dog whose landscape would come sharply to mind when I stepped ashore on Hermite Island, five thousand kilometres and three decades away.

The islands could hardly be more geographically distant and still be part of Australia. Big Dog lies in Bass Strait between Flinders and Cape Barren islands in the Furneaux Group, off the north-east coast of Tasmania. It's a granite mound of dunes, tussock grassland and small patches of acacia. A strong imagination is necessary to see any resemblance to a dog. It could as easily have been named after an anvil, a leopard or a pelican. In the novel I gave it the name Cat Face Island.

Not only is the setting physically similar – Hermite is a limestone mound of dunes, hummock grassland and small patches of acacia – they share a primal spirit which instantly sparked my imagination. Each has a grim history and wild weather. Even aside from its cyclones, Hermite's winds are the legendary Roaring Forties from across the Indian Ocean, scourge of East Indies traders. Big Dog's winds are the notorious Bass Strait ship-wreckers howling up from the Antarctic.

In each case, the ocean winds flattening and whistling through the bristly grass heighten the sense of desolation. If anything, this remoteness and uniqueness only sharpened my enthusiasm. New and difficult territory was the whole point.

Looking back to that morning in the mid-seventies when the young writer hired a boat on Flinders Island with the photographer Wesley Stacey and waded ashore on Big Dog, I recall a slate-coloured bay thick with kelp. There was no jetty. Deceived by the clarity of the bay, in my nervous eagerness I underestimated its depth and stepped off the boat into waist-deep water, half-submerging my backpack and soaking my notebooks and pens as well as my pants.

Wes and I had arranged a magazine assignment to pay for the trip. Our Plan B was that he would take photographs for an exhibition, and I'd perhaps get some authentic atmosphere for my novel's final chapter. I just hoped the island would match the *tour de force* ending I'd decided on (that was the way my thinking went): about a young man who was obsessed with the fate of the original Tasmanian Aborigines.

I wanted first-hand contact with the descendents of the people I was making up. I needed to go mutton-birding, to see Big Dog Island and what occurred there. The rest of the book had been written out of my imagination and research without my ever having set foot in Tasmania; maybe I could chisel and mould the background material until Big Dog resembled what I'd visualised. I was operating like a sculptor or potter as much as a would-be novelist.

One big difference between Big Dog and Hermite islands was their latitude and hence their temperatures. And Big Dog wasn't a desert island either: it contained a handful of people, if only for five weeks a year. As they had for generations, Aborigines came across from Cape Barren and Flinders islands every autumn to catch mutton birds. The presence of mutton birds – or short-tailed shearwaters, *yolla* in the old Tasmanian dialect – was the other striking difference.

Every year hundreds of thousands of shearwaters migrated from the shores of Siberia and Alaska to the Bass Strait islands, where they mated, laid their eggs in holes amongst the tussocks, and reared their chicks. The mutton-birders, weather-beaten Straitsmen, most descended from nineteenth century sealers and whalers and their stolen Tasmanian Aboriginal women, harvested the fledglings for their flesh and oil.

It was a simple process. A catcher knelt or lay on the ground and thrust an arm down a mutton-bird hole. His fingers felt for the downy feathers, gripped the struggling, pecking bird and pulled it out of the nest. A quick flick of the wrist broke its neck, and he dropped the twitching body on the ground for collection. The birder moved on to the next hole and his offsider came by and threaded the dead bird onto a wooden spit with all the others.

There was an element of risk. The birder could be beaten to the chick in the nest. Blindly reaching into the hole in the tussock grass, his fingers might grasp a copperhead or tiger snake instead.

The men and youths who did this work were a range of ages and physiques, and of skin shades ranging from white to blue-black. But all their faces had the contour lines of relief maps and their stained and thickened fingers made them look to be wearing wrinkled black leather gloves.

. . .

We waded ashore through the kelp and layers of shells. Brilliant lichens of orange, lemon, scarlet and green patterned the boulders of the shoreline. From the sea it reminded me of the vivid graffiti that was beginning to appear along the boardwalk at Bondi beach.

The light breeze carried mixed whiffs of rotting flesh, salt and barbers' shops. Wes was already snapping away. I sat on a heap of dry kelp, rolled down my sodden trouser legs and put on my boots. From the kelp rose a cloud of blowflies. The weed pile was strewn with mutton birds' heads and feet and strings of intestines.

Up the hillside from the bay two small buildings squatted together in the sand. (On Hermite thirty years later I'd remember this resemblance, too.) One was made of cement blocks, the other of galvanised iron sheets, and they would have enjoyed panoramic views of the bay if they'd had windows. The rusty tin shed, presumably the living and sleeping quarters, was deserted. A steamy heat mirage quivered around the cement shed, and the barber-shop aroma grew stronger as we walked up the hill towards it.

Outside this shed, a wiry boy aged about ten was smoking a cigarette and shuffling between wooden racks which held spit-loads of dead birds. Methodically, he took bird after bird from each spit, held it by its legs and squeezed bloody stomach oil out the open gullet into a 44-gallon drum. Streaky red oil, sickly sweet as brilliantine – Californian Poppy was the particular pink pomade I recalled – nearly filled the drum to the brim.

Inside the cement shed the atmosphere was even more humid and brilliantine-sweet. Greasy bird-fluff and tussock-grass matted the floor. Sitting around a boiling cauldron in the corner, two women with hot, oil-smudged faces were scalding plucked bird corpses and rubbing off the clinging down-feathers with pieces of sacking.

This backdrop was a gift to my imagination. It allowed me to tie up loose ends and gave meaning to my final chapter. Now it was up to me to make up the characters and their motivation, which was not merely the harvesting of mutton birds. This was by far the most enjoyable part of the whole novel, and the quickest to write. From the Blue Plum to old Grandfather Raintree sheltering from the elements amongst the feathers in the plucking shed, the individuals populating my fictitious Cat Face Island came easily to mind.

The young boy smoking the cigarette was the only real person. Of the people on Big Dog, he's the one I can still clearly picture: a small boy covered in blood, feathers and mutton-bird grease, smelling of Californian Poppy and puffing away on a Winfield Blue.

41
THE AURA

The atmosphere was one of fire and brimstone. Cremation. Sour milk. Decay. Bones and ash. I expected Alpha Island to have a bad aura, and in that sense I wasn't disappointed.

Arriving on the most notorious island in the Montebellos was like stepping onto an Armageddon film set: Hollywood's vision of a nuclear bomb site. It was a film cliché, right down to the prominent skeleton of a large goanna, lying on its side in the ashy dirt, shreds of dried skin fluttering in the breeze, a front leg clawing dramatically at the sky. From a production designer's point of view, that was overdoing it.

Brent and I arrived on Alpha in the camp's dinghy, a ten-minute spin over the bay from Hermite Island. My visit to Alpha was my reward for helping him map out another grid system in the heat of the afternoon. More lugging twenty metal stakes at a time, more stomping along in straight lines up and down the dunes, more crashing through the wire-wood and the Bushes of Doom.

I didn't mind. We were friends by now, and I couldn't remember the last time I worked in unison with someone on a physically taxing job. My work-ethic side enjoyed it, and I relished the countdown feeling of hammering each stake, especially the twentieth and last, into the ground. And I wanted to see Alpha Island.

Stepping ashore, we faced a sign on the beach warning us not to stay on the island longer than one hour. And not to disturb the soil or pick up metal fragments or remove any relics: they might still be radioactive. Following a second bomb test, codenamed *Mosaic G1*, on Trimouille Island in May 1956, it was here, a month later, that the biggest nuclear device on Australian soil was exploded.

For the *Mosaic G1* test, the *West Australian* had a reporter and photographer positioned on the mainland at Onslow. Under a photo of a dozen grinning men and three women, some of them standing on beer kegs and pointing into the distance, a caption reads: 'An atomic test on the Montebellos draws a crowd at the Onslow Hotel. A nuclear blast was seen as more of a drawcard than a threat by this crowd, which gathered, beers in hand, to watch as the British exploded a nuclear bomb on the Montebello Islands.'

The paper went on, 'Closer to the poisonous mushroom cloud, the officers and crew of the British destroyer HMS *Diana* were ordered to sail through the radioactive cloud that drifted across the ocean. For protection this time they were issued with Polaroid sunglasses, overshoes and face masks.'

That bomb was insignificant compared to the Alpha Island explosion which followed shortly after. *Mosaic G2* yielded 98 kilotons – an explosive force of 98,000 tons of TNT – and created a mushroom cloud 47,000 feet high, 10,000 feet higher than predicted. Not only was this the largest atomic test in Australia, it was five times more powerful than the atomic bomb dropped on Hiroshima in 1945.

For the first time an official Australian Atomic Weapons Tests Safety Committee was set up to monitor the safety of the tests. After the blasts the committee reported that the safety measures were 'completely adequate' and that the *Mosaic* tests 'proved no hazard to persons or livestock'. The report flew in the face of claims that the main cloud had passed completely over mainland Australia and that something had gone radically wrong with the tests.

From the devastated appearance of the island more than fifty years later, the blasts might have happened only months ago. Alpha's gravelly foreground and the bleak hills behind were still scorched and bleached of colour. Bits of twisted rusty metal and broken concrete bunkers poked up through the sand.

Growing up on Western Australia's endless limestone and coral coastline has etched its beaches and wind-lashed off-shore islands into my brain. Their glaring white sands and bare, salty scrub are always in my mind's eye. My fondness for the State's landscape is often romantic but I acknowledge its frequently ghostly barrenness. Occasionally it looks like the dead surface of the moon.

I can see how outsiders could find its atmosphere overwhelming. D.H. Lawrence, for one, was made anxious by the primal settings of Western Australia. His European eyes found a 'spirit of place' that evoked metaphysical terror.

In *Kangaroo,* Lawrence's character, Richard Somers, a thinly disguised portrait of himself, having decided that Europe 'is done for, played out, finished,' emigrates to 'the newest country: young Australia.' At first, Somers' sense of Western Australia is poetic-mystical:

The sky was pure, crystal pure and blue . . . the air was wonderful, new and unbreathed . . . but the bush . . . the grey charred bush. It scared him . . . It was so phantom-like, so ghostly, with its tall pale trees and many dead trees, like corpses partly charred by bush fires, and then the foliage so dark, like grey-green iron. And then it was so deathly still.

Exploring the bush alone on the outskirts of Perth, Somers, alias Lawrence, has a more alarming, visceral vision that stays with him through the remainder of his Australian adventure:

> He walked on, had walked a mile or so into the bush, and had just come to a clump of tall, nude, dead trees, shining almost phosphorescent with the moon, when the terror of the bush overcame him . . . There was a presence. He looked at weird, white, dead trees, and into the hollow distances of the bush. Nothing! Nothing at all . . . It must be the spirit of the place. Something fully evoked tonight by that unnatural West Australian moon.
>
> Provoked by the moon, the roused spirit of the bush . . . It was biding its time with a terrible ageless watchfulness, waiting for a far-off end, watching the myriad intruding white men.

Kangaroo shows that Lawrence was often spooked by Australia, and not only by the primal landscape. The skylarking physicality of its young denizens, especially those beach frolickers with muscular thighs on the south coast of New South Wales, caused a distaste close to fear.

But I understand what he meant about the moon. His Western Australia is ninety years away from mine, but I feel the same about a full moon. It might be a film cliché, occurring as it does only twelve days out of the 365, but just as I always associate daytime Western Australia with summer, whenever I imagine it by night I see a full moon.

This moon of my memory throws its sentimental beams on the Swan River estuary, across the white sands of Cottesloe and Scarborough and especially over the sensual bays of Rottnest Island.

Yet the nostalgic moon is also a prowler's moon. It swayed the sanity of at least one local serial killer. For his eight murders of total strangers – with scissors and axe, with fishing knife and rifles, with cars and blunt instruments – the Eric Cooke of my teenage acquaintance preferred the one bright night in thirty, this romantic coastal moon.

Whenever I consider this barren limestone coast and its off-shore islands, the word *moonscape* comes to mind. I think about how it took this landmass millions of years to make a single cardboard-coloured rock, millions of years for fierce westerly winds to break its crust and weather it down, millions of years to build it again.

And yet the rock was so soft my small daughter could break off a piece of cliff at Little Parrakeet Bay on Rottnest Island and let it trickle through her fingers like sugar.

. . .

Even considering the general starkness of the coastline, Alpha Island stood out, its ashy barrenness at the farthest extreme of West Australian harshness. By comparison, Hermite Island seemed almost verdant.

A grim obelisk on the Alpha detonation spot stated: 'A British atomic weapon was test-exploded above this point in 1956.' It's a peculiar sensation being photographed beside a nuclear marker. A casual smile, a jaunty thumbs-up to the camera ('Here's to you, Alpha, Beta and Gamma!') seem inappropriate.

The ground around the obelisk was still a circle of flattened dust. Not a rock or any foliage protruded from the ground for fifty metres in any direction. The outlying boulders looked like stage rocks made of melted and re-solidified plastic. A second sign warned against touching or removing anything. Further away still, there were sporadic patches of flat, sickly ground cover. They didn't remind me of any known vegetation. They were like scraps of old carpet squares left out to moulder in the weather.

Returning to Hermite Island in the dinghy, we detoured over the original Ground Zero, in the bay just off the western shore of Trimouille Island, where the first bomb was exploded in the hull of the *Plym* in 1952. There was nothing to see but the yellowy shallows abruptly dropping to deep inky purple, marking the kilometre-wide crater in the seabed where the battleship was vapourised. The bay seemed bottomless.

Named by Nicolas Baudin after a noble French family, Trimouille Island was previously known only for being the main turtle breeding ground in the archipelago. As we passed over the bomb crater, a flatback turtle swam languidly under the boat and, snorting, came up the other side. It didn't have three eyes or two heads like irradiated creatures in *The Simpsons*.

Even if nuclear-caused deformities had occurred back in the 1950s, they would hardly have registered. Environmental interest was negligible. Untold turtles, dugongs, dolphins, seabirds and fish died from the blast and fallout. Their deaths were not subject to any analysis, however, as their existence hadn't ever been considered.

In fact, no thought was given to the effects on the entire Montebello environment. Even decades afterwards, the rare post-bomb tests undertaken were those measuring residual radiation as it might affect future human visitors to the islands, and these were only randomly conducted by the navy when passing by. No tests were made for radiation effects, such as mutations, on any animals, birds or fish. Nor were people warned off eating them.

The results of the navy's casual surveys were eventually evaluated by the Australian and Western Australian governments in 1979 and 1990 – twenty-three and thirty-eight years later. They found that apart from the limited-access areas of the bomb sites there would now be 'no undue risk' for casual visitors to the other, non-nuclear, islands for a stay of up to one week. Visitors were however warned of possible ionising radiation exposure.

The term 'ionising radiation' covers everything from the effects of standing in the sun to being smothered by the fallout of a nuclear bomb. We're all exposed to low levels of ionising radiation all our lives. Radiation exposure varies from place to place, depending on such things as height above sea-level (cosmic radiation from the sun); soil and rocks containing uranium, thorium and potassium (Gamma and Beta radiation); and radon gas in the air (Alpha radiation). Additional exposure occurs during medical treatment, such as X-rays and Gamma radiation treatment for cancer.

I remember the childhood thrill of standing under the ubiquitous X-ray machines at Perth's biggest shoe store; not so much to see if my shiny new school shoes fitted properly, but to observe the nail-heads dotted around the shoes' front rim and to see my toe-bones wiggling in the eerie green glow of Ezywalkin's X-ray apparatus.

Radioactivity comes in two basic types: rays and particles. Gamma and X-rays are rays; Alpha and Beta radiation are charged particles. Different types of radiation have different powers of penetration. Alpha particles, which are atomic nuclei, can be stopped by a thin sheet of paper, and can't penetrate the skin. Gamma and X-rays will easily penetrate flesh, but can be stopped by massive materials such as lead, steel or concrete. Beta particles, which are high-energy electrons, can penetrate solids to a depth of a few millimetres.

The nuclear fallout of the Montebello tests contained every type of radiation: Gamma, Beta and Alpha.

Some cleanup attempts of the bomb sites were made by the Australian military, although given the amount of junk I saw there, obviously half-hearted ones. A commercial operator was permitted to salvage a large amount of radioactive scrap iron and steel. It was shipped to the mainland and either sold to Japan or recycled into general circulation.

42
SWEETLIP

One more island has featured prominently in my life. Hayman Island is an unlikely literary backdrop, but the luxurious tourist resort off the Queensland coast would end up occupying more of my writing time and energy than any other place or subject – almost the entire 1980s.

Even now, deep fatigue sweeps over me just writing the word *Sweetlip*. My *Sweetlip* years began when Terry Rowe, the fifty-year-old CEO of a big company, Reckitt and Colman, was found dead on the bathroom floor of his room during a business convention on Hayman Island. He was naked, his genitals covered with a wash cloth.

Foul play was not suspected. Just as well. The island owners (not the current ones, I must point out), the Queensland police on the mainland at Proserpine, the town coroner, and the Queensland Government then behaved in ways that were increasingly and amateurishly bizarre.

Before his death, six other businessmen in the company party, a quarter of the convention team, had already fallen ill on the island with vomiting and diarrohea. One had to be rushed by rescue helicopter to hospital on the mainland, paralysed down one side and vomiting profusely. And a week later one of the island staff died after a big meal of coral trout.

Reef fish, including the evocatively named sweetlip, were on the menu every noon and evening – at South Sea Island Night, King Neptune Night, Oriental Night, Roaring Twenties Night and Left Bank Night – and I would come to suspect either rampant food poisoning or the virulent tropical fish toxin ciguatera as the cause of everyone's illness.

Terry Rowe's body was taken to Proserpine where a GP inexperienced in autopsies performed a post-mortem examination. He said the heart 'looked OK'. He could not decide the cause of death so he removed the heart, brain, liver, kidneys and other organs, as well as the stomach contents, for further analysis.

These body parts he gave to the local police to send to the State Pathology Laboratories in Brisbane. At this stage the blackest of black comedies, already well in train, now proceeded apace.

Some time after the transferral of organs, the heart was lost, never to be found. Then, instead of putting the organs – properly preserved and contained – on a plane for immediate despatch, a cop transported them down to Brisbane in the boot of his police car, in the tropical summer, over a three-week period, during which he took the opportunity to stop off at various coastal towns to play in lawn-bowls tournaments, socialise in bowling clubs and fill the boot with crabs and lobsters he obtained on his travels.

The parlous state of the organs on arrival (only the liver and kidneys made it to the laboratories anyway; the brain had also been lost by now) made it impossible to analyse them.

Months passed while government and island authorities kept an all-encompassing silence. There was no autopsy report. The local coroner claimed he'd never heard of that particular death on Hayman Island. Everyone was stone-walling. Hayman Island was a major part of the coastal economy. No-one wanted to damage the Barrier Reef tourist trade or embarrass the local authorities. No inquest was scheduled and no death certificate could be issued, so Terry Rowe's wife Robyn couldn't get the life insurance or superannuation due to her.

All her inquiries came to nothing. The Queensland Government of Joh Bjelke-Petersen just wanted her to go away. She had seen her husband laid out in the funeral parlour 'so wonderfully tanned it was hard to believe he was dead'. And as far as Queensland was concerned, he wasn't.

To help her, I travelled to the island, sniffed around, stayed overnight (and also became sick after a reef fish meal) and wrote a story for the *Bulletin*. This embarrassed the government into holding an inquest. Or, rather, an 'inquest'. At the coroner's court hearing the island management was encouraged to stress the high standards of their food preparation, evidence which was heartily commended by the coroner. Then the State produced a government doctor from Brisbane (who had sighted neither the body nor any body parts) to declare positively that Terry Rowe had died of a heart attack.

The coroner accepted this assertion with relief, made his finding accordingly, and the island, the local police, the State Government and the Barrier Reef tourist industry breathed more easily.

At least Robyn Rowe was then able to obtain a death certificate, and the insurance due to her. In his decision, the coroner made a point of saying how properly everyone had acted, and he had no criticism of anyone involved in the debacle, choosing only to shoot the messenger and save his one criticism for me sitting at the Press table: 'the unwelcome muckraker from the south.'

I fashioned these inane and macabre events into a short story, 'Sweetlip' in *The Bodysurfers*. With my good friend, the eminent film director Ray Lawrence (an admirer, like myself, of quirky narratives), I eventually transformed the story into a film script of the same name. And the fun continued.

. . .

Films have influenced my fiction writing. I've always greatly admired directors. (I see Robert Altman's *Nashville* script, for example, or Quentin Tarantino's *Pulp Fiction,* or Ray Lawrence's *Lantana,* as interesting fictions.) I've also had personal dealings with the industry and seen it from three angles. Some books have been adapted for films or television. I've also been a film reviewer and written three screenplays.

It's a given that every novelist wants their books made into films. They might grizzle afterwards but even successful literary novelists earn meagre incomes and film adaptation money can keep you writing for several years. The following experience is pretty typical for an established author: one book of mine made it onto the big screen (Hollywood turned *Our Sunshine,* starring the late Heath Ledger, into *Ned Kelly*), and one other film was cancelled just days before the shoot (and thus before payment to me). Two books became successful ABC and BBC mini-series, and continue to be shown on cable around the world (at no return to me). And three screenwriting projects began encouragingly, swallowed months and years of my time and then spectacularly bit the dust.

Why is it that those three disasters remain set in my mind? It's because what happened in each case was outrageous, silly, completely unexpected, and out of the screenwriters' control. They were screenplays co-written with Ray in the decade between his two big hits, *Bliss* and *Lantana*. I think of this period as *Lawrence and Drewe: The Lost Years*. Or, considering the time Ray and I spent in Kings Cross long-lunch discussions – which often included the publisher James Fraser, Bruce Petty the cartoonist and film-maker, and Sandra Hall, the film critic – *The Bayswater Brasserie Years*.

Ray's and my longest-running unfilmed project was the aforementioned *Sweetlip*. It took us and the producer Tony Buckley several years of sweat, anguish and lunch just to get to the starting gates.

It involved film bureaucracies of three State and Federal administrations and co-producers of several countries, including one would-be mogul who affected the overcoat-draped-over-the-shoulders Orson Welles image and changed not only his financial position but also his nationality and accent from German to French halfway through our dealings.

This was twenty-five years ago. An expensive Australian film for the time, with a budget of $10 million (still minuscule by American standards), it was set on the Great Barrier Reef. (At one stage producers suggested Fiji should stand in for Queensland because Fiji was cheaper.) After seven years' manoeuvrings, many pride-swallowings and numerous script re-writes it was finally a definite starter. Yes, it would be set in Queensland after all. The lead actor would be Sam Neill, then at his most debonair and bankable.

Everyone was happy, including the bank. To celebrate Sam agreeing to do the film, Ray took him and me to lunch at Tre Scalini, a fashionable Sydney restaurant of the era. After the third bottle of wine we were all enthusiastically writing scenes on the tablecloth and Sam was enlightening us on how a screenplay was shaped like the letter W and had three acts. He was a terrific, likeable fellow. Then, as we left the restaurant, Ray cracked a sort of joke.

It was like a *Eureka* lightbulb moment in reverse. He winked at Sam, Australia's suavest actor – indeed, at that stage he was being called the new James Mason – and informed him, 'We're going to change your image entirely, mate. We're going to ruffle your hair. We're going to put your head down the toilet in this one.' Did I imagine a shadow pass across Sam's handsome features?

We all parted in apparent high spirits. Early next morning, just before the contracts were to be signed, the fax arrived, 'Dear Ray and Rob, I don't think I can see my way clear to do this film.' Was it the toilet-dousing joke? Bitter memories of schoolboy Royal Flushes? Anyway, the bank followed Sam out the door.

. . .

The second project, *Machete*, based on another of my stories, fell at the first hurdle when the lovely lead actress, who had a romantically sorrowful attitude to life, embarked on a Lady Chatterley affair.

Wistful and lonely, she was married to a wealthy Australian business-man who was often absent overseas. On the husband's return from one trip, the couple's fresh-faced young gardener not only took the oppor-tunity to announce their affair to his employer but sought his blessing. Strangely, this was unforthcoming. The husband instantly cancelled the gardener's employment, the marriage, and the cheque for $1 million in seed money he'd promised for our film.

The one prevailing characteristic of every film project anywhere has always been uncertainty. How does one anticipate the last-minute lunchtime toilet-frightening of the male star? How do you predict your female star's tryst with the lawnmower man?

But it was Ray's and my third venture, an adaptation of *Tracks*, Robyn Davidson's account of her personal journey by camel across Australia, that not only fell at the umpteenth hurdle but had to be put down.

The *Tracks* project had already been on the drawing-board for many years, passed from director to director, star to star, writer to writer. Indicative of its age was that *Tracks* had been around since Meryl Streep and Diane Keaton were ingenues. They'd both been proposed as Robyn the young Camel Woman and now it was to be Julia Roberts' turn to star, and Ray's to direct. We began work on the script.

In her best-selling book, Robyn the feminist heroine is shadowed throughout her outback trek by an unwelcome American magazine photographer and would-be scene-stealer. He wants to join the camel train and make it his *National Geographic* project; she wants to accom-plish her journey alone. Finally, he shrewdly throws himself at her mercy by getting himself air-dropped, without support, in the middle of the desert, and she's forced to include him.

In a nutshell, they're both young, single heterosexuals alone in the wilderness. In the 1970s. The real, urban world seems not to exist and before long they have sex.

Yes, the sex scene. As the whole point of the story was female fortitude, the scriptwriters thought it correct to portray this scene honestly and forthrightly and place the intrepid female character, who after all had just ridden a camel across the continent, in the dominant sexual position. So we wrote it that way.

Hollywood was outraged. The studio refused point-blank to have a sex scene where an American man was not on top. As the chief executive frothed, 'I'm not having you Aussie sons of bitches saying that American men are pussy-whipped!'

And that was *Tracks*. It never got over the hump.

. . .

A thin man in a beret asked me in a *Books to Film* session at a recent writers' festival when my first film-inspired sexual stirrings had occurred. Festivals are no place for faint-hearted authors; audience members feel free to ask you anything. Especially people wearing berets.

I hummed and hawed. Then suddenly I recalled a particular summer Saturday afternoon when, aged about eight, I first gazed upon the creamy skin, flaming hair and – because all this skin and hair was being vigorously flung about – feisty demeanour of Maureen O'Hara.

The Easterly wind baked the Perth suburbs and the sun beat down on the theatre's tin roof. My cronies and I sat spellbound, absent-mindedly peeling the sunburnt skin from our noses and cheeks and eating it, as Maureen (if I may be so bold) swashbuckled her way through *Sinbad the Sailor*.

I hadn't been so impressed by a female since my folk-dancing partner Elizabeth Garland, with whom, accompanied by Miss Serisier on the piano, I visited the Camptown Races (*doo-dah, doo-dah*) every Friday afternoon on the State-school veranda. Elizabeth it was who broke the school head-stand record, staying upside down on the playground gravel for an entire lunchtime, until she froze in position, blacked out, and an ambulance was called.

The film was already a decade old but the fact that Maureen was not out-swashed by two such exemplars of the art as Douglas Fairbanks Jr and Anthony Quinn so impressed the front rows of deck-chairs in Mr Palmer's cinema in Waratah Avenue that he made the projectionist halt the film until our noise stopped.

Sitting there on the hot canvas seats, wolf-whistling, stamping and cannibalising ourselves with excitement, we felt Maureen would approve of the hubbub. Maureen liked a good stoush. She was no simpering June Allyson, Debbie Reynolds or Doris Day – or schoolmarmish Katherine Hepburn, a boy's least favourite film star. She didn't share their sexlessness. We somehow recognised the presence of sex appeal – and its absence. She had, well, bosoms.

Some bitchier critics said Maureen had the perfect Technicolor complexion for John Ford's outdoor roles. (*How Green Was My Valley, The Quiet Man, Rio Grande.*) She'd later say that photographing well in colour had meant missing out on dramatic roles still being offered in black and white films. But Ford denied that her vivid screen presence outweighed her acting talent. He thought her more capable than the other major fifties' stars of a warmly sympathetic performance. (Joan Crawford? Bette Davis? Lana Turner? Hardly.)

It was that compassionate stage-Irish side of her, always eventually revealing itself after the obligatory fireworks with John Wayne or Henry Fonda or Tyrone Power had died down, that endeared her to me as a child.

Maureen usually gave sound advice, put up a flashing-eyed scrap when it wasn't followed, and then bathed the bloke's wounds when he messed up. As John Wayne said of her character in *The Quiet Man*: 'Some things a man doesn't get over so easy.'

It was impossible to imagine my parents in any such scene. 'Gee, watch it, Maureen!' I'd think, as she cheeked Wayne in film after film. ('There'll be no locks or bolts between us, Mary Kate. Except those in your own mercenary little heart': Wayne, barging in on his new wife in *The Quiet Man*.)

I could picture my father storming about and slamming doors, but not barging in like John Wayne. Instead, he'd speed off in the car, tyres screeching, to the pub.

And Maureen wasn't a sulker. It was hard to imagine her not speaking for days, impossible to envision her smoking cigarette after cigarette alone on the veranda on a summer's night, playing Nat King Cole's *Stardust* softly on the radiogram as she patted the dog over and over, and clung tenaciously to her hurt feelings, and we kids went to our rooms and a pall fell over the house.

Maureen was brave and strong and – the only word we boys could consider to describe our nascent sexual urges: 'pretty'. Maybe – of course we didn't know the word *Freudian* then – because she was also motherly.

After publicly recalling my crush on her to the thin man in the beret at the writers' festival, which was being taped for broadcasting, my admission was picked up by her fan club, which still exists and, glory be, relayed to Maureen O'Hara, who also still exists, aged 92, and living back in Ireland. And I received a warm and affectionate thank-you email from her.

Not a major event but I couldn't believe it. Maureen O'Hara had written to me. I felt shy and delighted all at once. My heart leapt. I was an eight-year-old in love.

43
MONTEBELLO

Wiping a trail of cobwebs off my face, I stood by the old Observation Post high on the Hermite Island dune so I could phone Tracy. The wind still rattled the window frames and lizards again investigated the intrusion.

I could imagine, just, the scene at eight a.m. on 3 October 1952, when a senior British scientist on Dr William Penney's team, Ian Maddocks, nicknamed the Count of Montebello, started the count-down and detonated Britain's first-ever nuclear bomb from here.

Straight ahead of me lay Ground Zero, the seabed still noticeably deeper and inkier than the surrounding waters. Here, 400 metres off Main Beach on the western side of Trimouille Island, the 25 kiloton plutonium device, similar to the *Fat Man* dropped on Nagasaki, exploded in the hold of HMS *Plym*.

The idea was to simulate a sneak bomb attack by the Russians on a Western harbour. The Montebellos were seen as an ideal testing ground for an attack on, say, the Port of London or Pearl Harbour. This sort of test, one of great secrecy and urgency, had not yet been undertaken by the Americans. Britain was avid for nuclear prestige, the test of the true superpower, and there was kudos in gaining this form of nuclear experience before America did.

Even more satisfyingly, they could magnanimously pass on the results, something the distrustful Americans were loath to do with their own nuclear secrets.

On the decks of the observing ships the British and Australian seamen assembled in groups. The Australian sailors were bare-chested, bare-headed, wearing only shorts and sandals. When the countdown began, the men on most of the ships other than Pat Coverley's, where no 'safety' instructions were given, were ordered to turn their backs to Ground Zero and to press the palms of their hands hard into their eye sockets.

On the count of 'Zero!' a brilliant flash of blue-white light passed through the men's heads. It was so bright they could see the bones of their hands pressed into their eyes, as if highlighted by X-rays. This flash was followed by a wave of intense heat – 'like standing against an open oven'. Seconds later, the men were told to turn and view the explosion and brace themselves for the shock wave.

According to one naval officer, 'The blinding electric blue light was of an intensity I hadn't seen before or since. I was pressing my hands hard to my eyes and this terrific light power was passing through my head and body and hands for ten to twelve seconds, and I saw my bones. Then came the pressure wave, with the feeling of being trapped deep underwater. This was followed by a vacuum suction wave, and my whole body felt it was billowing out like a balloon.'

Ten seconds after the detonation, the photographers ran to their cameras. It was an awesome but ugly sight: the bomb was sucking up millions of tons of mud in a water column. And every-one was confused by the shape of the cloud. Like Pat Coverley said, it wasn't the traditional mushroom cloud they had seen on American films of atomic explosions. It was huge and billowing and moving sideways.

The blast vaporised most of *Plym* and sucked those millions of tons of seawater and sediment and turtles and dolphins and fish and seabirds into the air. Trimouille was the region's main turtle breeding ground; October was the start of the nesting season when thousands of females came in from the sea.

After one second the nuclear cloud rose 1500 feet into the sky; after four minutes it was billowing higher than 10,000 feet. Some pieces of the frigate were turned into molten blobs of steel, other parts of the ship were now grey treacle liquefied into mist.

Even by the standards of the time, the test was considered 'dirty'. The seawater and mud and animal matter raised by the supersonic pressure wave was contaminated with fission products from the plutonium device. Much of this fell onto Trimouille Island. Islands to the north-west of Trimouille, including North West, Primrose, Bluebell, Carnation, Kingcup, Gardenia and Jonquil islands were contaminated. Much of the contamination fell in surrounding waters, both within the Montebello lagoons and into the Indian Ocean to the north, north-west and north-east of Trimouille.

It was later recognised by the hastily formed Australian Atomic Weapon Trials Safety Committee that before and after this blast and the next, *Operation Mosaic,* the meteorological measurements were unsatisfactory. Weather conditions were inaccurately forecast before the tests, or else dangerous risks were knowingly taken.

'Wrong weather' produced unexpected fallout across the country. The British scientists didn't realise how windy the West Australian coast could be, especially islands capable of recording the highest winds in the world.

The committee dismissed the monitoring of the pattern of fallout clouds as 'inadequate and highly dangerous.' It was highly critical of air force pilots having been been ordered to fly through the main nuclear cloud to collect samples of radioactive airborne fallout.

The pilots had to follow the clouds to see which direction the fallout was travelling. It was going east.

. . .

On our last afternoon in the Montebellos, Andy and I went out in the dinghy to troll for coral trout and emperors. Out of necessity I'd put my fishing conscience aside. Our food supplies were low by now – even the Four Bean Mix and Jatz crackers were long gone – and we wanted a memorable final meal that night. Already we were anticipating the delicious freshly caught and grilled fish. We surged through the Hole in the Wall where Don the Ancient Mariner never missed catching a couple of big fish every time he went out. We motored up and down for an hour or so, but we caught nothing; we saw nothing. Only a tiger shark a metre longer than our boat.

We held a farewell party anyway, down on the sea-level rock shelf on Hermite Island where the barge had moored and from where the helicopter would take us off next morning. We finished our remaining alcohol and food supplies but there wasn't much left except tinned tuna and salami. For once, no bandicoots scurried around our feet; they were made timid by the lack of ground cover on the rock shelf; nowhere to escape to.

Fish jumped and flopped and fled in the lagoon nearby. Big fish were feeding on little fish. It was a moonlit night and in the distance you could just make out the ghostly shape of the yacht that had belonged to the dead man and whose propensity for high drama would turn out not to be over.

In their laconic way, the conservationists were delighted with the result of the animal translocations. They had the microchip details and figures and their professional observations to prove that the immigrant animals were thriving and enthusiastically reproducing. The Joint

Government and Mining Company environmental model was working. The White Hats and the Black Hats, the Angels and the Bogeymen, seemed to have pulled it off. This second Ark, the Montebellos, was a viable experiment which was saving whole species.

No-one made dramatic statements or pointed out the obvious, that these islands had endured some of the greatest negative impacts of any place on earth and yet their recovery and renewal seemed possible. What Andy said was, 'Another drink, everyone?' and produced a hidden cask of celebratory red wine.

The project's success meant that the next migration of endangered animals could take place. From Barrow Island would come the smallest Australian marsupial of all: a five-gram, nocturnal, carnivorous and secretive animal called the planigale; as well as the boodie, or burrowing betong: a tiny burrowing kangaroo thought for many years to be extinct.

They would also bring across the western chestnut mouse, the leopard or spotted skink, the critically threatened central rock rat – not *rattus rattus* – and a creature whose name did not trip off the tongue as readily: the pseudoantechinus or fat-tailed antechinus, a small grey carnivorous marsupial, ten centimetres long, that was red behind the ears and whose tail was, well, fat.

In this mellow mood of project success and welcome fatigue I could nevertheless see the conservationists considering something. A question was looming. What was I going to write about the islands, about their endeavour? About them? They phrased their questions delicately, and all turned to me simultaneously. What had been the high point of my stay? And the low point?

This was complicated. My response seemed overly sentimental and made me blush with embarrassment in the darkness. I said the high point was when I held on my chest the expelled new-born wallaby, Jar Jar Binks, whose survival had aroused a range of unexpected emotions. The low point was probably the Bushes of Doom.

They seemed relieved that I didn't mention something else. The bandicoot accident perhaps? I didn't want to bring down the mood of the evening, but the small explosion of the plump bandicoot, the way it dramatically went *pop* when stepped upon, certainly sprang to mind.

. . .

We packed up to leave the islands. The dinghy and the quad-bike had to be safely stored in the cyclone-proof container-huts on Hermite Island. Hurricane Hut needed to be swept out and locked up and the toilet lashed down. Our beer cans were crushed for easy packing and removal. (There was a surprising number of them.) All disposable rubbish was carefully burned down on the rocky shore by the sea. A camp of professional environmentalists probably shouldn't start a bushfire or leave any rubbish behind.

After the helicopter took off, Brent asked the pilot to show us the whole archipelago. I was sitting next to the pilot in the cockpit and it was stimulating to swoop languidly low over all the islands. The land-and-sea-scape was all around me, and under my legs as well. From the air the sharp-edged colours and contours of the Montebellos seemed brilliantly enriched, even exaggerated. The relief map was almost too vivid to be true.

Into the deep indigo pit of the first bomb blast off Trimouille Island, from the open sea, swam twenty or thirty turtles. They were returning to the island to nest, swimming in from the Indian Ocean to lay their eggs, as they had always done.

The idealistic thirteen-year-old who wished to be a friend to all peoples, to play *La Vie En Rose* to girls on the trumpet and ban the bomb, would have preferred there to be a stern lesson for mankind here: a definite change in turtle breeding habits, a turning-away from Trimouille, an instinctive animal resistance to past nuclear shores and annihilations. So he didn't know whether to be pleased at this or as confused as ever.

44
CYCLING

A light wash of rain blew in our faces as Tracy and I cycled across the island. I was a year back from the Montebellos and I wanted to share Little Parrakeet Bay with her, too. She was now a widow. It was our first trip away together, finally our first time alone, and I was pleased by her suggestion for us to go to Rottnest.

The salt lakes gave off whiffs of organic matter and on their shores ducks and seagulls crowded together for warmth against the wind. Great clumps of lake foam blew across the road and through our wheels and the froth clung momentarily to the spokes and pedals and to our legs.

We rode side by side and occasionally one or the other would speed ahead, then wait for the other to catch up. The bikes had back-pedal brakes and no gears and we walked together up the steeper hills. This grey first day of spring, 1 September, we were the only cyclists on the road. It was the anniversary of my Registry Office wedding to Ruth and the beginning of the long-ago Rottnest honeymoon. Yet another coincidence that fiction disfavoured but real life seemed to be encouraging with ever-increasing gusto.

In the cool weather at this time of year, and mid-week, there had been no trouble getting a room in the island's hotel. We had the place to ourselves though rarely left our room except to take the air and some exercise in the morning and evening.

Wherever we went for meals or a drink we were one of only three or four couples; the others were roadies and their girlfriends setting up equipment for a weekend pop concert. Their sound-checks boomed out all day but we weren't bothered by them. We had many years to make up and many things to say and hear.

Little Parrakeet Bay reflected the non-colour of agate as a milky glare showed through the clouds. Choppy waves broke on its reefs and rolled long banks of kelp onto the shore and the sea had that ominous look that Australians on any coast like to describe as 'sharky'. Drizzly rain soaked us as we tramped across the sand and shed our clothes. We found a weedless patch of sea and Tracy ran ahead and boldly dived in before me. We swam, but not for long or too far out.

As we rode off again she pedalled into the lead and the clouds lifted more and the sun and wind began to dry our clothes. We were returning to the hotel by the hilly coastal route. She was full of energy as she sped ahead of me down the slopes and through side-streets of deserted holiday cottages. We didn't want to wear our helmets. We were lawless exhilarated teenagers again, yahooing and sounding our bicycle bells as we raced faster and faster around the bends and down the suddenly familiar hills of my adolescence.

I admired her speed and spirit, and was touched by her efforts, and my yells and exhilaration were meant for her and all about her. As she crouched low over the handlebars to go even quicker I could see the sunlight shining on her head. Her scalp gleamed now that the chemotherapy sessions were taking effect – she was too straight-forward a person to wear a wig – and she'd had her remaining hair strands clipped close to her skull.

There seemed to be no-one else on the entire island. We yelled into the sea breeze and rang our bike bells all the way down to the bottom of the hill until we reached another bay that was sheltered from the wind, where a few boats bobbed placidly on their moorings, and then I caught up with her and we pedalled slowly back to the settlement side by side and talking quietly.

ACKNOWLEDGEMENTS

Firstly I want to thank Gerri Sutton, whose generous assistance made this book possible.

Special thanks for their patience and hospitality to Brent Johnson, former Principal Technical Officer, Fauna Conservation, and Dr Andy Smith, former Senior Research Scientist (Fauna Translocations), Wildlife Research Centre, Department of Environment and Conservation, Western Australia. And for their willingness to share their specialist conservation knowledge and Montebello experiences, I'm immensely grateful to Dr Andrew Burbidge and Peter Kendrick.

For their help, time and assorted kindnesses, I'm indebted to Dirk Avery; Carmel Bird; Robbie Burns; Dana Burrows; Patrick and Maxine Coverley; Tracy Coverley, Bill Drewe; Tony Gibson; Jack and Nancy Harrison; Janet Hocken; Mark Holden; Chris Mews; Nelson and Julie Mews; Rusty Miller and Tricia Shantz; Kim Newman; Ross Nobel; Jan Purcell; Sagaro at Lightforce Computers; Dr Catherine Samson; Moya Sayer-Jones; Brian Sierakowski; Peter Temple; and Stephen Van Mil.

For their publishing support, thanks as always to Julie Gibbs, Fiona Inglis, Jocelyn Hungerford and Bob Sessions.

Some early fragments of this book were first published in *Granta; When the Wild Comes Leaping Up: Personal Encounters with Nature* (edited by David

Suzuki); *Best Australian Essays 2006; Best Australian Short Stories 2008; Sand* (with John Kinsella); *Westerly*; the *Saturday Age*; *West Weekend*; *Sunday Life*; the *Bulletin*; and the *Weekend Australian Magazine*.

The following works are acknowledged: For literature and history: *New Voyage Round the World*, by William Dampier; *William Dampier in New Holland*, by Alex S. George; 'Youth', by Joseph Conrad; *Kangaroo*, by D.H. Lawrence; *The Island of Dr Moreau*, by H.G. Wells; *My Family and Other Animals*, by Gerald Durrell; *Prospero's Cell* and *Reflections on a Marine Venus*, by Lawrence Durrell; *Henry Lawson – The People's Poet: Women and the Bush: Forces of Desire in the Australian Cultural Tradition*, by Kay Schaffer; *Herzog*, by Saul Bellow; *A Move Abroad*, by Ian McEwan; *Point Omega*, by Don DeLillo; *Monster of God: The Man-Eating Predator in the Jungles of History and the Mind*, by David Quammen; *Time and Tide: History of Byron Bay*, by S.J. Dening; and *Byron Bay: The History, Beauty and Spirit,* by Peter Duke.

On conservation matters: *Landscope* (Department of the Environment and Conservation, W.A.); *The Western Australian Naturalist*, Vol. 24, No. 2, 2003: *Mass Deaths of Sea Turtles on the Montebello Islands, October 1953, Following Operation Hurricane*, by Peter Kendrick; *Exploiting Green and Hawksbill Turtles in Western Australia: A Case Study of Commercial Marine Turtle Fishing 1869– 1973*, by Brooke Halkyard; *Radiation Management Plan, Montebello Islands Conservation Park*, and *Management Proposals for the Montebello Islands and Surrounding Waters* (Department of Conservation and Land Management, W.A.).

On nuclear testing: Max Kimber's ABC interviews; *Beyond Belief,* by Roger Cross and Avon Hudson; *Atomic Fallout*, publication of the Atomic Ex-Servicemen's Association; *Wayward Governance: Illegality and Its Control in the Public Sector:* Chapter 16: *A Toxic Legacy – British Nuclear Weapons Testing in Australia*, by P.N. Grabowsky (Australian Institute of Criminology); *The Story of Operation Hurricane*, a 1977 paper by J.J. McEnhill (National Archives of Australia); *Radiation Hazard Assessment and Monitoring Programme for the Montebello Islands* (Western Radiation Services).

Credits: *Blueberry Hill* was recorded by Fats Domino in 1956 and written by Vincent Rose, Al Lewis and Larry Stock in 1940; *Groundhog Day* (1993) was directed by Harold Ramis and written by Danny Rubin and Harold Ramis; and *Hiroshima Mon Amour* (1959) was directed by Alain Resnais and written by Marguerite Duras.

HAMISH HAMILTON

UK | USA | Canada | Ireland | Australia
India | New Zealand | South Africa | China

Penguin Books is part of the Penguin Random House group of companies
whose addresses can be found at global.penguinrandomhouse.com.

Penguin
Random House
Australia

First published by Penguin Australia Pty Ltd, 2012

Cover design by Emily O'Neill © Penguin Group (Australia)
Cover photograph by Judy Dunlop
Text design by Emily O'Neill © Penguin Group (Australia)
Typeset in 11.5/16.5pt Fairfield Light by Post Pre-Press, Brisbane
Printed and bound in Australia by Griffin Press, an accredited ISO AS/NZS 14001
Environmental Management Systems printer.

National Library of Australia
Cataloguing-in-Publication data:

Drewe, Robert
Montebello / Robert Drewe.
9780143569046 (pbk.)
Drewe, Robert
Authors, Australian – 20th century – Biography.
Western Australia – Social life and customs – 1945–
Western Australia – Social conditions – 20th century.
364.15230994

penguin.com.au